HARLEQUIN SHERIDAN
THE MAN AND THE LEGENDS

By R. Crompton Rhodes

The Stagery of Shakespeare
Shakespeare's First Folio
Black Sheep: A Comedy

Blowing up the PIC NIC's — or — Harlequin Quixotte attacking the Puppets. Vide Tottenham Street Pantomine

SHERIDAN AND PRIVATE THEATRICALS, 1805

Frontispiece

HARLEQUIN SHERIDAN

THE MAN AND THE LEGENDS

With a Bibliography and Appendices by

R. CROMPTON RHODES

Editor of The Plays and Poems of
Richard Brinsley Sheridan

OXFORD: BASIL BLACKWELL
1933

Printed in Great Britain for BASIL BLACKWELL & MOTT LTD.
by the KEMP HALL PRESS LTD. in the City of Oxford

TO JOHN DRINKWATER AND BARRY VINCENT
JACKSON

FEBRUARY 15TH 1913—FEBRUARY 15TH 1933

PREFACE

1

IT is seven years since this biography was planned, at the same time as the edition of *The Plays and Poems of Richard Brinsley Sheridan*, which appeared in three volumes in 1928. From all my precursors, from John Watkins in 1816 to E. M. Butler in 1931, I have exacted contributions, going to them, however, for documents and facts rather than opinions and interpretations. To these I have added what is known as "new material" being the further evidence of contemporary sources, printed or unprinted, upon which they have not drawn. It is my hope to have shown Sheridan in the round, as he appeared to his own generation, not only from his letters and plays and speeches, but surrounded by squibs and lampoons, newspaper-paragraphs and election-results, accusations and exculpations, libels and lies.

Sheridan was caricatured and lampooned under many soubriquets like "Dick Merryman" and "Bardolph" and "Old Sherry," but Harlequin is the one nickname that linked up his character with his theatrical avocations.

2

Sheridan, as he always insisted, was a man of the theatre in spite of himself. It was the paradox of his life. At Harrow, where players were despised, he was taunted with being "a player's son," and the insult rankled to the last. When he came to marry, his wife was a public performer, and he insisted upon her retirement as her profession was inconsistent with his own of being a gentleman. He was forced by poverty into the only occupation that offered a rapid advancement for his talents, and within a year he was acclaimed as the author of "the two best comedies of his age." Then the opportunity for his financial ambitions presented itself for him to become a proprietor and manager of a theatre. Of the routine duties of theatrical management he was speedily tired, and before he was thirty he was anxious to relinquish them. He was an opponent of monopolies, yet it was from his share in the theatrical monopoly that he derived his income for thirty years, and all his numerous financial embarrassments proceeded from his anxiety to preserve his property against opposition. He hated to be reminded of his theatrical connection, and in the House of Commons on no point was he more sensitive.

Yet in the strangest ways he was always thrown back on the theatre. When he was Treasurer of the Navy, holding one of the richest of Ministerial appointments, with a residence in Somerset House, for his gentlemen out of livery he pressed into service the inferior officers of the theatre. When he won his seat at Westminster as the successor to Charles Fox he staged his triumph, as Cobbett said, with a procession through the streets like that in *Blue Beard*. At the end of every passage in his life, there was somebody to cry "Harlequin."

The notion that he wasted his life by entering the House of Commons appears to me as purely a literary prejudice. Stated in the concrete, he might perhaps have completed his comedy of *Affectation* as a second *School for Scandal* and his opera of *The Foresters* as a second *Duenna*, at the cost of his Begum Speeches at the trial of Warren Hastings, or of his long advocacy of Catholic Emancipation. In both these political causes he fought on the losing side. While history has confirmed the judgment of the House of Lords in its honourable acquittal of Warren Hastings, this impeachment—however much it owed to the venom of Philip Francis—determined the course of British administration in India for future generations, and set a new standard of public service. The cause of Catholic Emancipation was not won till after his death, but that does not make his advocacy of it, though its inexpediency alienated him from his friends, the less noble or the less disinterested. It may be that *sub specie aeternitatis* it is much greater to be a writer of comedies than to be for a quarter of a century a leader of His Majesty's Opposition, with two years of minor office as a member of His Majesty's Government. It depends entirely upon one's sense of values.

And, after all, if Sheridan had wanted to write plays, he could have written them, for his Parliamentary duties gave him abundant leisure. Perhaps he had exhausted his mine with *The School for Scandal*, for when he wrote *The Critic* he had narrowed his satire from life itself to the life of the theatre, and it is possible to interpret his burlesque into a confession that he was wasting his life as a dramatist and theatrical manager. After that, his contributions to the theatre were negligible— the pantomime of *Robinson Crusoe, or, Harlequin Friday* in 1781 was the only one of them that was not actuated by a patriotic or political motive.

He wrote an interlude called *The Storming of Fort Omoa* in 1780, in celebration of a naval victory, and in 1794 he arranged an entertainment called *The Glorious First of June* for the benefit of the widows and orphans of the men who fell in the engagements under Lord Howe, and he altered this in 1797 to another piece called *Cape St. Vincent, or, British Valour Triumphant*. His adaptation of *Pizarro, or, The Spaniards in Peru* from the German of Kotzebue he valued above all his other writings, because it was interpreted, and intended to be interpreted, as an exhortation of Britain in defiance of Revolutionary France. He paraphrased it from literal translations, and added oratorical decorations of which he was intensely proud, with the gratified pride of a politician.

His play-making ended with the *programme* or scenario of *The Forty Thieves* in 1806. At this point, however, it is convenient to dispose of the "attributed plays" which Coventry Patmore discovered and presented to the British Museum. One of these MSS. is *The Statesman*, bearing Patmore's note "Almost certainly by Sheridan; it is clever enough for him, and the blanks left by the copyist have all been filled in by his hand." Mr. Sichel has confidently presented some excerpts as Sheridan's: but *The Gazeteer and New Daily Advertiser* on December 21st, 1781, announced that "a new farce of two acts called *The Statesman* is in rehearsal and will be performed in the course of a few days." In spite of this it was never acted, and a reference to the obvious source, *Biographia Dramatica*, shows that the author was John Dent. The other plays *Renaud d'Aste*, *King Arthur* and *The Cobler of Preston*—an alteration from Charles Johnson—must be dismissed without ceremony. After his entry into Parliament, Sheridan did not even write prologues and epilogues, or use his pen in any way for the assistance of his theatrical property. At the close of his life he could not recall ever sitting at the theatre through a single play—his own excepted, and those only at rehearsal.

"I do not know," wrote Lord Byron to Thomas Moore, then beginning his own seven years' task ,"any good model for a life of Sheridan but that of Savage. Recollect, however, that the life of such a man may be made far more amusing than if he had been a Wilberforce." Miss Butler, however, complains that Watkins passed his mantle of dullness to the long line of his successors—Thomas Moore, Fraser Rae, and Walter Sichel, "three highly intelligent men with the facts before them who should have found no difficulty in compiling interesting lives, seem to have been stifled with tedium and are certainly suffocatingly wearisome throughout the course of their works." It would not become me, having profited by the labours of others, to complain that they are a set of dull dogs. Moore's *Sheridan* is—I must repeat—"a much better book than his later biographers have admitted, or even understood." While his memoir was written "at the request of the family," Moore was by no means subservient in dealing with the literary and political aspects, he was constrained to a polite reticence as to certain matters he knew well, as is testified by many notes in his *Journal*, and even by this letter of Byron's, which, while exhorting him to be "amusing," yet added a rider as to discretion over such matters as Sheridan's debts and his drunkenness—"Were his intrigues," he demanded, "more notorious than those of his contemporaries? And is his memory to be blasted and theirs respected?"

It has been my endeavour to reduce such traits as these to their proper proportions, without emphasis or evasion. This biography assembles for the first time, briefly and dispassionately, the evidence as to the strange tangle in the lives of Sheridan and his first wife with Lord Edward Fitzgerald and Pamela Seymour, the supposed daughter of Mme. de Genlis and the *ci-devant* Duc d'Orleans. While any scandal propagated by the Princess of Wales is suspect, it seems probable that she was correct in telling Lord Glenbervie that Lord Edward was the father of Mrs. Sheridan's last child, Mary, who died so soon after her mother. What effect this discovery may have had upon Sheridan is a matter for speculation, but there can be no doubt that within eight weeks of his wife's death he had proposed marriage to, and been accepted by Pamela, who nevertheless shortly afterwards married Lord Edward in France.

Again, for the first time I am able to give an impartial account of Sheridan's relations with the Prince of Wales, afterwards King George the Fourth. This friendship was entirely honourable to both of them, for Sheridan gave the Prince his disinterested advice: and the Prince had sufficient magnanimity to be grateful for it, even though it was often directly opposed to his own wishes. He treated Sheridan with the deepest affection, and even indulgence, until the last unfortunate incident which led to their estrangement.

Since Moore, all Sheridan's biographers have fallen at the last hurdle. He wrote bitterly against the Prince's "desertion" of Sheridan in 1812. Later writers have so expanded this legend that the Prince is condemned of "duplicity," "ingratitude," and "treachery" to Sheridan as early as 1804, when he appointed him as Receiver-General of the Duchy of Cornwall. It is my privilege, by the kindness of H.R.H. the Prince of Wales, to print from the records of the Duchy of Cornwall the facts as to Sheridan's tenure of this office, which explodes this legend, and acquits the Prince of these charges. As a corollary, I have disposed of Moore's charge that the Prince refused to find Sheridan a seat in Parliament after his defeat at Stafford, except under implied and ignominious conditions of subservience. Among the "new material" is something which certainly should not be "new," yet no previous biographer of Sheridan has ever troubled to read the 5th Edition of Moore's *Life of Sheridan*, with its preface and its reluctant postscript which shows that all his censures of the Prince had been blown sky-high.

It has been my fortune to recover from many sources information as to passages in Sheridan's life which have hitherto been obscure. For instance, scarcely anything has been written of the events of 1806, but I have discovered in the Birmingham Reference Library Sheridan's *Eulogium on the Death of Mr. Fox*, now reprinted for the first time from an unrecorded pamphlet, and by the kindness of Mr. Percival F. Hinton I have availed myself of a *History of the Westminster Election*, which places him at the hustings, the central figure in a picture of Hogarthian vigour. Again, at the William Salt Library, Stafford, I have found, among other documents, the draft of his furious manifesto against the electors of Stafford who deserted him in 1812—which now appears for the first time in print, faithfully reproducing his spelling, his punctuation, and his incomplete sentences. From some MSS. notes made by John Graham on a set of *Sheridan's Speeches* I have found a few lively touches, such as his account of Sheridan recovering, after a quarter of a century, his MS. of the Begum speech in Westminster Hall. Mr. T. P. Lefanu, the great-grandson of Sheridan's elder sister, Alicia—Mrs. Joseph Lefanu—has generously placed at my disposal the letters written to her between 1784 and 1790 by her younger sister, Elizabeth—Mrs. Henry Lefanu. To this *Journal of Betsy Sheridan*, as it is called, I owe a great deal of "background," many quotations, and above all, the account of Mrs. Sturt's ball at Hammersmith which gives so lively a picture of "the raree show of the great world" in 1789. Other acknowledgments are made in detail elsewhere.

3

It has been my object to work *de novo* over the mass of contemporary material: to place evidence before comment: and to select such details, without falsifying the whole, as will present in the compass of a single volume the most graphic illustrations of Sheridan's career.

R. CROMPTON RHODES.

February 15th, 1933.

ACKNOWLEDGMENTS

MY cordial thanks for the use of material previously unpublished are due to:

H.R.H. the Prince of Wales
and Sir Walter Peacock, Counsellor of the Duchy of Cornwall,
> *for the records of Sheridan's tenure of the office of Receiver-General of the Duchy.*

The William Salt Library, Stafford, and Miss Henrietta Garbett, Librarian,
> *for documents and letters to, from, and concerning Sheridan.*

The Municipal Library, Bath, and Mr. Reginald W. M. Wright, Director,
> *for documents and much other assistance.*

The Catholic Record Society and Mr. R. Cecil Wilton, Hon. Sec.,
> *for four letters from Sheridan in the Norfolk MSS.*

The Birmingham Reference Library and Mr. H. M. Cashmore, Chief Librarian,
> *for Sheridan's Eulogium on the Death of Charles Fox.*

The Garrick Club,
> *for permission to search the library for Sheridan material.*

Mr. T. P. Lefanu, C.B.,
> *for a complete transcript of* The Journal of Betsy Sheridan *being the letters of Sheridan's younger sister, Elizabeth (Mrs. Henry Lefanu) to his elder sister, Alicia (Mrs. Joseph Lefanu), between* 1784 *and* 1790.

Mr. Percival F. Hinton,
> *for the loan of numerous books from his Sheridan collection,*
> *including a set of* Sheridan's Speeches *with contemporary*
> *MS. biographical notes by John Graham.*

Mr. F. W. Bateson,
> *for information as to Sheridan MS. and editions in American*
> *Libraries.*

Messrs. Birrell and Garnett,
> *for four letters from Sheridan to Burgess and others.*

CONTENTS

CONTENTS

List of Illustrations

CHAPTER THE FIRST
The Family Tree

What parchment have we here?—"Richard heir to Thomas"
—oh, our genealogy in full.

The School for Scandal.

I

THE SHERIDAN FAMILY has been furnished
with a most imposing pedigree, which at a first glance
seems to prove the descent of Richard Brinsley Sheridan
from Donald O'Sheridan, who was, *tempo Eliz.*, "of Clough-
loughter Castle, and Balliconnel Castle in County Cavan." But
a closer scrutiny reveals that between the descendants of
Donald and the ancestors of Richard there is a hiatus or two.
The European Magazine, in 1782, printed "A Memoir of
Richard Brinsley Sheridan, Esq., Member of Parliament for
the Borough of Stafford," which affirmed that he was "the son
of Thomas Sheridan, late manager of the Theatre in Dublin,
by Frances, his lady, who was the author of several dramatic
works: and grandson to the Rev. Dr. Thomas Sheridan, the
celebrated friend of Dean Swift." Beyond these indisputable
progenitors his ancestry was not traced, though the article
ended with a promise, never fulfilled, of a genealogical
account, interspersed with anecdotes, of the Sheridan family.

John Watkins roused the wrath of Sheridan's sisters by
describing him as "a man possessing neither pedigree nor
property": and at their instigation, his niece Alicia Lefanu
made a vigorous but vague rejoinder in her *Memoirs of Mrs.
Frances Sheridan*. It was true, she admitted, that even at the
beginning of the seventeenth century, the Sheridans were
"no longer possessed of the large estates assigned to them by

the ancient geographers"—the dirty acres, in the words of Sir
Lucius O'Trigger, had slipped through their fingers; but the
family honour, she thanked Heaven, was as fresh as ever;—
they boasted, she said, that they were "in direct and unbroken
descent from a family renowned in Ireland equally for its antiquity and respectability."

Such indeed was the boast of many other Irish families in
County Cavan. Count O'Rourke favoured the world in 1782
with a table of his descent, through forty-three generations,
from "Achey Moymedon, King of Ireland from the 358th to
the 366th year of the Christian aera." *The European Magazine*,
in printing this pedigree, interpolated that the regal pretensions
of the O'Rourkes were disputed by the O'Reillys, the O'Gradys
and the O'Sheridans: yet, the most learned and subtle anti-
quaries being unable to decide between the contending families,
the question as to which candidate was entitled to be considered heir to the ancient princely throne of Cavan was regarded as being in honourable suspense. Nevertheless, in token
of their several claims, the various families prefixed the distinguishing O to their names, "as a proof of the royalty and antiquity of their blood." This explanation of the patronymic,
though hardly in accordance with historical philology, still
suffices to show that the "dark Milesian pedigrees," so passionately flaunted by their owners, were regarded with considerable levity by the rest of the world.

Sheridan in his later years often talked of his descent from
the O'Sheridans. He used to protest that, while proud of being
a scion of so ancient and honourable a family, he thought it
better, out of modesty, to drop the O: "But who has a greater
right to the O than we have?" enquired his son Tom. "We *owe*
everybody." Sheridan often expatiated upon the antiquity of
Irish families; while affirming that no man had less family pride
than himself, he was still an O'Sheridan, whose sires were the
ancient princes of Ireland. When presiding at a dinner of the
Theatrical Fund, he descanted with great eloquence upon this
theme, till Joe Munden, at last weary of it, said, "Mr. Sheridan,
I have not the least doubt of what you say. I daresay you are

descended from princes. The laſt time I saw your father, he
was the Prince of Denmark."[1]

Alicia Lefanu could not flourish a genealogical tree so luxuriant as those of Count O'Rourke and his rival, Count O'Reilly.
She did not produce the name of any anceſtor before her great-
grandfather, Dr. Thomas the schoolmaſter, though under pro-
vocation she asserted that his grandfather was a younger son of
William Sheridan, Bishop of Kildare and Armagh in the reign
of King Charles the Second. The *Alumni Dublinenses* records
Thomas Sheridan as admitted to Trinity College in 1707, the
son of Patrick, *colonus*, a farmer. Beyond this point, the pedigree is speculative, though Watkins asserted that Dr. Sheridan's father, whom he called Thomas, was a country gentleman possessed of a small eſtate in Cavan, who, like two or three
other families of the same name in the neighbourhood, claimed
to be related to the Bishop of Kilmore. And, no doubt, all the
Sheridans of County Cavan could have satisfied the definition
of Irish cousins as given in *The Beaux Stratagem*—"Your foſter-
moder's son was married to my nurse's siſter, joy: and so we are
Irish cussens."

2

The romantic tendency has elevated Quilca into the ances-
tral seat of the Sheridans, under the resonant titles of Quilcagh
House and Quilca Mansion. "It is said"—affirms Rae, not
vouchsafing by whom—"that the house was built by James
Sheridan who, like his brothers William the Bishop and
Thomas the Secretary of Ireland, was an ardent Jacobite, and
his eſtates were confiscated for his loyalty to King James the
Second: Quilca was then granted to Charles Macfadden for
his devotion to the cause of William of Orange." When his
daughter Elizabeth married Dr. Sheridan, "the happy accident
of a marriage led to the reſtoration of the old ſtock to the old
home."[2] James Sheridan was not, as Rae supposes, the father
of Dr. Sheridan; the confiscation is mere supposition; and there
is nothing to show that Quilca, or the land it was built upon,

[1]Angelo, *Picnic*, 143.　　　　[2]Rae, I, 3.

had ever belonged to the ancestors of Dr. Sheridan; the obituary of his son the actor in *The European Magazine* affirmed that this small estate passed to his father by marriage, and appeared to be the only landed property his family ever possessed, for his grandfather, also a native of Cavan, lived in obscurity.

When Sheridan was thirteen, the first account of his father appeared in *The Companion to the Playhouse*—the earliest form of the *Biographia Dramatica*, whose author, David Baker, said that Thomas Sheridan, A.M., the second son of Dr. Thomas Sheridan, was ("I believe") born at Quilca, a little place in the County of Cavan in Ireland, which came into his family in right of his mother, the daughter of one "Mr. McPherson, who became possessed of it during the troubles in Ireland"—that is, after the Revolution of 1689. Thomas Sheridan the actor was born in Dublin and his mother's name was not McPherson, but Macfadden; or, as Swift spells it, Mackfadin; or as Alicia Lefanu spells it, Macfoddin.

Dean Swift, Dr. Sheridan's friend, spent many months in the year at Quilca, writing *Gulliver's Travels* there in 1724. But *more suo* he used to ridicule his friend's pretensions. The most celebrated instance was when the Bishop of Meath told Swift and Sheridan that as his palace was undergoing repair, he was without a house. Swift at once offered to lend his vicarage at Laracor, and Sheridan began to descant upon the superior advantages and beauties of Quilca. Swift, to put an end to this, exclaimed, "My Lord, do you hear that vapouring scab? I will show you an exact picture of the place which he has painted in such fine colours." He then produced a sarcastic description of Quilca, which he had written with the intention of mortifying Dr. Sheridan's vanity upon a suitable occasion:—

"Let me thy properties explain;
A rotten cabin, dropping rain,
Chimneys with scorn rejecting smoke,
Stools, tables, chairs, and bedsteads broke.
Here elements have lost their uses,
Air ripens not, nor earth produces.

In vain we make poor Shelah toil,
Fire will not roaſt, nor water boil.
Through all the valleys, hills, and plains,
The goddess *Want* in triumph reigns;
And her chief officers of ſtate,
Sloth, *Dirt*, and *Theft* around her wait."

Of course, this satire is not to be taken literally, and though Dr. Sheridan spent extravagantly in attempting to convert Quilca into a *ferme ornée*, it remained nothing but a cottage, with a coved roof, like a barn. Nevertheless, Dr. Sheridan's daughter Elizabeth was a firm believer in the "Banshi, or female dæmon attached to certain ancient Irish families." She seriously maintained that the Banshi of the Sheridan family was heard wailing beneath the windows of Quilca before the news arrived from France of the death of Frances Sheridan at Blois. Her niece made her very angry by observing that as Mrs. Sheridan was by birth a Chamberlaine, a family of English extraction, she had no right to the guardianship of an Irish fairy, and therefore the Banshi had made a miſtake.[1] Except for its dæmon, there was nothing of the anceſtral mansion about Quilca. After Dr.Sheridan's death, it passed, no doubt heavily mortgaged, to his elder son Richard, from whom it was purchased by Thomas Sheridan.

3

Thomas Sheridan, the actor, was the third son of the Rev. Dr. Sheridan, and born in Dublin about 1720: being admitted to Weſtminster School in February 1732-3 as "aged eleven," and to Trinity College, Dublin, in May 1735 as "aged sixteen." His godfather was Dr. Swift, who said that when Thomas was sent to Weſtminſter School by his father, who could ill afford it, he was elected a King's Scholar by pure merit. Unfortunately, his father could not find fourteen pounds to enable him to finish the year, and he was recalled to Dublin, and after entering Trinity College as a Pensioner (that is, one who paid fees) he was elected a scholar in 1738, and graduated B.A., in 1739. While he was

[1]Lefanu, 33.

still at college, he wrote a farce entitled *Captain O'Blunder or The Brave Irishman*, which was greatly approved in Ireland, because the Irish gentleman was, despite his absurdities, depicted in an attractive and engaging manner. Isaac Sparkes, an Irish actor, was the favourite actor of *Captain O'Blunder*, and in Dublin there were many signs hanging in the street with his portrait in this character. *Captain O'Blunder* was acted in Dublin about 1738, and was printed in 1754, but not with the author's consent; he declared that the copy had been lost and that what was printed had been put together from memory by people who had appeared in it.

About this time—on October 10th, 1738—Dr. Sheridan died at Rathfarnham near Dublin, in poverty and disappointment. It was expected that his son would either become a clergyman or a schoolmaster, but in January 1743, he made his appearance on the stage at Smock Alley as King Richard III, and then played in *Mithridates, King of Pontus*, at once establishing himself as an actor. His influence over the Dublin audience was so great that James Quin, who arrived in the city during the first glow of Sheridan's prosperity, quitted it in disgust. The Irish theatre had never known so much applause given to an actor, or such full houses.

On January 19th, 1746, during a performance of Vanbrugh's comedy of *Æsop*, a dissolute young man from Galway forced his way behind the scenes, despite Sheridan's orders, and insulted Mrs. Bellamy. Being ejected, a few days later he headed a party to demolish the theatre during a performance of *The Fair Penitent*. This resulted in a lawsuit, in which Sheridan was victorious, but the disturbances had been very disastrous. During the controversy a fable in verse called *The Owls* appeared in a Dublin newspaper, addressed "to Mr. Sheridan on his late affair at the Theatre." It began:—

> "Envy will Merit still pursue,
>   As shade succeeds to light;
> And though a shade obstructs the view,
>   It proves the substance right.

"If Worth appears, and gets its due,
(But oh! how rare that gain!)
The satyrs and the mimic crew
Shall grin behind the scene."[1]

He discovered that the writer of these complimentary verses, and an equally complimentary pamphlet, was Frances Chamberlaine. She was twenty-two, the daughter of the Rev. Dr. Philip Chamberlaine, rector of St. Nicholas Without, who had died a year or two previously. Thomas Sheridan found her conversation as captivating as her writing, and they were married in 1747 at Dublin by her brother, the Rev. Walter Chamberlaine.

4

Richard Brinsley Sheridan was the third son of Thomas and Frances Sheridan. In 1750 the eldest brother, Thomas, died at three years old; in June of that year, Charles Francis, the second child was born. The accepted legend is that the third son was christened Richard Brinsley Butler. Alicia Lefanu made this curious statement in her *Memoirs of Mrs. Frances Sheridan* in 1824, and Thomas Moore adopted it in his *Memoirs of Sheridan* in 1825, when, having remarked that he was baptized Richard Brinsley, he added a footnote that he was christened "also by the name of Butler, after the Earl of Lanesborough." This name was not given him at baptism, nor until then had it been associated with him; he never signed "Butler" or its initial letter in any bill, warrant, quittance or obligation whatsoever. The Earl of Lanesborough of 1751 was Humphrey Butler; but both the father whom he succeeded and the son who succeeded him were named Brinsley Butler; and Alicia Lefanu had merely confused two names in the family tradition. It is not known whether the sponsor was Humphrey, naming him Brinsley after his own father, or Brinsley, then Lord Newton Abbott, M.P., for Cavan, naming him after himself; and there is no evidence that Butler ever took the slightest interest in his godson. Moreover, Sheridan certainly was not baptized by the

[1]Lefanu, 23.

name of Butler, nor even Richard. The entry in the registers of
St. Mary's Church, Dublin, says:—

"1751. Novr. 4th. Thos. Brinsley, son of Mr. and Mrs.
Sheridan."

Thomas was the name of his father, his grandfather, and his
eldest brother. It is unlikely that the clergyman made a mistake,
and wrote "Thos. Brinsley" for "Richard Brinsley Butler":
probably the parents afterwards changed their minds, and
called him Richard after one of his uncles, his father's brother,
Richard Sheridan of Dublin, or his mother's brother, Richard
Chamberlaine of London.

The date of Sheridan's birth is unknown; the various positive statements are unsupported deductions from the time of
baptism, November 4th. Alicia Lefanu, who gives in her accounts of the family only the month of birth, says "in September," which is repeated by Moore. The rest is guessing.[1]

Quilca in County Cavan was frequently stated to have been
the birthplace of Sheridan and his son Richard Brinsley. The
"Memoirs of the late Thomas Sheridan, Esq.," which appeared
in *The European Magazine* for 1788 say:

"Thomas Sheridan was the eldest son of Dr. Thomas
Sheridan, an eminent divine and schoolmaster, but more
celebrated as the friend and companion of Dean Swift, by
Miss Macpherson, daughter of a Scots gentleman. He was
born at Quilca, a place which to future times will acquire a
degree of importance, as the residence of Swift, and the
birth-place of most of Mr. Sheridan's family; particularly
the author of *The School for Scandal*."

Samuel Whyte, the intimate friend of Thomas and Frances
Sheridan, doubted the authenticity of these facts, and with
their nephew Richard Sheridan, K.C., he made enquiries from
Dr. Sheridan's only surviving child, Hester Knowles. She told
them that Thomas Sheridan was the third son of his father and

[1] Graham's MS. notes say October 21st.

that his mother, who was named Macfadden, and not Macpherson, was not of Scotch extraction, but Irish. She added that the ascription of Quilca as the birthplace of her brother Thomas was devoid of all foundation, for she said, "both her mother and sister [in law] were remarkably timid on these occasions, and invariably fixed on the Capital, where they were in the way of more immediate and better assistance than could be expected in the country." She and her brother were born in Capel Street, in King James's Mint-House, as it was called, where her father kept his school; and Thomas's third son, Richard Brinsley, was born at his father's house in Dorset Street. This account, said Whyte, "is confirmed by the Register, to be seen in the Church books of St. Mary's, Dublin, which could not well have been the case had they been born at Quilca; a journey of about fifty English miles from Dublin, and not, as asserted, in its neighbourhood."[1] Strangely enough, the only reference that Sheridan is known to have made to his birthplace has been entirely missed; in his obituary in *The Gentleman's Magazine* of 1816, it was stated that he was born in Dublin, but the editor, John Nichols, added a footnote—"I have heard Mr. Sheridan say that he believed he was born at Quilca, a short distance from Dublin, where his father had a small estate." The evidence of his Aunt Hester, however, establishes his birthplace as No. 12 Dorset Street, Dublin.

[1] Whyte: *Miscellanea Nova*, 38-40.

CHAPTER THE SECOND

Harlequin Schoolboy

Grief seldom join'd with blooming Youth is seen.
Howard, *The Indian Queen.*

I

SHERIDAN remembered his schooldays at Harrow only for their misery. He entered at the beginning of 1762, when his mother wrote Whyte that "Dick has been at Harrow School since Christmas; as he may probably fall into a bustling life, we have a mind to accustom him early to shift for himself; Charles's domestic and sedentary turn is best suited to a home education."[1]

"Dick" was certainly accustomed early to "shift for himself." Some six weeks before his death, he had a long conversation at his house in Saville Row with John Graham, who recorded some fragments of it on the fly-leaf of his set of Sheridan's *Speeches*:—

"He told me it was his practice when a boy to study in the Fields with no other refreshment than a Sausage and a bit of Bread, and the Water from any Brook or Pond that came in his way—the Ballad he recited to me a short time previous to his Decease (the story of King Henry and Queen Eleanor) he learnt by listening to an old Cobler when he was at Harrow."

When he was staying at Brighton with the Prince of Wales in the autumn of 1805, he spoke of his unhappiness to Thomas Creevey, who was also a guest at the Pavilion:

[1]Mrs. Sheridan to Whyte, February 25th, 1762. *Miscellanea Nova*, 104.

"He was at school at Harrow, and, as he told me, never had any scholastic fame while he was there, nor did he appear to have formed any friendships there. He said he was a very low-spirited boy, much given to crying when alone; and he attributed this very much to being neglected by his father, to his being left without money, and often not taken home at the regular holidays."[1]

Lord Holland in his *Further Memoirs of the Whig Party* spoke of "the irregularities and mortifications of his early life and education"—

"The salary for Richard Brinsley's education at Harrow, where he had been left, was irregularly paid. He was slighted by the masters and tormented by the boys, as a poor player's son. I have heard him relate, with tears in his eyes, that he never met with kindness at school but from Dr. Parr." Lord Holland added "He assured me, at the same time, that his treatment had created in his mind such an aversion for the stage, that he had never even seen a play when he wrote *The Duenna*; that he engaged in that work from absolute indigence; and that, throughout his life, he had never seen a representation from beginning to end, except of his own pieces at rehearsals."[2]

Lord Holland found this incredible, or at least exaggerated, but even about 1809, when he saw his own *Rivals* acted at the Marquis of Abercorn's private theatre, Sheridan told his wife that he did not remember ever previously sitting out any play in his whole life. These were Sheridan's impressions of Harrow, and, psychologically, they are of much greater importance than the recollections of other people, written after his death.

2

The main source of information is Dr. Samuel Parr, who was at Harrow for only two years of Richard's seven, the first

---

[1]*The Creevey Papers,* 53-54.   [2]Holland, *Further Memoirs,* 1816, 240-241.

as head boy, and the last as an assistant master. He was closely allied to Sheridan in the later years, for it was to him at Hatton in Warwickshire, that Sheridan sent his Tom to school, and he was a great Whig. Parr wrote several letters to Thomas Moore and others, confessing, however, that "there was little in his boyhood worth communication: he never reached the Sixth Form, and was inferior to many of his schoolfellows in the ordinary business of a school." As master, however, Parr had little or no knowledge of Sheridan, except that in taking his form for a brief spell in the absence of Dr. Robert Sumner, the headmaster, he found him very defective in Greek Grammar, and harassed him into preparing his lessons:

> "But you will take notice that he did not incur any corporal punishment for his idleness: his industry was just sufficient to protect him from disgrace. All the while Sumner and I saw in him vestiges of a superior intellect. His eye, his countenance, his general manner, were striking. His answers to any common question were prompt and acute. We knew the esteem, and even admiration, which somehow or other all his school-fellows felt for him. He was mischievous enough, but his pranks were accompanied by a sort of vivacity and cheerfulness, which delighted Sumner and myself. I had much talk with him about his apple-loft, for the supply of which all the gardens in the neighbourhood were taxed, and some of the lower boys were employed to furnish it. I threatened, but without asperity, to trace the depredators through his associates up to their leader. He with perfect good-humour set me at defiance, and I never could bring the charge home to him. All boys and masters were pleased with him."[1]

But these reminiscences, in Parr's vein of ponderous triviality, are hardly to be taken seriously. Fifty years had passed, and Parr was anxious to associate his memory with that of a great man. In the same way, when invited to supply an epitaph for a memorial to Thomas Sheridan, Parr added among his praises,

[1]Moore, 6.

"He had been the school-fellow, and was through life the companion, of the amiable Archbishop Markham. He was the friend of the learned Dr. Sumner of Harrow School, and the *well-known Dr. Parr.*"

Alicia Lefanu, Sheridan's niece, gave a roseate account of the Harrow days. According to this, he was beloved by masters, school-fellows, and acquaintances. His vacations were spent with a friend of his father's, named Aikenhead, "a splendid West Indian," "an amateur of fashion in the literary and theatrical history of the day," who owned a villa at Richmond and a house in London. The care of his pecuniary concerns devolved upon his maternal uncle, Richard Chamberlaine,[1] who, of course, "allowed him every reasonable indulgence." Dr. Sumner, the headmaster, his father's friend, was ever remembered by Sheridan with sentiments of the highest gratitude, regard and veneration, and he bewailed his early death with the affection he owed to a second parent.

It is possible, and indeed likely, that it was his earlier years at Harrow that Sheridan remembered so bitterly. It is strange that none of these reminiscences mention his cousin William Chamberlaine, a year his junior, who entered Harrow in 1764, and afterwards followed his uncle Richard's profession of surgeon and apothecary in London.[2]

The two letters cited as written at Harrow by Sheridan to

[1]Of Sheridan's uncle little is known. Lefanu, 3, says that he was educated for a surgeon, and served in that capacity on board a man-of-war: on the death of his uncle, Solomon Whyte, Deputy Governor of Birmingham Tower, he "inherited a considerable estate in County Longford," and dying without children, this estate "devolved upon Charles Sheridan" as heir-at-law. Samuel Whyte, *Miscellanea Nova*, 51, calls him "a surgeon eminent in his profession, for many a long year the Oracle of the Grecian coffee-house, and the delight of the young Templars, particularly from Ireland." His name not being found in Murray's *Medical Registers* for 1779, and 1780, he was then presumably dead. *The Gentleman's Magazine* for 1784 says briefly: "Died, March 17. Mrs. Chamberlaine widow of R. C. Esq., lately deceased" which may refer to him.

[2]According to *A Biographical Dictionary of Living Authors*, 1816, William Chamberlaine, born at Dublin in 1752, entered Harrow School in 1764, finishing his education at Trinity College, Dublin. After serving his apprenticeship to surgery, he resided for nine years in Jamaica, and in 1784 settled in London as an apothecary and surgeon. The *Alumni Dublinenses* records his entry "age nineteen," at Trinity in 1774; his B.A., was not taken until 1783. He published a medical treatise in London in 1784, and became Secretary to the Medical Society. He died in London on August 3rd, 1822, "aged 75."

this uncle are curious productions: the first, dated March 2nd, 1765, begins:—

"Dear Uncle, As it is not more than three weeks to the holydays, I should be greatly obliged to you, if you could get me some new cloaths as soon as possible, for those which I have at present are very bad and I have no others; I am almost ashamed to wear them on a sunday. I fancy I shall spend my holydays again at Harrow, for I have not seen nor heard from Mr. Akenhead since August. Though I had rather stay at Harrow than go to Richmond. Mr. Somner asked me the other day if I had heard lately from my brother and says he has not heard from them this long time."[1]

In the second, written a year later, this Harrow boy of fourteen, who never to the end of his life learned to spell, regrets the "mellancholly knews" of his poor mother's death, and desires his uncle to order him a suit of black, "a new hat with crape, black stockins and buckles."

The Duke of Grafton, who was born in 1760, told Moore that in 1818 he, "had succeeded Sheridan within a few years at Harrow, where he found his name preserved very affectionately, his poems repeated, and a room called after his name."[2]

3

Sheridan left school with "small Latin and less Greek." To the end of his days, he could grace an oration with some passage from a Greek or Roman poet, and he delighted to be regarded as a classical scholar. John Graham noted that "he certainly had a knowledge of the Greek tongue, although it has been said he never rose higher than the Fourth Form at Harrow School. He always maintained that Fox was a better scholar than Pitt."

One of the stories current after his death was that Lord Belgrave, afterwards Earl Grosvenor, once ended a speech in the House of Commons, with a quotation from *Demosthenes*.

[1] Rae, I, 72.   [2] Moore, *Journal*, II, 148.

Sheridan, in reply, pointed out that while the quotation was applicable so far as it went, the noble Lord had omitted to complete it. If he had continued the passage a little further, he would have seen that it applied the other way. Sheridan then spouted something, *ore rotundo*, which had all the *ais*, *ois*, *ous*, *ton* and *tous*, that give the world the assurance of a Greek quotation. Thereupon Lord Belgrave, very promptly and handsomely complimented him on his readiness of recollection, and admitted that this continuation had the force which Sheridan ascribed to it. At the breaking up of the House, Fox asked, "Sheridan, how came you to be so ready with that passage? It certainly is as you say, but I was not aware of it before you quoted it."[1] It is, of course, quite absurd to think that Charles Fox would have been taken in by bogus Greek; Sheridan's correction, which occurred during a debate on the Regency Bill, in 1789, was a proper one, and from that day he never lost an opportunity of making fun of Lord Belgrave's Greek. As in 1799, Belgrave complained that some petition had no weight because schoolboys had been forced to sign it, "a most iniquitous proceeding."—"Monstrous," replied Sheridan, "to take them from learning their Greek." He was always intensely proud of his victory over Lord Belgrave, and, as Lady Holland said, reminded the House of it on every opportunity.

At Harrow he cultivated the acquaintance of Nathaniel Brassey Halhed, whom he joined in translating some lyrics from Theocritus, and afterwards in publishing a poetical paraphrase of the *Love Epistles of Aristænetus*, but Halhed was an accomplished scholar, and a natural linguist who gained great distinction by his studies in the Oriental tongues. He sent his translation complete to Sheridan, who had to purchase a Greek grammar before he could venture upon the subject, so that he appears to have done little more than modify a few passages: certainly the fundamental scholarship was Halhed's.

4

Harrow, unlike Westminster, had an aversion for play-acting.

[1] *Sheridaniana*, 290–1.

It was interdicted in 1752 by an ordinance of the Governors; for some years previously it had been the annual custom to perform a play for three nights before the Christmas holidays, the piece being selected by the headmaster, Dr. Thackeray. In 1752, Tate Wilkinson, then thirteen, acted Lady Townley in *The Provoked Husband* and Romeo in *Romeo and Juliet*, with such success that the whole neighbourhood found it a topic of conversation. The Governors, alarmed that the school might gain a reputation for "breeding up actors in lieu of scholars," abolished the annual performances, and their prohibition was still active and unbroken forty years later, when Tate Wilkinson wrote his *Memoirs*.[1]

The theatrical habits had formerly been borrowed from John Rich, of Covent Garden Theatre, but when the declamations on Speech Day were instituted, in 1772, though scenes from English plays were added, it was enacted that the performers wore ordinary full dress of the day, and not theatrical costume.

In Sheridan's time at Harrow the great event was the annual archery contest. In 1731 it was described as an "ancient custom" in *The Gentleman's Magazine*, which declared that "the diversion was the gift of John Lyon, Esq., the Founder of the School, a Silver Arrow, value three pounds, being shot for by six youths of the Free School, in archery habits." These dresses singularly graceful and elaborate, were of satin, white, green, or red, fringed with silk and decked with spangles, with green silk sashes and caps. Alicia Lefanu said that Sheridan wished to enter for the shooting, but his uncle Richard prohibited him on account of the expense of the uniform. He was, however, required on that occasion to deliver an oration, which was supposed to be spoken by a military commander of ancient Greece. Sheridan, considering that this necessitated a military uniform, ordered the complete regimentals of scarlet and gold as worn by an English general in the army of King George the Third, in which costume he delivered his oration with great effect. When Dr. Chamberlaine received the tailor's bill, he severely remonstrated with Sheridan upon this unexpected piece of

[1] Tate Wilkinson, *Memoirs of his Own Life*, Dublin (1791), I, 44-5.

extravagance: to which his nephew replied that "as the speech was to be delivered in a martial character, he did not think the effect would have been complete without an appropriate dress; indeed, so deeply was he himself impressed with that feeling, that he was sure if he had not been properly habited, he could not have delivered a word of the oration."

Alicia Lefanu regarded this as a pleasant example of Sheridan's early propensity for hoaxing, but the hoax was in the story, not in the event. It is quite unlikely that, if any such oration had been delivered, it would have been assigned to a youth in the Fourth or Fifth Form, especially one who was notoriously defective in Greek grammar. There was, moreover, no Speech Day at Harrow until 1772, when Benjamin Heath, who followed Robert Sumner as headmaster, decided to abolish the shootings, "on account of the number of idle and dissolute people who journeyed from London to see it, and of the number of exemptions from the regular business of the school, which were claimed as a right, and not as a privilege by those who were practising as competitors for the prize." Instead of this contest, Heath instituted the practice of declamations. Besides, expensive as an archer's habit must have been, it was much less so than that of an English General, which no tailor would have made to the order of a sixteen-year-old boy.

5

Another Sheridan legend appeared in the Life which was prefixed to an undated and unauthorized collection of *Sheridan's Works* published in London about 1800. In this he figures as the leader of a rebellion at Harrow School, where Dr. Parr

"continued assistant until the death of Dr. Sumner, which happened about the year 1767. He was not then above twenty-one, which was the main objection to his being appointed the principal master. The boys, knowing him to be a most excellent scholar, were extremely desirous he should be the supreme teacher. Mr. Parr was a candidate, but was rejected on account of his youth. He accordingly resigned

C

his subordinate situation, and set up a private academy at
Stanmore, in the county of Middlesex. Meanwhile his disappointment at Harrow was so severely resented by his
friends and admirers the scholars, that a rebellion broke out
on the occasion. In this disturbance young Sheridan took a
very active part, and was indeed one of the leaders. Richard
was now taken away from that school, and sent to his friend
Mr. Parr's seminary, where he remained until he became a
very thorough classical scholar."

The whole story is nonsense, for Dr. Sumner did not die till
two years after Sheridan had left the school, and whatever was
the extent of this "rebellion" Sheridan had no part in it, and
was certainly never a pupil at Stanmore.[1]

Sheridan remained at Harrow till 1768, or 1769, being removed "in his seventeenth year."

His father, Thomas, was not only an actor; he was an edu-
cationist, strongly opposed to the methods of teaching in
vogue, and regarding the practice of oratory as a necessary preparation for the millennium. He was a Master of Arts of three
universities; he had graduated at Trinity College, Dublin, and
was admitted by incorporation to his degree at Oxford and
Cambridge; at Glasgow he was made a Freeman of the City.
At the end of 1768, he returned from France to England and
published "A Plan of Education for the Nobility and Gentry of
Great Britain," which was "most humbly ascribed to the Father
of his People," King George the Third. He contended that the
sole end of education as then practised was to make good Latin
and Greek scholars, to the neglect of those things which contribute most to public and private prosperity, "that is to say,
religion, morality and the English language." In his Dedication to the King, he offered to devote the remainder of his
life to conducting an academy, provided he was allowed an

---

[1]Sheridan sent neither of his sons to Harrow: Tom, the elder, he put under the
tuition of Parr at Hatton in Warwickshire; and Charles, the younger, he sent to Winchester. In 1795, after dining with the headmaster of Winchester, he persuaded the
Prince of Wales to offer a gold medal for declamation. Sichel (1, 260) says that through
Sheridan's influence, William Linley entered Harrow, but it was St. Paul's.

appointment equal to what he was then able to make in less laborious pursuits—that is, he was willing to give up acting, providing his pension was increased. But the "Father of his People" was not moved by his loyal addresses, which, by the way, were in the main, very sensible, and much in advance of their time.

With these theories, he could not do otherwise than take Richard away from Harrow, to live with him first at Chelsea, and afterwards in Frith Street, Soho, where they were joined by Charles and his two sisters. Thomas proceeded to educate his two sons according to his own oratorical system, giving them daily instruction in his favourite subjects, and he also engaged a tutor, Lewis Ker, a physician incapacitated from following his own profession, who instructed Richard in mathematics, and Charles in Latin. Again, in exchange for the lessons that the elder Sheridan gave Henry Angelo, who had recently left Eton, Charles and Richard both became pupils in Angelo's riding and fencing academy in Soho. Dr. Parr attributed all Richard's infirmities in his later life to these undisciplined years, and this desultory education "to the scanty and precarious allowance from his father, the want of a regular plan in some profession, and above all, the act of throwing him upon the town when he ought to have been pursuing his studies at the University."

CHAPTER THE THIRD

The Maid of Bath

> But bright Cecilia raised the Wonder higher,
> When to her vocal organ breath was given.
> An Angel heard, and straight appeared
> Mistaking earth for Heaven.
>> Dryden, *Ode upon St. Cecilia's Day.*

I

THOMAS SHERIDAN moved to Bath at the close of 1770 for the purpose of establishing an Academy of Oratory, and began by giving a series of Attic Entertainments, when his lecturing and declamation was diversified by the singing of Elizabeth Linley, then a beautiful girl of sixteen. In spite of her youth, she had a voice of "angelic" purity; at the first of these entertainments on November 24th she sang such ballads as "Black-Ey'd Susan" and "Eileen Aroon," while he followed with his celebrated recitation of the "Ode Upon St. Cecilia's Day." From that time onward, Elizabeth Linley was known as "St. Cecilia." Nine Attic Entertainments were given in the next two months, after which Mr. Sheridan's public performances in Bath were discontinued.

Elizabeth Ann Linley, the second of twelve children of Thomas Linley, was baptized at St. Michael's, Bath, on September 25th, 1754. She was born at a small house in Abbey Square, shortly before her parents removed to 5 Pierpont Street, which was the birthplace of her brothers and sisters, who were baptized in the parish church of St. James's. Her father, born at Badminton in 1733, was the son of a carpenter and builder who removed to Bath about 1744. He became a pupil of Thomas Chilcot, the organist of Bath Abbey, and studied music in London under Paradisi. By 1764 when Thomas Sheridan first lectured on oratory at Bath and Bristol, Linley was a musician of high repute, and Mrs. Sheridan then took lessons in singing from him, and "the peculiar expression and pathos that marked the Linley and Jackson school opened a new world of harmony to her senses."[1]

Of all his pupils, his daughters were his finest singers. At the age of eleven, Mary Linley, a younger daughter, had played little Sally Cross in Colman's *Man and Wife, or, The Stratford Jubilee* at Covent Garden in 1769. Elizabeth is believed to have been the Singing Fairy in a masque called *The Fairy Favour*, by Thomas Hull, which was performed with music by her father, at Covent Garden in 1769 "before Their Majesties" and for the especial delight of the Prince of Wales, a boy of twelve.[2] Both sisters afterwards attended a boarding school at Bristol, near Brandon Hill and the Clifton Downs.

The Linleys became the friends of the Sheridans. In December 1770 Mr. Sheridan notified through *The Bath Chronicle* that he had established "an Academy for the regular instruction of Young Gentlemen in the art of reading and reciting and grammatical knowledge of the English tongue," and was ready "to receive the commands of any ladies and gentlemen at Bowers'" in Kingsmead Street." They lodged therefore, with William Bowers, who occupied a small house in Kingsmead Street, in the part called shortly afterwards New King Street.

In the conduct of the academy, Thomas was to be assisted by his two sons, Charles, aged twenty, and Richard, aged nineteen. He was accompanied by his two daughters, Alicia, or Lissy, then seventeen, and Elizabeth or Betsy, then thirteen. How many pupils entered the academy is not known; thirty years afterwards Richard Sheridan told Creevy that the undertaking, in which he was to be rhetorical usher, was "speedily laughed off the stage." At all events, in October 1771 Thomas Sheridan was once more acting in Dublin, and the only pupil whose name survives is George Grenville, afterwards Marquis of Buckingham.

[1] Lefanu, 246.   [2] Sichel, I, 191, cf. *London Magazine*, 1767 and 1769.

2

In November 1770, Elizabeth Linley, then just seventeen, went to Oxford for the Music Meeting, and Nathaniel Halhed wrote Sheridan: "I have just been to hear Miss Linley rehearse. I am petrified; my very faculties are annihilated with wonder. My conception could not form such a power of voice—such a melody—such a soft, yet so audible a tone." She had carried to him from Sheridan a "packet by the fairest hands that ever inspired a harpsichord with sentiment and feelings." He became her adorer, though he wrote a few days later, "I dare not examine too closely whether I am in love with her or not."

This was in reply to Sheridan, who had enquired about the young men who were supposed to be in love with her at Oxford—Norris the singer, James Watts of Combe Abbey, a wealthy young landowner in Warwickshire, and Sir Thomas Clarges. Of them, Halhed wrote Sheridan, "Norris the singer is here, *qui est, ut ita dicam, vox et præterea Nihil*, for I own I see no other accomplishment in him. His behaviour I think low, and his affectation abominable, but the ladies may see with other eyes. As for my friend Watts, he is a gentleman-commoner worth money, but I need not fear him. The animal is quite tame, and a very pigeon in gall: indeed, in Oxford he sleeps away most of his time, and he is not very well furnished with that commodity so necessary among the ladies called small talk. I believe Fame has for once spoken truth in saying he admires Miss Linley."

Whether James Watts proposed marriage to her or not, on December 18th, when Elizabeth had returned to Bath, Halhed wrote from Oxford to Sheridan, saying, "it is currently reported here that Miss has gone to Scotland with a young man of £3,000 per annum; you never saw such faces as we have here about it, but I fancy it is only Watts's story a little exaggerated." The news must have reached Oxford that Elizabeth was cancelling her engagements, as she was about to be married.

But her betrothal was not to a young man of Oxford: it was to an old Wiltshire squire, of sixty years of age, Walter Long. He is described in contemporary accounts as a man of vast estates and ancient lineage, which he was; and, as a baronet, which he was not. Until the age of thirty he had lived in humble circumstances with his father, Thomas Long of Rowdon, who had then inherited unexpectedly the estates of a distant relation, Sir Walter Long of Whaddon, the last baronet of a family who had for generations been landowners in Wiltshire.

His estates were valued at a quarter of a million pounds, but the habits of his early years clung to him, and he was mean, ill-bred, and avaricious. Nevertheless, he paid his court to Miss Linley, who was the indentured apprentice of her father, according to the custom of the time. Under pressure of her friends, she consented to the marriage, and in turn he agreed to pay her father one thousand pounds in compensation for the loss of her services, and she at once ceased to sing in public.

3

Just before the marriage was to take place, Squire Long broke off the match. Thomas Linley, incensed at his conduct, demanded compensation for the loss of his daughter's services, and also for breach of promise. Long firmly refused. According to the version of the story by Samuel Foote, who was staying in Bath at the time, he had broken the engagement because she had refused to pass the night at his lodgings before marriage. Therefore "Aristophanes" determined to stage the events as a play, in order to expose on the stage Long's "avarice, cunning, and folly."

This play has been brushed aside as a mere invention by Foote, but this ignores the fact that it had the support of Garrick and Cumberland, whose testimony is not lightly to be disregarded. Richard Cumberland, a man of high principles, wrote the Epilogue declaring:—

> "Ask us 'Why bring a private cause to view?'
> We answer, with a sigh,—because 'tis true.
> For tho' invention is our poet's trade
> Here he but copies parts which others play'd."

Again, David Garrick wrote the Prologue, which compared

Foote to Jack the Giant-Killer, and Long to a monster who sought to devour a young and tender virgin :—

"Tally-ho!—a rank old *fox* we now pursue,
So strong the scent, you'll run him full in view:
If we can't kill such *brutes* in human shape,
Let's fright 'em, that your *chickens* may escape:
Rouse 'em, when o'er their tender prey they're grumbling,
And rub their gums at least to mar their mumbling."

Foote staged the play under the title of *The Maid of Bath* at the Haymarket Theatre, with Elizabeth Linley represented as Kitty Linnet and Walter Long as Solomon Flint. Accepting it in the main as a truthful delineation of the affair; the passages of relevance will give the story better than any paraphrase.

At the Linnets' house in Bath lodges Sir Christopher Cripple, a neighbouring landowner—

"The rake of sixty, crippled hand and knee
Who sins on claret, and repents on tea."

He denounces his co-eval Master Solomon Flint, as a "fusty, shabby, shuffling, money-loving, water-drinking, mirth-marring, amorous old hunks." Sir Christopher, with Major Racket, a young macaroni officer, and the other members of the Claret Club at the Bear Inn, forms a plot to frighten old Flint by describing what happens to old men who marry young girls— continual quarrels, squandered fortunes, broken health. At last, Flint, alarmed by these terrible pictures, says that he will go and break matters off that very minute. He consults Billy Button, the tailor:—

Flint. And yet, Button, she is a vast pretty girl—I should be heartily sorry to lose her—dost think one could not get her on easier terms than on marriage?
Button. It is but trying, however.
Flint. To tell truth, Billy, I have always had that in my head; and, at all events, I have thought of a project that will answer my purpose.

Button. Ay, Squire, what is it?

Flint. No matter—And, do you hear, Billy? should I get her consent, if you will take her off my hands, and marry her when I begin to grow tired, I'll settle ten pounds a year upon you, for both your lives.

Though it is late at night, he stumps off to Linnet's, and demands to see Kitty. He tells her that while he belongs to one of the most ancient families in the country round, and is matched by few people in those parts for money and lands— but, not to speak in a disparaging way, her friends are low folks, and her fortune just nothing:—

Miss Linnet. True, Sir; but this is no new discovery, you have known this——

Flint. Hear me out. Now, as I bring all these good things on my side, and you have nothing to give me in return but your love, I ought to be pretty sure of the possession of that.

Miss Linnet. I hope the properly discharging all the duties of that condition, which I am shortly to owe to your favour, will give you convincing proofs of my gratitude.

Flint. Your gratitude, Miss!—but we talk of your love! And of that I must have plain and positive proofs.

Miss Linnet. Proofs! of what kind?

Flint. To steal away directly with me to my lodgings——

Miss Linnet. Your lodgings!

Flint. There pass the night, and in the morning, the very minute we rise, we will march away to the Abbey.

Miss Linnet. Sir!

Flint. In short, Miss, I must have this token of love, or not a syllable more of the marriage.

Miss Linnet. Give me patience!

Kitty Linnet concludes her denunciation:—

Miss Linnet. You have wealth, I confess; but where could have been the advantage to me, as a reward for becoming your drudge? I might perhaps have received a scanty subsistence, for I can hardly suppose you would grant the free use of that to your wife, which your meanness has deny'd to yourself.

Flint. So, so, so! By and by she will alarm the whole house!

Miss Linnet. The whole house? the whole town shall be told! Sure the greatest misfortune that Poverty brings in its train, is the subjecting us to the insults of wretches like this, who have no other merit but that their riches bestow on them.

Flint. What a damnable vixen!

Miss Linnet. Go, sir, leave the house!

When her friends enter at the sound of the dispute, she exposes his proposal to them—her mother, the Scots Lady Catherine Coldstream, Billy Button the tailor, Sir Christopher and Major Racket. Flint stoutly persists that on no condition will he marry her:—

Lady Catherine. Well, but Maister Flint, are you willing to make Miss a pecuniary acknowledgement for the damage?

Flint. I have done her no damage, and I'll make no reparation.

Major Rackit. Twelve honest men of your country may happen to differ in judgment.

Flint. Let her try, if she will——

Sir Christopher. And I promise you she shan't be to seek for the means.

Lady Catherine. If you be nae afraid o' the laws, ha you nae sense o' shame?

Rackit. He sense of shame?

Lady Catherine. Gad's wull, it shall cum to the proof; you mun ken, good folk, at Edinburgh last winter, I got acquainted with Maister Foote the play-actor—I will get him to bring the filthy loon on the stage——

Sir Christopher. And expose him to the contempt of the world; he richly deserves it.

Flint. Ay, he may write, you may rail, and the people may

hiss, and what care I? I have that at home that will keep up my spirits——

Lady Catherine. At home?

Rackit. The wretch means his money.

Flint. And what better friend can any man have? Tell me the place where its influence failed? Ask that gentleman how he got his cockade. Money! I know its worth, and therefore can't too carefully keep it. At this instant I have a proof of its value; it enables me to laugh at that squeamish impertinent girl, and despise the weak efforts of your impotent malice —Call me forth to your courts when you please, that will procure me able defenders; and good witnesses too, if they are wanted.

Squire Flint then takes his departure, but Sir Christopher says to Major Racket, who would have been one of her suitors if she had possessed any fortune—

"I don't think I can better begin my plan of reforming than by a compliment paid to her virtue—then take her, and with her two thousand guineas in hand."

But even this dowry does not tempt her; since Major Racket has already carried away from Bath a milliner's apprentice, Patty Prim from the Grove. Miss Linnet prefers to "remain in her own station," with "public protection for her talents."

4

The identity of the chief characters was instantly announced by the periodicals, for Foote left no doubt as to whom he had satirized. While his opponents censured its personality, and complained against the Lord Chamberlain giving his licence for the comedy, such papers as *The London Magazine* soberly defended it, holding that it was the proper province of the dramatic satirist to hold a poetical Court of Justice for the punishment of profligacy. But a year later, in *An Account of the Maid of Bath*, the same paper attributed the termination of the engagement to Elizabeth herself:

"The necessary preparations for the celebration of the nuptials were making, and the expected day almost arrived, when an unexpected accident happened; it was, the absolute refusal of the lady to consent to the match. The thought of being dragged from the kind eye of the public, who had so often caressed and applauded her, and of resigning all her hopes, her pleasures, to be eternally imprisoned in an obscure country-house—nothing but baleful yew-trees and dreary avenues—without; nothing but an old husband—within—these thoughts were insupportable, and she told her father so; and added, with a truly English spirit, 'that if she married at all, she would marry only to be *free*.' This stroke fell upon him like thunder; it overturned the gaudy structure which ambition had raised in his imagination, and with it fell all his hopes. She was now too resolute to be compelled, and his prudence therefore advised him to 'make the best of a bad bargain.'

"In the matrimonial treaties between the lover and the father it had been settled, that, as Miss L. was an apprentice to her father, her lover should pay the trifling sum of one thousand pounds, as a compensation for the loss her father should sustain by resigning the remainder of her time. Now, though the match was entirely broke off, the prudent old man still insisted that this part of the treaty should be fulfilled, because his daughter had not been allowed to appear in public since her connections with Mr. L-ng began—a circumstance by which he was considerably a loser. Mr. L-ng refused to acquiesce, and the matter was finally left to the discussion of certain friends, who adjudged that the money should be paid to the young lady, and placed in trust in her father's hands till she arrived at age. Matters being thus settled, Miss L. did not appear in public during some months after; her father's income felt the defection, and he obliged her to resume her profession."

Although this account agrees with Mrs. Henry Lefanu's, in 1816, it is more likely that Foote's presentation of Long's character, supported as it was by Cumberland and Garrick is the truer one. He was frightened into the payment of compensation, for *Lloyd's Evening Post* of July 29th announced: "Miss L . . . of Bath has commenced an action for damages against Mr. . . . , as he has also against Mr. Foote." A little later the same paper recorded that the suit had been withdrawn on his giving Linley £3,000 and Elizabeth jewels to the value of £1,000 besides other valuable presents.[1]

5

But Long's attempt to "undermine the virtue" of Elizabeth was not an isolated attack. At this period, it was assumed that a woman who sang or acted in public was a purchasable beauty, and it was taken as a matter of course that she should be exposed to the solicitation of any man who had enough wealth to propose a settlement. In the same issue that announced her marriage to Sheridan, *The Bath Chronicle* published two letters "confidently said" to have passed between Elizabeth Linley and Lord Grosvenor. He was a rake of forty who in 1764 had married Henrietta Vernon, and in 1770 had prosecuted the Duke of Cumberland, the King's brother, for *crim. con.* with his wife, obtaining ten thousand pounds damages. Nevertheless, he either could not or would not divorce her. His letter was given as:—

"ADORABLE CREATURE,

"Permit me to assure you in the most tender and affectionate manner that the united force of your charms and qualifications have made so complete a prisoner of my heart that I despair of its being set at liberty but through your means.

"Under this situation I have it ever to lament that the laws will not permit me to offer you my hand. Here I cannot assist fate; but what I can dispose of, my *heart* and my *fortune*, are entirely at your devotion, thinking myself the happiest of mankind should either be acceptable.

[1]M. M. Belden, *Samuel Foote*, 138, 145.

"Lady A—— who will deliver this and who obligingly vouchsafes to be my mediator, will, I flatter myself, urge the sincerity of my heart on this occasion so as to obtain a permission for me to throw myself at your feet to-morrow evening. In momentary expectation of which
I am your devoted admirer,
"G——R."

"Wednesday evening, 4 o'clock."

Her reply is:—

"My Lord,
"Lest my silence should bear the most distant interpretation of listening to your proposals, I condescend to answer your infamous letter. You lament the laws will not permit you to offer me your hand. I lament it too, my lord, but on a different principle—to convince your dissipated heart that I have a soul capable of *refusing* a coronet when the owner is not the object of my affections—despising it when the offer of an unworthy possessor.

"The reception your *honourable* messenger met with in the execution of her embassy saves me the trouble of replying to the other parts of your letter, and (if you have any feelings left) will explain to you the *baseness* as well as the *inefficacy* of your design.
"L——Y."[1]

This correspondence was introduced thus:

"The following letters are confidently said to have passed between Lord G——r and the celebrated English syren Miss L——y. I send them to you for publication not with any view to increase the volume of literary scandal which I am sorry to say at present needs no assistance, but with the more laudable intent of setting example for our modern belles by holding out the character of a young woman who, notwithstanding the solicitations of her profession and the

---

[1] *The Bath Chronicle*, April 15th, 1773.

flattering example of higher ranks, has added *incorruptible virtue* to a number of the most elegant qualifications.

"HORATIO."

"Grosvenor Square."

Moore, who cited only the preamble, describes the "correspondence," without giving any reasons, as "pretty evidently a fabrication;" the letters may, nevertheless, be genuine.[1] He added that they "yet prove the high opinion that was entertained of her character," but they prove equally the type of insolent solicitations to which her profession exposed her. Whoever wrote this letter, it expressed the views which were held by many men of the period—among them, it is said, Captain Thomas Mathews. The account in *The London Magazine* of 1772, in alluding to the suitors of the Maid of Bath, however, asserted:

> "Among the earliest of these attendants of Miss L. was Mr. M—ws, a circumstance which was far from being favourable to her fame, for this gentleman was at the time married, and whether he admired her for her personal or professional perfections, he was her constant attendant. The censorious, as usual, took the alarm, and became very anxious for her virtue, without knowing whether it was in danger."

6

Thomas Mathews is the villain of the Sheridan romance, against whom have been made all sorts of accusations—that he posed as "a gay bachelor," or was indeed unmarried when first he paid attentions to Elizabeth; that he was a sham captain; that he was a coward who tried by every means in his power to avoid a duel with Sheridan; that his conduct exposed him to universal execration till public opinion drove him from Bath.

The general opinion that he was the original of Major

---

[1] Sichel (I, 433) decides that they are genuine because in "Miss Linley's dignified reply" he finds "traces of her husband's style." Clementina Black in *The Linley's of Bath* suggests that they were sent by Sheridan, who called himself Horatio in his poem *The Grotto*.

Racket in *The Maid of Bath* is absurd. They had nothing in common but a military title; the one essential of Racket's dramatic importance is that he is a bachelor and a suitor in marriage of Kitty Linnet. It was perfectly known in Bath that Mathews was married, and had been for seven years, and *The London Magazine* for November 1763 testifies among its marriages:

> "Lately, Thomas Mathews Esq; grandson of the late brave Admiral, to Miss Diana Jones"

of Fonmon Castle in Glamorganshire. In October 1770 *The Bath Chronicle* listed among the arrivals in the city "Mr. and Mrs. Mathews." Therefore he could not have posed as a bachelor, and whatever attentions he paid to Elizabeth Linley, they were paid as a married man.

Thomas Mathews was the son of Major Thomas Mathews, who died in 1768, and the grandson of Admiral Thomas Mathews of Llandaff Court. Commissioned as ensign in the 86th Foot in 1762, he exchanged into the 54th Foot in 1766; a general demobilization followed in 1767, when his name does not appear in the Army List. Possibly he had not purchased his promotion, and whether "Captain" was a courtesy title on retirement, or (as I think) a rank in the county militia, he was generally known by it in military circles.

"He was a man of elegant exterior, kindly disposition, lively manners, agreeable conversation, and by no means deficient in intellectual power" wrote Sigmond in 1848, on the authority of "many now living in Bath" who had heard Mathews give a consistent narrative of his relations with Sheridan which was largely at variance with the facts stated by Moore. Unfortunately, however, Sigmond's account incorporated a forged narrative, "written by Miss Linley herself to Miss Sanders," which makes Mathews a very theatrical villain. Sigmond certainly interpolated "if that letter be genuine," and neglected to say whether it was his own supposition or part of this consistent narrative which declared that Mathews became her professional admirer, "led away by the opinion that prevailed at that time that every woman who came prominently before the public was open to the attention of any man of sufficient fortune to make a handsome settlement."

However it was, Sheridan joined those who censured Elizabeth for permitting the attentions of Mathews, and persuaded her that the only way to avoid such importunities was to leave her profession, break all the contracts her father had made for her, and enter a French convent which accepted Protestant boarders. Accordingly, she disappeared with him, and *The London Chronicle* of March 24th said:

"Bath. 23rd March. On Wednesday, the eldest Miss Linley of this city, justly celebrated for her musical abilities, set off with Mr. Sheridan, jun., on a matrimonial excursion to Scotland."

D

CHAPTER THE FOURTH
Rare Doings at Bath

Sir Benjamin. Then, madam, they began to fight with swords.
Crabtree. With pistols, nephew—pistols. I have it from undoubted
      authority.

The School for Scandal.

I

ABOUT 1817, forty-five years after the event, a long
and romantic account of the elopement to France, the
clandestine marriage, and the duel with Mathews was
written for Thomas Moore by Sheridan's younger sister, Mrs.
Henry Lefanu. She was then living again in Bath, but her recollections[1] contain many errors of fact. She says that "Major"
Mathews persecuted Elizabeth Linley, who was afraid to
speak to her father, but she

> "was at length induced to consult Richard Sheridan, whose
> intimacy with Major Mathews at the time, she thought,
> might warrant his interference. Her father, she was certain,
> would at the risk of ruin to himself and his family have
> called the Major to account, if she ventured to consult him.
> R. B. Sheridan sounded Mathews on the subject, and at
> length prevailed on him to give up the pursuit.
>   "Miss Linley, now completely disgusted with a profes-
> sion she never liked, conceived the idea of retiring to a Con-
> vent in France till she came of age, meaning to indemnify
> her father by giving up a part of the money settled upon her
> by Long. She advised with her young friend Sheridan on the

[1]The quotations are from the original MS.: Rae, I, 165–8. Moore paraphrased
this with corrections.

subject, and he communicated the scheme to his elder sister, who, thinking it meritorious to assist a young person situated as Miss Linley was in getting out of the difficulties that surrounded her, offered to give her letters of introduction to some ladies she had known in France, where she had resided some years, and Sheridan offered to be her conductor to St. Quentin, where these friends lived. The arranging the whole plan of course produced frequent meetings between the young couple, and tho' Sheridan was then strongly attached to Miss Linley, he claimed only the title of friend, and his sister had no idea that the projected excursion was to lead to an immediate marriage.

"At length they fixed on an evening when Mr. Linley, his eldest son, and Miss M. Linley were engaged at the Concert (Miss Linley being excused on the plea of illness)."

What concert? *The Bath Chronicle* shows that Thomas Linley had arranged the performance of three Oratorios at Bath for the Lent of 1772, beginning with *Judas Maccabaeus* on April 3rd, "the vocal parts by the Misses Linley." An advertisement in these terms was printed in *The Bath Chronicle* for March 12th and March 19th, but on March 26th Elizabeth's name was withdrawn, and only Mary's remained. It is obvious that no public performance by the Linleys was given on March 18th, and it is possible that Mrs. Henry Lefanu was confusing them with some rehearsals for the oratorios, whose production was jeopardized by Elizabeth's elopement.

Mrs. Henry Lefanu continued:

"Sheridan brought a sedan-chair to Mr. Linley's house in the Crescent, in which he had Miss Linley conveyed to a postchaise that was waiting for them on the London Road. A woman was in the chaise who had been hired by Sheridan to accompany them on this extraordinary elopement. They reached London early the next day, when Sheridan introduced Miss Linley to a friend and relation [Richard Chamberlaine], then in Town, as an Heiress who had consented to be united to him in France. Another friend [Simon Ewart], the son of a respectable brandy-merchant in the City, [John Ewart] suggested the idea of their sailing from the Port of London to Dunkirk, to which place his father had a vessel ready to sail immediately. This plan, as making pursuit more difficult, was immediately adopted, and the old gentleman not being entirely let into the secret, accompanied the young couple on board his ship, recommending them to the care of the Captain as if they had been his own children. He gave them letters of introduction to his correspondent at Dunkirk, and they were from thence given recommendations to several persons at Lille."

Surely no more genteel an elopement could be pictured!

2

Before resuming the narrative, it is necessary to remove from the legend the element of confusion which begins with carelessness. Moore had identified the brandy-merchant as Ewart, whom Rae converted into the friend and relation, thus leaving the "old gentleman" without a name; Sichel, discovering a passage in Charles Lamb, promptly supplied the deficiency by a positive statement that this "respectable brandy-merchant in the City" was "none other than Lamb's godfather, Field,"—that "most gentlemanly of oilmen, grandiloquent yet courteous," whose sole remuneration for "many years' nightly illumination of the orchestra and various avenues" of Drury Lane theatre was "a pretty liberal supply of those cheap billets" —the orders for free admission—"in Brinsley's easy autograph." The *London Directories* from 1770–1775 show that John Ewart of 31 Lower Thames Street was a brandy-merchant.

In *The London Magazine* of December 1821 Lamb told how in 1781, as a boy of seven, he went to his first play at Old Drury, "with orders, which my godfather F. had sent us. He kept the oil-shop (now Davies's) at the corner of Featherstone Buildings in Holborn. It was to his house in Holborn that young Brinsley brought his first wife on her elopement from boarding school at Bath—the beautiful Maria Linley. My parents were present (over a quadrille table) when he arrived in the evening with his harmonious charge."

Lamb's story has the ring of truth, even though its details are wrong. Francis Field does not appear as an oilman in Featherstone Buildings before 1781, so it may have been another house. Maria is a slip, though as Sheridan did not introduce Miss Linley under her own name but as an heiress, the "boarding school at Bath" may obviously have been part of his story. It is most likely that Sheridan would avoid taking Elizabeth to an inn, where she might be recognized, choosing a lodging in an obscure house whose "respectability" was beyond doubt.[1]

3

Moore tried to get the family version from William Linley, who was not very informative, but out of his prolixity and his confusion comes this statement:—"The Captain was a surly, ill-behaved fellow, and used Mr. Sheridan and my sister very shamefully. They were detained by a contrary wind, and there was not a morsel to eat or drink on board. Sheridan was determined that he should suffer for it, so he wrote an epigram, which is the severest thing I ever saw. It did for him completely." Having thus raised Moore's expectations, Linley confessed in agony that he could not recall one word of the epigram. But *The Morning Post* in 1787, printed a note on the elopement which explained that they were driven into Margate by stress of weather, and went ashore, while the boatman whom they had engaged to take them back to the ship went off without them because he had been offered more money by other people. Sheridan thereupon wrote this epigram on the chimneypiece of the inn at Margate:

[1]*Lamb's Essays*, 1929, i, 144. The kindness of Dr. S. L. Douthwaite supplies these particulars from the directories in the Guildhall Library: "In the 1821 directory, the name J. Davies, Oilman, is given at the address 62 High Holborn. The occupancy of No. 62 from 1781 onwards is given in the directories as follows:—1781–1793, Francis Field; Fielde in 1792; 1794–1795, Fielde and Lewis; 1796–1801, Robert Lewis; 1802–21, John Davies. All these were Oilmen. Field's name does not appear before 1781." The incorporation of "Godfather Field" into the Sheridan legend and his promotion from oilman to brandy-merchant and shipowner is too exquisite to be ignored: E. M. Butler, *Sheridan*, 1931, says that "Charles Lamb's godfather, Mr. Field, obtained a passage for them on one of his father's ships!"

"When Christ once hired a boat to cross the sea,
O Cooley, had that boat been hired from thee,
Had Satan offered but a sixpence more,
Our blessed Lord had soon been left on shore."[1]

The epigram has been dismissed, perhaps justly, as fraudulent, yet, although Mrs. Lefanu's account omits any reference to it, on the Sunday before March 27th there was a storm of exceptional violence, the worst for years. *The Town and Country Magazine* for 1772 records that it raged over London, while in Kent and Essex great trees were uprooted, houses blown down, and people killed by lightning.

In 1792, when his wife lay ill at Southampton, Sheridan wrote to the Duchess of Devonshire:

"How many years have passed since on these unreasoning, restless waters, which this night I have been gazing at and listening to, I bore poor E., who is now so near me fading in sickness, from all her natural attachments and affections, and then loved her so that, had she died as I once thought she would in the Passage, I should assuredly have plunged with her body to the Grave."[2]

This crossing gave Elizabeth Sheridan a horror and hatred of the sea which never left her throughout her life: after her return from France, she never ventured again out of England.

As for the "woman hired to accompany them on this extraordinary elopement," no more is heard of her elsewhere, so she may have stayed in London, or perhaps never have existed. In reporting the rumour of Sheridan's death on July 4th, 1772, *The General Evening Post* declared that "nothing criminal passed between Mr. S., the young gentleman said to have been killed in a duel with Captain M., and the Maid of Bath during their late tour in France. At every place they put up at, he requested the landlady's company, and took care to have Miss Linley constantly provided with a bedfellow."[3]

---

[1]Fitzgerald, I, 93.   [2]Sichel, II, 435.   [3]Green, 56.

The only definite evidence of what occurred during a whole month is contained in a letter written on April 15th from Sheridan to his brother Charles:

"Everything on our side has at last succeeded. Miss L., is now fixing in a Convent, where she has been entered some time. This has been a much more difficult point than you could have imagined, and we have, I find, been extremely fortunate. She has been ill, but is now recovered; this, too, has delayed me. We would have wrote, but have been kept in the most tormenting expectation from day to day of receiving your letters; but, as everything is now so happily settled here, I will delay no longer in giving you that information, though probably I shall set out for England without knowing a syllable of what has happened with you.

"All is well, I hope; and I hope, too that though you may have been ignorant for some time of our proceedings, it never could have been uneasy lest anything should tempt me to depart, even in a thought, from the honour and consistency which engaged me at first."[1]

Mrs. Lefanu's account, if true, would strongly refute Sheridan's claim to "honour and consistency." She says:

" After quitting Dunkirk, Mr. Sheridan was more explicit with Miss Linley as to his views in accompanying her to France. He told her he could not be content to leave her in a Convent unless she consented to a previous marriage, which all along had been the object of his hopes, and she must be aware that, after the step she had taken, she could not appear in England but as his wife. Miss Linley, who really preferred him greatly to any person, was not difficult to persuade, and at a village not far from Calais the marriage ceremony was performed by a priest who was known to be often employed on such occasions."

No other statement exists that such a ceremony did take

[1]Rae, I, 169–70.

place; nor can it be reconciled with Sheridan's anxiety some months later as to rumours of her marriage with Sir Thomas Clarges.

Mrs. Lefanu continued:

"They then proceeded to Lille, where Miss Linley determined to stop in preference to proceeding to St. Quentin. She immediately secured an apartment in a Convent, where it was settled she was to remain either till Sheridan came of age or till he was in a situation to support a wife. He remained a few days at Lille to be satisfied she was settled to her satisfaction, but whether from agitation of mind or fatigue she was taken ill, and an English physician, Dr. Dolman of York, was called in to attend her. From what he perceived of her case he wished to have her more immediately under his care than he could in the Convent, and he and Mrs. Dolman most kindly invited her to their house."[1]

Mrs. Lefanu concluded this part of her narrative by saying:

"After some private conversations with Mr. Sheridan, he appeared quite reconciled to his daughter, but insisted on her returning to England with him to fulfil several engagements he had entered into on her account. The whole party set out together the next day, Mr. Linley having previously promised to allow his daughter to return to Lille when her engagements were over."

Sheridan, whether with them or not, arrived in England on Tuesday, April 28th. Thus ended the trip to France, but not its consequences.

4

"Young Sheridan" had two *rencontres* with Captain Mathews, the first by candlelight on Monday, May 4th, 1772, at the Castle Tavern in Covent Garden, and the second in the light of early dawn on Wednesday, July 1st, 1772, on Kingsdown, about four miles from Bath. He was still fighting them

---

[1]In York there was no "Doctor Dolman."

on paper at Waltham Abbey during the January of the next year, and accusing Mathews of cowardice, and the seconds of falsity and misrepresentation. It is only just to examine the accounts not as scenes in the theatrical romance of the Maid of Bath, but as "points of honour" in which an officer of the eighteenth century was called upon to vindicate his conduct as a gentleman, against the charges of a hot-headed and courageous youth.

On March 18th Sheridan left an explanation of Elizabeth's elopement to France for Linley, which Captain Mathews did not see, but whatever it contained, it was magnified into an accusation that he had seduced her. He wrote Sheridan at least four letters, two to be forwarded through Charles Sheridan, and two to await him in London with Simon Ewart. They were in effect challenges, and receiving no reply after a lapse of three weeks, he took the unusual course of "posting"[1] Sheridan as a "lyar and treacherous scoundrel" in *The Bath Chronicle* of April 9th, 1772:

"Bath, Wednesday, April 8, 1772.
"Mr. Richard S******* having attempted, in a Letter left him for that Purpose, to account for his scandalous Method of running away from this Place, by Insinuations, derogating from *my* character, and that of a young Lady, *innocent* as far as relates to *me*, or *my knowledge*; since which he neither has taken any Notice of Letters, or even informed his own Family of the Place where he has hid himself;—I can no longer think he deserves the Treatment of a Gentleman, and therefore shall trouble myself no further about him than, in this public Method, to post him a L***, and a *treacherous* S********.

"And as I am convinced there have been many malevolent incendiaries concerned in the Propagation of this infamous Lie, if any of them, unprotected by *Age*, *Infirmities*, or *Profession*, will dare to acknowledge the Part they have

[1]"Posting" in coffee-houses was an occasional way of making a duel inevitable, but I know no other instance of using the newspapers.

acted, and affirm *to*, what they have [affirmed] *of* me, they may depend on receiving the proper reward of their Villainy, in the most public Manner. The World will be candid enough to judge properly (I make no Doubt) of any *private* Abuse on this subject for the future; as nobody can defend himself from an accusation he is ignorant of.

"THOMAS MATHEWS."

This was not merely addressed against Sheridan, but a general challenge to all calumniators; "unprotected by age, infirmities, and profession," that is, old men, cripples, and parsons. It was the letter of an angry man, but certainly not of a coward.

But a month later, in its issue of May 7th, *The Bath Chronicle* contained these paragraphs:

"Being convinced that the Expressions I made Use of to Mr. Sheridan's Disadvantage were the effects of Passion and Misrepresentation, I retract what I have said to that Gentleman's Disadvantage, and particularly beg his pardon for my Advertisement in the Bath Chronicle.

"THOMAS MATHEWS."

"We can with authority contradict the account in the London Evening Post of last night of a duel between Mr. M—t—ws and Mr. S—r—n as to the time and event of their meeting, Mr. S. being at this place on Saturday, and both these gentlemen being here at present."

The account of *The London Evening Post* for Tuesday, May 5th, was:

"On Saturday morning Th——s M—th—s, Esq., and Mr. Sh—r-d-n met in Crutched Friars and came to a decision in their well-known quarrel, when the latter was run through the body and carried to Mr. E——s, Thames Street, where it appears the wound is not mortal. Mr. M—— has gone to France with Capt. K——t, his second."

These newspaper paragraphs naturally demanded some explanation. From references to Colonel Gould, it is probable that the missing link in the story is that he was the commanding officer in a regiment of militia, in which Mathews had a company.[1] When therefore he was required to show that his apology was not an act of cowardice, Mathews explained that after the duel, in which his opponent had the advantage, he refused it; but on Sheridan ceasing to demand it, he gave it as a point of generosity. Then for some reason or other it became known in Bath that Sheridan had broken Mathews' sword, and flung the pieces across the room, an unheard-of proceeding which savoured of theatrical heroics. Sheridan had agreed that this indignity, hotly resented by Captain Mathews, should not be disclosed—"providing," he claimed to have said, "that the affair was not misrepresented." He alleged that this condition had been broken, for he wished it to be believed that this apology was won at the point of the sword, and he asserted that Captain Mathews had "begged his life," which was denied by Captain Knight, his uncle and second—a circumstance which would have made Sheridan immune from accepting a further challenge from him, without any imputation of cowardice.

It appears that Sheridan had given his version while Mathews was absent from Bath, at his estates in Glamorganshire. Under these charges of cowardly conduct, he returned to Bath, and it was inevitable that he should either receive a statement from Sheridan, testifying as to his behaviour in the duel, or they should have another engagement.

5

Accordingly, a second duel followed which was reported extensively in the newspapers. *The Bath Chronicle* of Thursday, July 2nd, 1772, said:

"This morning" [that is, Wednesday, the day of going to press] "about three o'clock, a second duel was fought with

[1] I have been unable to verify this deduction, but there were many military officers in Bath, and also a regimental mess: Wilkes records in his Diary: "11 January, 1773. Dined at the mess of Captain Rice in Orange Court with Captains Rice, Mathews, Messrs. Oliver, Fonnereau, and Day." (Green.) If Mathews had been adjudged a coward, he would have been compelled to resign any commission, and also excluded from their society.

swords, between Captain Mathews and Mr. R. Sheridan, on
Kingsdown, near this city, in consequence of their former
dispute respecting an amiable young lady, which Mr. M.
considered as improperly adjusted; Mr. S. having, since
their first rencontre, declared his sentiments respecting Mr.
M. in a manner that the former thought required satisfaction.
Mr. Sheridan received three or four wounds in his breast
and sides, and now lies very ill. Mr. M. was only slightly
wounded, and left this city soon after the affair was over."

The *St. James's Chronicle* of July 4th said:

"Bath, Wednesday July 1st.
"Young Sheridan and Capt. Mathews of this town, who
lately had a rencontre in a tavern in London, upon account
of the Maid of Bath, Miss Linley, have had another this
morning upon Kingsdown, about four miles hence. Sheridan
is much wounded but whether mortally or not is yet unknown. Both their swords breaking upon the first lunge,
they threw each other down and with the broken pieces
hacked at each other rolling upon the ground, the seconds
standing by, quiet spectators. Mathews is little, if at all,
wounded, and is since gone off."

Another cutting declares:[1]

"Bath, Wednesday, July 8th.
"The last affair between Mr. Mathews and Mr. Sheridan
we are now assured was occasioned by Mr. S.'s refusal to
sign a paper, testifying the spirit and propriety of Mr. M.'s
behaviour in their former rencounter. This refusal induced
Mr. M. to send him a challenge, which was accepted, and
Kingsdown was the place appointed for the decision of their
quarrel. After a few passes both their swords were broken,
Mr. Sheridan's almost to the hilt, who thereupon closed with
Mr. Mathews, and they both fell—Mr. Mathews having
then considerably the advantage called on Sheridan to beg

[1]Apparently the source is the *St. James's Chronicle*, but the same information was
given in *The London General Evening Post* of July 9th and other papers. (Cf. Green,
40–55.)

his life, which he refused (having in the former duel given Mathews his life) upon which Mathews picked up a broken piece of his sword, gave him the wounds of which he laſt Wednesday lay dangerously ill, and immediately left the City. The seconds ſtood by, quiet speſtators."

On June 30th, William Barnett, the reputed original of Sir Lucius O'Trigger, had invited Sheridan to supper at the White Hart Inn, Bath, in the course of which he presented an account of the firſt duel affirmed by Captain Mathews, and authenticated by his second, Captain Knight. Sheridan was asked to sign this in testimony of the propriety of his opponent's conduſt. He denied almoſt every article of it, and dismissed it as "misrepresentation, equivocation, and falsity" not only then, but in a letter which he drafted—but, as no other duel followed, he probably never sent—to Captain Knight after his recovery.

6

However, with the reminder that his version was entirely repudiated by Knight, as well as Mathews, it deserves to be reproduced: at the Castle Tavern:

"Mr. Ewart took lights up in his hand, and almoſt immediately on our entering the room we engaged. I ſtruck Mr. Mathews's point so much out of the line, that I ſtepped up and caught hold of his wriſt, or the hilt of his sword, while the point of mine was at his breaſt. You ran in and caught hold of my arm, exclaiming, '*don't kill him.*' I ſtruggled to disengage my arm, and said his sword was in my power. Mr. Mathews called out twice or thrice, '*I beg my life.*'—We were parted. You immediately said, '*there, he has begged his life, and now there is an end of it*'; and, on Mr. Ewart's saying that, when his sword was in my power, as I attempted no more you should not have interfered, you replied that you *were wrong*, but that you had *done it haſtily, and to prevent mischief*—or words to that effeſt. Mr. Mathews then hinted that I was rather *obliged to your interposition* for the advantage; you declared that '*before* you did so, both the swords were in Mr. Sheridan's power.' Mr. Mathews still seemed resolved to give it another turn, and observed that *he had never quitted his sword.*—Provoked at this, I then swore (with too much heat perhaps) that he should either give up his sword and I would break it, or go to his guard again. He refused—but, on my persisting, either gave it into my hand, or flung it on the table, or the ground (*which*, I will not absolutely affirm). I broke it, and flung the hilt to the other end of the room. He exclaimed at this. I took a mourning sword from Mr. Ewart, and presenting him with mine, gave my honour that what had passed should never be mentioned by me, and he might now right himself again. He replied that he '*would never draw a sword against the man who had given him his life:*'—but, on his still exclaiming against the indignity of breaking his sword (which he had brought upon himself) Mr. Ewart offered him the pistols, and some altercation passed between them. Mr. Mathews said, that he *could never shew his face, if it were known how his sword was broke—that such a thing had never been done—that it cancelled all obligations, &c. &c.* You seemed to think it was wrong, and we both proposed, that if he never misrepresented the affair, it should not be mentioned by us."[1]

The *naïveté* of his declaration that Captain Knight "seemed to think it wrong" for him to break Mathews's sword, shows that Sheridan had but little acquaintance with "points of honour." But he so persisted in his charges as to the second duel that in October Mathews was compelled to ask his second, William Barnett, for an account which he sent by Major William Brereton to Sheridan's second, Captain Paumier, who agreed that it was "true and impartial," and differing from his own opinion in "a few immaterial circumstances only." For some reason, it had not reached Sheridan at Waltham Abbey, (where he had been exiled by his father) on December 8th when he wrote to Thomas Grenville: "I have this day had an account

[1]Moore, 59–60.

of the basest, meanest, and most ungrateful piece of treachery
that ever disgraced human nature. Mathews is come to Bath,
and bullying Paumier, by attempting to call him out, has made
him sign some infamous falsehoods which I am told are
credited."

A few days later Sheridan confessed to Grenville that "the
representation I had given me was highly exaggerated and
malicious." But he accused Paumier of "equivocal excuses and
self-sufficient assertions which always betray a consciousness
of demerit," and in a draft to Barnett traversed all his statements with quibbles. But the account given by the seconds was
properly accepted: on the very day Sheridan wrote this letter,
Colonel and Mrs. Gould and John Wilkes were dining with
Captain and Mrs. Mathews at their house. Therefore, to his
brother officers at Bath, Mathews had vindicated himself as a
man of "honour, courage, and intrepidity." So had Richard
Sheridan. It is one of the strange accidents of time that "Mr.
Sheridan's bill" from November 21st, 1771, to September 9th,
1772, should have survived, for foils, new hollow blades and
the rest of the duellist's equipment, together with the hair-
locket and picture-case which were memorials and *gages
d'amour* of the Maid of Bath.

Mr. Sheridan.   Bath. 21st Nov. 1771.

BOUGHT OF WILLIAM EVILL.
In the Market Place.

	To 1 pair neat Foyls ...		10	6
Dec. 12	To 1 pair do. do. ...		10	6
Jany. 23/72	To 1 neat Toothpick Case ...	4	4	0
June 10	To 1 neat Hair Locket ...	1	11	6
	To 1 neat fancy Ring ...	2	12	6
	To 2 do seals ...		9	0
	To fitting a Picture in a Case ...		3	6
Aug. 25	To 1 neat Gilt Watch Key ...		1	6
	To 1 pair neat Garnet Buttons ...	1	15	0
	To mending Gold Seal ...		1	0

Sept. 9   To 2 neat German hollow Blades
to Swords with vellum Scab-
bards, neat Steel and Gold Loc-
ket & Chape and Mounted to   3   13   6
2 Steel and Gold Helts & re-
pairing the Helts . . .
To 1 neat Morocco Belts for
Swivels

$\pounds$15   12   6[1]

7

Lord John Townshend, as Lord Thanet told Moore, went to Bath for the purpose of getting acquainted with Mathews, and making enquiries about his affair with Sheridan. Mathews described the duel as "a mere hoax—in fact it was no duel at all," and said that Sheridan came drunk, and that he could have killed him with the greatest ease if he had chosen.[2] To this Moore made a scornful comment—"a precious fellow this Mathews was," without troubling further. Sigmond, from enquiries at Bath declared, in the edition of Sheridan's plays he published in 1848, that Mathews's version was essentially different from Sheridan's. He invited Sheridan to sup with him and the seconds on the night before the duel; Sheridan remained at table drinking claret until the time of the appointment. When he left it, he walked up Milsom Street, where he saw Mathews's chaise waiting, reeled into it, insisted upon the seconds following him, and drove off, leaving Mathews to follow in Paumier's. How far this does represent Mathews's version it is difficult to say, but it reiterates that Sheridan was in "a high state of excitement from potations deep."

From this welter the author of *The School for Scandal* at last emerges, *The General Evening Post* of London recorded in an account, afterwards corrected, of the duel:

"Reports are arrived from Bath that the son of a celebrated actor, who though very young, had all the romance of

---

[1]Bath Public Library MS.   [2]Moore, *Journal*.

\honour in his character which is attributed to the heroes of antiquity, fell two days ago in that city defending a young lady's honour against the aspersions cast upon it by a certain military gentleman."

When he was recovering from his wounds, it was one of his amusements to read the daily accounts of himself in the papers and say, "Let me see what they report of me to-day: I wish to know whether I am dead or alive."[1]

The Public Advertiser of November 19th, 1772, said:

"Mr. Sheridan junr, who last summer fought a duel with Captain Mathews about the Maid of Bath, is entirely recovered of his wounds, but has lost the use of his right arm from receiving a shot between the bones at the joint."

[1]Lefanu, 406.

E

CHAPTER THE FIFTH

London

I

HENRY ANGELO, who was staying with the Sheridans at Bath when Richard eloped with Elizabeth, recalled that it "incensed the two fathers so much that when they first met they were like the two Spanish fathers in the play of *The Wonder*. Old Sheridan was enraged that his son should marry the daughter of a fiddler, the other furious at the thought that his daughter, the Cecilia of her age, should be allied to the son of an actor."

In the Lent of 1773 the Maid of Bath enchanted London. Her appearance in the Oratorios at Drury Lane had been preceded by reports of her beauty, her grace, and her charm; and by romantic accounts of her numerous suitors, from old Walter Long to young Richard Sheridan, which were summarized by *The London Magazine*—"She has been sung by bards and fought for by heroes." Fanny Burney wrote at the time in her Diary:

"she is believed to be very romantic. She has been very celebrated for her singing, though never till within this month has she been in London. She has met with a great variety of adventures, and has had more lovers and admirers than any nymph of these times: she has been addressed by men of all ranks,—I dare not pretend to say honourably, which is doubtful; but what is certain is that whatever were their designs, she has rejected them all. She is attracted to a Mr. Sheridan, whom it is expected shortly she will marry."

HIS ROYAL HIGHNESS GEORGE PRINCE OF WALES

R. Cosway R.A. pinx.   L. Sailliar Sc.

R.dus Cosway. R.A. et Primarius Pictor Serenifsimi Walliæ Principis delin. et Excu.

THE PRINCE OF WALES, 1787

To face page 51

The praises of Bath and Oxford, where musical reputations were not made lightly, anticipated an English singer of the first order. On February 19th, 1773, her sister Mary sang in Handel's *Judas Maccabaeus*, her brother Thomas contributed a "concerto on the violin." Fanny Burney, who was present, wrote:

"She is really beautiful, her complexion a clear, lovely, animated brown, with a bloomy colour on her cheeks, her nose that most elegant of shapes, Grecian;—fine, luxurious, easy-sitting hair, a charming forehead, pretty mouth, and most beautiful eyes."

She captivated all the amateurs of music, among them King George the Third. *The Bath Chronicle* recorded that:

"April 2nd, Mr. Linley, his son, and eldest daughter, were at the Queen's concert at Buckingham House; Miss Mary Linley, being ill, could not attend. The King and Queen were particularly affable; His Majesty told Mr. Linley that he never in his life heard so fine a voice as his daughter's nor one so well instructed; that she was a great credit to him, and presented him with a £100 bank note. No one attended the concert but their Majesties, the children, and one lady. It continued five hours, yet no one sat, except the two performers who played on the harpsichord and the violincello."

A fortnight later *The Morning Chronicle* of April 16th, 1773, said:

"Tuesday was married at Marylebone Church by the Rev. Dr. Booth the celebrated Miss Linley to Mr. Sheridan. After the ceremony they set out with her family and friends, and dined at the Star and Garter on Richmond Hill; in the evening they had a ball after which the family and friends returned to town, and left the young couple at a gentleman's house at Mitcham to consummate their nuptials."

2

After their marriage, they lived in a cottage at Burnham Grove and Elizabeth terminated her engagements as a public performer. She had previously retired on the signing of the marriage-contract with Walter Long of Whaddon, and she would certainly have retired if she had married Sir Thomas Clarges, or Mr. Watts of Combe Abbey, so it was no matter of surprise —except that her husband happened to be without a penny in the world.

Pressure was brought upon Sheridan to permit her to fulfil two contracts that her father had made for her to sing at Oxford in July, and at Worcester in September. It was urged upon him as a point of honour, but he replied that she had not made the contracts, and those who had made them knew that her marriage would terminate her father's powers over her as naturally as her death would have done. He added—this was on May 13th, 1773, a month after their marriage—that when he declined to allow her to appear at Oxford, he had been waited upon by the Professor of Music, Dr. Hayes, who told him that if he permitted his wife to sing there it would be a compliment to the University; moreover, he was charged with a message from Lord North, who was to be installed as Chancellor of the University, that he would regard it as the highest compliment to himself.[1]

After some persuasion from Linley, Sheridan at last consented to her appearance at Oxford. Accordingly, at the installation among the splendid entertainments, said *The London Magazine*, was a grand miscellaneous concert conducted by Dr. Hayes on July 7th in which "the celebrated Mrs. Sheridan and Miss Linley" sang, as they did the next day in the oratorio of *The Prodigal Son*. Lord North, in thanking him, said that the University had conferred degrees *honoris causa*, and Sheridan should have received one *uxoris causa*.[2] Sheridan is supposed to have been highly gratified by this "witty and graceful" phrase, but it must have hardened his heart against any other public

[1]Moore, 86. [2]Moore, *Journal*, IV, 33.

appearance by his wife: he was not destined to be "Mrs. Sheridan's husband."

However, Lord Coventry had also persuaded him to allow his wife to sing at the Worcester Festival—the profits of which were given to charity—in September, and invited them to stay with him as his guests at Croome Court. Mrs. Sheridan's fee was a bank-note for one hundred pounds, which she put into the plate at the Cathedral as a donation to the expenses of the meeting.

After this superb gesture, Mrs. Sheridan never sang again in public; and her husband was equally determined that she should not be invited to private houses as an unpaid performer. Sir Joshua Reynolds asked them to dinner, and in the expectation that she would entertain his guests, he bought a new pianoforte, and invited a large company. To his mortification, when he hinted that a song by Mrs. Sheridan would be received as a great favour, her husband replied that, *with his assent*, she had resolved never to sing again in a public company. This polite rebuke angered Sir Joshua, who enquired next day from James Northcote, "What reason could they think I had in inviting them to dinner, unless it was to hear her sing?— for she cannot talk."[1] But Sir Joshua was soon mollified, and became one of their greatest friends. He painted Mrs. Sheridan as St. Cecilia, seated singing at her harpsichord, with the two little daughters of Bartholomew Coote as cherubs. When this picture was exhibited at the Royal Academy in May 1775, Horace Walpole praised it as "most simple and beautiful."

In July 1773, Samuel Arnold, the composer, offered Mrs. Sheridan more than three thousand pounds for a series of some twenty appearances in oratorio at the Pantheon, and at Giardini's Concerts. She refused. Her husband was obdurate. The King desired Mrs. Sheridan to sing at Drury Lane in the Lent of 1775. In November 1774, Sheridan wrote to Linley that Thomas Stanley, the Master of the King's Musick had

---

[1] Northcote, *Reynolds*, II, 85.

consulted him about the oratorios. His partner, John Christopher Smith, was retiring to Bath:

"Mr. Stanley informed me that on his applying to the King for the continuance of his favour, he was desired by His Majesty to make an offer of Mr. Smith's situation and partnership in them, and that he should continue his protection, &c.—I declined the matter very civilly and very peremptorily. I should imagine that Mr. Stanley would apply to you: I started the subject to him, and said you had twenty Mrs. Sheridan's more."

Linley succeeded J. C. Smith, and directed the Oratorios for many years, but Elizabeth never sang in them.

Sheridan's independence was much discussed. Johnson, at Cambridge's house, in the April of 1775, talked of "a young gentleman's marriage with an eminent singer, and his determination that she should not sing in public, though her father was very earnest that she should." It was argued that "the young gentleman, who had not a shilling in the world, but was blest with uncommon talents, was foolishly delicate and foolishly proud." But Johnson, in his high Roman spirit, said, "He has resolved wisely and nobly, to be sure. He is a brave man. Would a gentleman not be disgraced by having his wife sing publicly for hire? No, Sir, there can be no doubt there. I know not if I should not prepare myself for a public singer as readily as let my wife be one."[1]

Sheridan, however, was actuated by his ambition to appear a "gentleman." He would not add "the singer's husband" to the "player's son."

In the spring of 1774, they removed to a house which Thomas Linley furnished for them in Orchard Street, between Oxford Street and Portman Square; *The Morning Post* on February 4th, 1774, said that they were "fitting up" a music room, "where concerts would be given twice a week for the nobility." These private concerts, however, were the least expensive

[1]Boswell, *Johnson*, April 17th, 1775.

entertainments they could give as a return for the civilities and hospitality they had received from "persons of fashion and consequence."[1] The performers were the Linleys, and Dr. Burney considered it an honour to be invited by Mrs. Sheridan to accompany her singing.

The concerts were the rage of London. In 1775, as Fanny Burney recalled, "the highest circles of society were attracted to them by the talents, beauty and fashion of Mrs. Sheridan. Entrance to them was sought not only by all the votaries of taste and admirers of musical excellence, but by the leaders of the *ton* and their followers and slaves."

3

The Rivals was written in six or eight weeks during the summer of 1774, produced at Covent Garden on January 17th, 1775, nearly damned on the first night, withdrawn, re-written, and again produced in a new version on January 28th, 1775.[2]

Sheridan is supposed to have borrowed the character of Mrs. Malaprop from a comedy by his mother, *A Journey to Bath*, or *A Trip to Bath*. Watkins indeed insinuated that *The Rivals* was one and the same play with his mother's: he said that *A Trip to Bath*, written in France, was cordially approved by Garrick, by Murphy, and by Johnson

"But, notwithstanding their approval, it never made its appearance before the public; which was the more unaccountable considering the peculiar circumstances and professional pursuits of Mr. Sheridan, who caused the two remaining volumes of *Sidney Biddulph* to be printed, but totally neglected the other literary remains of the author. Into whose hands her papers afterwards fell, is not clearly known, though it is probable that by the recent death of her youngest son, some information may be obtained upon the subject."

Thomas Sheridan mentioned this play twice in his letters to Samuel Whyte. In October 1763, he said his wife "had finished

[1]Lefanu, 402.   [2]For a full account, see *Plays & Poems*, 1, 5-18: 117-130.

a comedy" which he thought "excellent—spick and span and new throughout." In August 1766 he said that among the labours she had been engaged upon during their residence at Blois was "a comedy called *A Trip to Bath* in which many judges find a great deal of merit."[1] But so far from Garrick having approved the play, there is direct evidence to the contrary. Frances Sheridan wrote a letter to Mrs. Benjamin Victor, whose husband had been appointed prompter in Drury Lane in 1763, which showed that she had submitted a play to Garrick, whose verdict upon it she summed up ironically in these words: "imprimis, the play is without fable; secondly, all the scenes are detached; thirdly, there is nothing to interest the audience; and lastly, it has no humour." To this she replied at some length, traversing each of his statements.[2]

The title of this comedy was not given, but it cannot have been *The Dupe*, performed in December 1763 while the Sheridans were still in London. Possibly in spite of her protestations as to its merits, Mrs. Sheridan started to alter it, for it was described long afterwards as "unfinished" by her daughter, who as Mrs. Henry Lefanu wrote to her friend Lady Morgan: "My mother's sketch of a comedy, unfinished, was put into my brother Richard's hands by my father at Bath, when we were resident there, but my father never even hinted that he had made any use of it in *The Rivals*."[3]

During Thomas Sheridan's quarrels with his son, he would undoubtedly have expatiated upon any plagiarism in *The Rivals*, yet since 1864—when Coventry Patmore gave the British Museum a manuscript entitled *A Journey to Bath*—it has never been doubted that from his mother's unacted comedy Sheridan annexed Mrs. Malaprop. On the surface evidence seems complete and irrefutable. In this comedy, a certain Mrs.

---

[1] *Miscellanea Nova*, 127.

[2] *Garrick Correspondence*, I, 15–18, where the letter is dated "Blois, Nov. 16th, 1743." Frances Chamberlaine did not marry Thomas Sheridan till 1747; they did not go to Blois till 1764, where she died on September 22nd, 1766. Garrick being absent from England between September 1763 and April 1765, the year was 1765.

[3] Fitzgerald, I, 417.

Tryfort speaks of "a progeny of learning," and "contagious countries," and declares that "so much taciturnity doesn't become a young man," all of which are echoed by Mrs. Malaprop. There is another very striking similarity. Sir Johnathan Bull, the English baronet of *A Trip to Bath*, declares: "If I had your ladyship at Bull Hall, I could show you a line of anceſtry that would convince you we are not a people of yeſterday. . . . Why, the land and mansion house has slipped through our fingers, but, thank Heaven, the family piĉtures are ſtill extant." Sir Lucius O'Trigger, the Irish baronet of *The Rivals* declares: "Oh, my little friend! if I had the Blunderbuss Hall here —I could show you a range of anceſtry in the O'Trigger line that would furnish the New Rooms, every one of whom has killed his man!—For though the mansion house and dirty acres have slipt through our fingers, I thank Heaven, our honour and the family piĉtures are as fresh as ever."

Sheridan, it is clear, in attempting a revision of his mother's *A Trip to Bath* as *A Journey to Bath*, added these lines himself, and out of them grew the charaĉters of Mrs. Malaprop and Sir Lucius O'Trigger, whom he transferred to his own comedy. He was his own plagiary.

St. Patrick's Day was written in forty-eight hours, and presented to Lawrence Clinch, in gratitude for his impersonation of Sir Lucius O'Trigger on the second night of *The Rivals*, when he replaced Lee. The original bill announced that "For Mr. Clinch's Benefit" on May 2nd, 1775, there would be aĉted "*Alexander the Great*, with (for that night only) a new farce called *St. Patrick's Day, or, The Scheming Lieutenant*." It was, however, advertised as "for the sixth time" on June 1ſt. *The London Magazine*, which was particularly pedantic about this time—said that in *St. Patrick's Day*, the author's canvas is certainly filled with the likeness of no one human creature in exiſtence—"The prologue promises a high feaſt for the sons and daughters of fun, and it cannot be denied that the writer of the farce has contrived to keep his word with them, though it is not so clear as might be wished whether the laughter his scenes excite is a laugh of applause or ridicule."

4

"So now-a-days, As 'twas in Gay's,
The world's run mad agen-a:
From morn to night, Its whole delight
To cry up *The Duenna*."

Street song of 1776.

It was the comic opera of *The Duenna*, produced at Covent
Garden on November 21st, 1775, which made the reputation of
Richard Brinsley Sheridan. "We cannot do justice to this piece,"
declared *The London Magazine*, "by speaking of it as an opera
only, for there is more character and plot in it than in most
comedies." It was written, according to John Graham, at Waltham Abbey, that is to say, before Sheridan's marriage. If this is
true, *The Duenna* was written as a comedy, or rather, having
only three acts, as what was then called a farce.

Its conversion into an opera was the work of Sheridan's wife,
for he had no musical knowledge. Thomas Linley gave his
assistance, but it was his daughter Elizabeth who prompted
Sheridan in his letters. On September 28th, 1775, Linley
wrote from Bath to David Garrick:

"As often as I am called upon, I have promised to assist
Sheridan in compiling—I believe is the properest term—an
opera; which, I understand from him, he has engaged to
produce at Covent-Garden this winter. I have already set
some airs which he has given me, and he intends writing new
words to some other tunes of mine. My son has likewise
written some tunes for him, and I understand he is to have
others from Mr. Jackson of Exeter. This is a mode of proceeding in regard to his composition I by no means approve
of. I think he ought first to have finished his opera with the
songs he intends to introduce in it, and have got it entirely
new set. No musician can set a song properly unless he un-
derstands the character,—and knows the performer who is
to exhibit it. For my part, I shall be very unwilling for either
my name, or my son's, to appear in this business; and it is
my present resolution to forbid it: for I have great reason to

be diffident of my own abilities and genius; and my son has not had experience in theatrical composition, though I think well of his invention and musical skill."[1]

Thomas Linley's assistance in this "compilation" has been greatly exaggerated. The playbill for the first performance promised "the music partly new, and partly selected from the most eminent composers, with a new overture." In October Sheridan wrote him that "Betsy intended to have troubled you with some music for correction, and I with some stanzas," which may mean that she had composed or adapted the airs.

Garrick must have shown Linley's letter to Sheridan; for the later correspondence shows that instead of merely sending words to be set to music Sheridan tried to give Linley, still without sending him the dialogue as a whole, some idea of "the character" and "the person who is to exhibit it." He wrote:

"My intention was to have closed the first act with a song, but I find it is not thought so well. Hence I trouble you with one of the inclosed papers; and, at the same time, you must excuse my impertinence in adding my idea of the cast I would wish the music to have; as I think I have heard you say you never heard Leoni, and I cannot briefly explain to you the character and situation of the persons on the stage with him. The first (a dialogue between Quick and Mrs. Mattocks), I would wish to be a pert, sprightly air; for, though some of the words mayn't seem suited to it, I should mention that they are neither of them in earnest in what they say."

This was the Duet he enclosed:—

Isaac.   "My mistress expects me, and I must go to her,
[Quick]   Or how can I hope for a smile?
Louisa.   Soon may you return a prosperous wooer,
[Mattocks] But think what I suffer the while:

[1] *The Private Correspondence of David Garrick*, II, 102. The tone of this letter shows that Linley was already hoping to purchase a share of the Drury Lane patent from David Garrick.

Alone and away from the man whom I love,
In strangers I'm forced to confide,

Isaac.   Dear lady, my friend you may trust, and he'll
prove,
Your servant, protector, and guide."

He continued:

"Leoni takes it up seriously [as Don Carlos] and I want
him to show himself advantageously in the six lines, beginning 'Gentle maid.' I should tell you that he sings nothing
well but in a plaintive or pastoral style; his voice is such as
appears to me always to be hurt by much accompaniment. I
have observed, too, that he never gets so much applause as
when he makes a cadence. Therefore my idea is that he
should make a flourish at 'Shall I grieve thee?' and return to
'Gentle maid,' and so sing that part of the tune again."

These were the words:

"Gentle maid, ah! why suspect me?
Let me serve thee—then reject me,
Canst thou trust, and I deceive thee?
Art thou sad, and shall I grieve thee?"

To Louisa's reply:

"Never may'st thou happy be,
If in ought thou'rt false to me."

Sheridan added these instructions:

"After that, the two last lines, sung by the three, with the
persons only varied, may get them off with as much spirit as
possible. The second act ends with a *slow* glee, therefore I
should think the two last lines in question had better be
brisk, especially as Quick and Mrs. Mattocks are concerned
in it."

5

The hand was the hand of Richard, but the voice was the
voice of Elizabeth. It was her knowledge of music which was

behind the composition of *The Duenna*. Her brother wrote the overture, but which songs were composed by him and which by his father is mostly beyond conjecture, and Jackson of Exeter can have given little, if any assistance. However, it is possible, though nobody has attempted it, to assign certain songs to their composers.

As *The London Magazine* said, several of the songs were adapted from Scots and Irish airs, and it was in singing ballads of this kind that Elizabeth excelled. Sheridan wrote to Linley that "the songs you have set up of 'Banna's Banks' and 'Deil Take the Wars' I had made words for before they arrived, which answer excessively well." "Banna's Banks" was commonly known as "Gramachree Molly," under which title as "a favourite Irish Air," it had been printed with the music in *The London Magazine* in 1774. It was the "matchless air," as Moore called it, to which he set his own lovely words, "The harp that once through Tara's Halls." "Gramachree Molly" ran:

> "By Banna's Banks I strayed
>   One Evening in May;
> The little Birds in liveliest Notes
>   Made vocal ev'ry Spray;
> They sung their little tales of Love,
>   They sung them o'er and o'er,
> Ah, Gramachree, ma Cholleen ouge,
>   Ma Molly asthore."

To this Sheridan wrote these words, sung by Don Carlos:

> "Had I a heart for falsehood fram'd
>   I ne'er could injure you:
> For though your tongue no promise claim'd
>   Your charms would make me true,
> To you no soul shall bear deceit,
>   No stranger offer wrong,
> But friends in all the aged you'll meet
>   And lovers in the young."

"Deil tak' the wars, that hurried Billy from me," printed in Playford's book of Scots tunes in 1698, was the air used for Clara's song "When sable night, each drooping plant restoring." There were several other annexations; for the favourite, "Ah, sure a pair was never seen," was set to an air called variously "Highland Laddie" and "Highland Lassie,"—not the old Scots melody for which Alan Ramsay wrote the two songs under those titles, but a new air for his words written by Dr. Thomas Arne. To Jackson's setting of Parnell's pretty song, "My days have been so wondrous free," Sheridan wrote "Ah cruel maid!", which Moore praised as having "for deep impassioned feeling and natural eloquence not perhaps its rival in through the whole range of lyrical poetry."

"By him we love offended" was adapted to "*Fuggiam da questo loco*," by Vincenzo Rauzinni; while Fisher's joyous "*Bel idol mio*" with its hautboy accompaniment was charmingly adapted for Louisa's farewell to the convent:

> "Adieu, thou dreary pile, where never dies,
> The sullen echo of repentant sighs:
> Ye sister mourners of each lonely cell,
> Inured to hymns and sorrow, fare ye well;
> For happier scenes I fly this darksome grove,
> To saints a prison, but a tomb of love."

Two of Dr. Hayes's glees were used—"Wind, gentle evergreen" for "Soft pity never leaves the gentle breast"; and "Gently touch the warbling lyre" for "Oft does Hymen smile to hear." One of Linley's songs, "Prithee, prithee, pretty man" was adapted for "Oh the days when I was young."[1] Spranger

---

[1] These identifications are partly deduced from Sheridan's letters to Linley (Moore, 122-136). The use of "*Fuggiam da questo loco*" is noted by Kelly (I, 11) and that of Arne's "Highland Laddie" by Alex Whitelaw in *The Book of Scottish Song*, 1849. Some contemporary MS. notes in Mr. Iolo A. Williams' *Songs of the Duenna*, 1st edition, 1775, identify seven airs, but this copy, through the binder cutting the margin, gives the air of "How oft, Louisa" as "Ber/ of er/ May," which defies me: "Oh had my love" is also marked "Scotch Air." On "the first page of his MSS." Sheridan wrote "Go rose, and die where I would be." Sichel (I, 506) says that this "strikes the keynote of Cavalier minstrelsy"; but I suspect that it was the name of an air that Sheridan used or intended using; it was set to music by Dr. Arne.

Barry, then growing old, heard at rehearsal such sad and solemn airs as "Oft does Hymen," "O had my love," "What Bard, O Time discover" and "Gentle Maid," and told old Sheridan it would not succeed because there was "too much church music."

But Sheridan's impulse to composition came from his own elopement to France, and the convent necessitated a Catholic country, and Spain must have been suggested by *The Spanish Friar*; beyond which his knowledge of Spanish manners and customs did not extend. Indeed, the picture of a monastic refectory, with its absurd caricatures of friars, was undoubtedly copied from Dryden. Their "licentiousness and hypocrisy" were offensive to Catholics, for when in 1779, *The Duenna* was adapted into an Italian opera, for performance at the Opera House, the Italian performers refused to appear in it unless this scene was deleted.

The London Magazine in 1775 objected: "Such a scene might have had a very proper effect towards the latter end of King Charles, or during the reign of James the Second, but at present we think this pious fraud totally unnecessary. It now appears as an excrescence, shot out by excess of the author's zeal against Popery, or the exuberance of his invention: it may indeed fit any other play as well as *The Duenna* when the scene is laid in a Popish country." Sheridan had no motive of religious animosity: he merely desired to find a convenient excuse for putting a catch-club on the stage.

The great successes among the players were made by Quick as Isaac Mendoza the Jew, "cunning little Isaac," by Leoni as Don Carlos, and by Miss Brown as Donna Clara. The street-ballad about *The Duenna* declared:

> "One half the Town Still talks of Brown,
> The other of Leoni,
> While those sly curs, The Managers,
> Keep pocketing the money."

The London Magazine for January 1776, annotated that Brown was "a young actress who first appeared in a principal character of the piece, to whom her part seeming so pleasing and natural that she soon converted her sham elopement into a real one"; and Leoni was "a famous Jew singer, in whom the playhouse goes snacks with the synagogue." Miss Brown, afterwards Mrs. Cargill, had levanted with Miles Peter Andrewes, who then "first brought himself into notice of the town"—"you have heard of our losing Miss Brown," wrote Sheridan to Linley, "however, we have missed her so little in *The Duenna* that the managers have not tried to regain her, which I believe they might have done." Leoni "made up his want of everything else by singing in a manner sufficient to create jealousy and envy in the breasts of some of the most celebrated *castrati* at the Haymarket"; he was cantor at the synagogue in Bevis Marks, under his own name of Meyer Lyon, and "was permitted to appear at the theatre so long as it did not interfere with his duties." *The Duenna*, says Moore, was acted no less than seventy-five times during the season, the only intermissions being a few days at Christmas—when Fisher's pantomime of *Harlequin Prometheus* was performed—and "the Fridays in every week, the latter on account of Leoni, who being a Jew could not act on those nights."[1]

6

It is impossible to say how much Sheridan received for *The Rivals* and *The Duenna*. It was the custom for an author to be paid the profits of the third, sixth, and ninth performance, which, in round figures, then amounted to five hundred pounds.

For *The Rivals*, the first performance being regarded as a *dies non*, the author's nights were the fourth, seventh and tenth, which explains his new prologue for the tenth night. In addition to this, the author sold his copyright to a bookseller, which reverted to him at the end of fourteen years. It was the custom of the time for the bookseller to pay a fixed sum of one hundred pounds, until Debrett, as an exception which was not

[1]The reason would be plainer if Moore had explained that the Jewish Sabbath begins at sunset on Friday, and lasts till sunset on Saturday.

a precedent, gave General Burgoyne two hundred pounds for *The Heiress* in 1786. But Wilkie of St. Paul's Churchyard told Anthony Pasquin, who noted it in an appendix to his *Life of Edwin* (1791), that he gave Sheridan two hundred pounds for the copyright of *The Rivals*, "though he afterwards confessed to me that he was a considerable loser by the purchase." The explanation seems to be that Wilkie paid one hundred pounds for the Covent Garden version, which was printed in the first and second editions, and another hundred pounds for the shorter Drury Lane version of 1776, which was first printed as "the third edition corrected."

In the case of *The Duenna*, Sheridan sold the copyright to Harris of Covent Garden, as "part of his original bargain," and the price, according to the custom of the time, would be the bookseller's fee of £100. The profits on the "Songs," however, were generally secured to the author, and the books, which were sold in the theatre at sixpence, were in their twenty-seventh edition in 1776. Moore, in his *Journal*, noted that he was told by the younger Wilkie that Sheridan succeeded "with his usual ingenuity, in appropriating the fees which would have gone to the composer. He made an excellent bargain with Thompson the music-seller who printed it, to pay him thirty pounds for every three successive nights." Wilkie added that he made "a great deal of money" by the sale of the music—which was published at half-a-guinea a copy. Unless the Christmas intermission broke the contract, Sheridan received about £700, being, through his wife, undoubtedly entitled to these fees.

Sheridan's unusual bargain with Thompson suggests that he may have made a similar bargain with Harris, for the extension of the author's nights beyond the customary ninth. It is idle to speculate what he received, but it must have been many times greater than any author had previously received for a play in the history of the stage.

F

CHAPTER THE SIXTH

Manager of Drury Lane

Writes himself—I know he does.
The Critic.

I

WHEN David Garrick decided to retire from the management of the Theatre Royal, Drury Lane, there were many who wished to succeed him. But after George Colman, to whom he offered the first refusal, the person whom Garrick favoured was Richard Brinsley Sheridan, whose father-in-law, Thomas Linley, had previously attempted to obtain a share in Covent Garden Theatre.

The "mystery" of how Sheridan found £20,000 has occupied much ingenuity. He borrowed it at more than 5 per cent. The security was ample, though there was some degree of risk, as he said, in case of fire. The only other danger was the granting of a patent for a third theatre, for during eight months of the year the drama was a monopoly of the two winter houses, the Theatres Royal of Drury Lane and Covent Garden. The Little Theatre in the Haymarket was licensed only for the summer months, and the King's Theatre in the Haymarket, or the Opera House, was licensed only for Italian and French Opera, and for Ballet. Having contributed £1,300 from himself and his wife, Sheridan raised the money by payment of two annuities of £500 per annum.

In June 1776, the contract with Garrick was perfected, and the moiety was divided into seven shares of £10,000, of which Sheridan held two, Linley two, and Ford three, John Ewart having relinquished his intention of becoming a purchaser. James Ford was a fashionable physician, and accoucheur to the nobility, wherefore on January 23rd, 1776, Kitty Clive wrote to David Garrick:

"What a strange jumble of people they have put in the papers as the purchasers of the patent! I thought I should have died with laughing when I saw a man-midwife among them: I suppose they have taken him in to prevent *miscarriages*! I have some opinion of Mr. Sheridan, as I hear everybody say that he is very sensible: he has a divine wife, and I loved his mother dearly."[1]

It was intended to appoint Thomas Sheridan as acting-manager, but he refused the terms. Richard Sheridan's department was to be that of business manager, and Thomas Linley became director of music.

Sheridan entered upon management in the September of 1776 with a revival of *Jane Shore*, accompanied by an occasional prelude written by George Colman under the title of *New Brooms*. It was, indeed, no bed of roses that he had chosen. In an epigram of the time, "three actresses drove Garrick from the stage," and it was not long before these same Mesdames Yates, Abington, and Younge were tormenting the new manager with their jealousies, and their refusals to play this part or that.

2

Sheridan's industry during the first season was copious. He revised old plays, and sought for new ones, and he was eager to find new performers, with youth and grace and beauty. By the beginning of December, though still in difficulties with the caprices of his actresses, he was fairly in his stride, and the record of a single week will show his activities. On December 5th, Linley came into play with a new dramatic romance called *Selima and Azor* with magnificent scenery by De Loutherbourg, and Mrs. Baddeley enchanting as Selima—"she looked like an angel and sang the flower-song like a syren." It was taken from the French of Favart, but it owed its success to the music arranged and composed by Thomas Linley the younger, under

[1]*Garrick Correspondence*, II, 128–9.

the direction of his father. On December 10th a very full and brilliant house assembled to see "a young gentlewoman (a Mrs. Robinson)" make her first appearance on the stage in the character of Juliet, to the Romeo of William Brereton. Her husband, a young profligate who had been a coeval of Sheridan's at Harrow, was the friend of such young men of fashion as "the wicked" Lord Lyttleton and Captain Edward Ayscough. She was under twenty, and very beautiful. The rehearsals of *Romeo and Juliet* had been conducted with the assistance of Garrick, who had taught her the part, frequently going through the whole of Romeo until he was exhausted by fatigue. At the first performance Sheridan stood in the wings to give her encouragement, while Garrick sat in the centre of the orchestra, from which "his keen and penetrating eyes darted their lustre." So she wrote thirty years later, when she recalled how "the night was concluded with peals of clamourous approbation."

On December 12th he produced *Semiramis* by Captain Ayscough, who was described as a nephew of the "great and amiable" Lord Lyttleton, which was a reflection upon his cousin, the holder of the title. This tragedy was a legacy from Garrick, and Sheridan nobly fulfilled his obligation to his predecessor by writing a prologue to grace the work of his protégé.

When Mr. Dangle in *The Critic* spoke of the nicety of the modern audience, which admitted no *double entendre*, no smart innuendo, "even Congreve and Vanbrugh obliged to undergo a bungling reformation," it was one of Sheridan's jokes against himself, and the efforts of his first season. When he himself revised both Congreve and Vanbrugh, perhaps on Garrick's advice, but more likely by his own inclination, he revived three of Congreve's comedies, which had not been acted for several years. *The Old Batchelor*, on November 19th; *Love for Love* on November 24th; *The Way of the World*, on December 31st. He eliminated expressions which were considered too licentious, and made some slight additions. The extent of these alterations has never been ascertained, but Fanny Burney's Evelina still found *Love for Love* "exceedingly gross and unrefined." As he himself told Michael Kelly, towards the end of his life, it was barbarous to mangle Congreve's plays, for *Love for Love* had been quite spoiled by its concession to "the delicate ears of modern audiences." Moreover, the revivals were not appreciated, as *The London Magazine* declared: "*Love for Love* and *The Old Batchelor* brought some tolerable houses, but on the whole both the town and the managers were disappointed. The parts were not judiciously cast, nor was the whole strength of the company put forth." He also altered *A Trip to Scarborough* from Vanbrugh's *Relapse*.

3

Among the schemes was one that Mary Linley should turn actress. In 1785, after seeing Mrs. Jordan make her first appearance in London as Peggy in *The Country Girl* she wrote to Mrs. Sheridan, "I could not help looking back at past days, during the play, as, if you have any recollection of the circumstances, it was in this play, altered purposely by Garrick, that a certain *friend* of yours was to have made an honourable and delicate *entrée* into the World." This means, of course, that she herself was intended for Peggy, which part in his own comedy Garrick was to alter, no doubt by adding songs which would give her an opportunity of displaying her own especial talent. Perhaps he may have thought of transforming it, with the aid of Thomas Linley, into a ballad-opera. The theory that "a certain friend of yours" meant Sheridan is, from the nature of the piece, untenable, and his own weight must have been thrown against the appearance of his wife's sister as an actress in his theatre.

4

Sheridan was regarded as the destined successor to Garrick in the art of writing prologues and epilogues. During his first season at Drury Lane he gave his assistance in this way to Covent Garden, writing a prologue to *Sir Thomas Overbury*, a tragedy altered by William Woodfall from a play by Savage. It was not, however, what it has always been assumed, an alteration of the piece performed in 1723. Its history is much more curious. At the first appearance of his tragedy, Savage had acted the leading part, but being "destitute of voice, look, and gesture," he failed wretchedly as an actor, and his play with him. Several years later, he resolved to write a second tragedy upon the same story, in which he retained only a few lines of the former, altering its plan totally, adding new incidents and new characters. He wrote his last two acts of it in Swansea, but when he died at Bristol in 1743 he had never succeeded in obtaining enough money to make the journey to place it with the managers in London. So far Johnson has told in his *Life of Savage*, but the sequel has remained hidden in the General Index of *The London Magazine*, in the preface which John Nicholls wrote in 1821. It appears that while Savage was in prison for debt in Bristol, he pawned the play with his gaoler, who sold it after his death for five guineas to Thomas Cadell, the Bristol bookseller. Passing to Cave, the proprietor of *The Gentleman's Magazine*, it lay among his papers for over thirty years, until it was put in the hands of William Woodfall, who made a number of alterations, with some advice and assistance from Garrick and Colman. It was this unacted piece of Savage's that was produced at Covent Garden, so it is small wonder that Johnson was there to see the first performance of a tragedy that had been lost for thirty years.

It was little more than an accident that Sheridan wrote this prologue. Richard Cumberland was first invited, but he had no sympathy with a wicked man like Savage. On January 18th, he wrote Garrick:

"What can I do about *Sir Thomas Overbury?* What I cannot do I well know, and that is that I cannot refuse your request; but I must see the tragedy. I will send for it to Mr. Woodfall, and endeavour at a Prologue; though, I think, upon reading Dr. Johnson's account of Rivers, that he was a bad man, and one for whose memory I have no idolatory."[1]

Sheridan therefore had only a week or so to think over the Prologue, which ended what Boswell called "an elegant compliment" to Johnson on his Dictionary:

[1] *Garrick Correspondence*, II, 207.

"So pleads the tale, that gives to future times
The son's misfortunes, and the parent's crimes;
There shall his fame (if own'd to-night) survive,
Fix'd by the hand that bids our language live."

"The tale," as the original footnote to the printed copies says, is *"The Life of Richard Savage*, by Dr. Samuel Johnson." "Mr. Sheridan," said Boswell, "here at once did honour to his taste and his liberality of sentiment, by shewing that he was not prejudiced by the unlucky difference that had taken place between his worthy father and Dr. Johnson."

In acknowledgment of this compliment, Johnson proposed Sheridan as a member of the Literary Club, observing, (says Boswell) that "he who has written the two best comedies of his age is surely a considerable man." This election took place on March 14th, before *The School for Scandal* had been produced, so Johnson was bestowing this praise upon *The Duenna* and *The Rivals*, exalting them even above *She Stoops to Conquer*. Boswell reflected, "accordingly, he had the honour to be elected, for an honour it undoubtedly must be allowed to be, when it is considered of whom that Society consists, and that a single black ball excludes a candidate."

5

The School for Scandal, produced at Drury Lane on May 5th, 1777, was partly a satire upon contemporary journalism, which dealt lavishly in scandal. It is by no means the earliest play with this interest, for Colman in *The English Merchant* drew a companion portrait to Snake in his Spatter. The Snakes, indeed, spawned in abundance. In his play, *The Capuchin*, Foote depicted a clerical journalist, the Rev. Dr. Viper, the editor of *The Scandalous Chronicle*, who was a caricature of an Irishman, the Rev. Dr. William Jackson, editor of *The Public Ledger*. When *The Capuchin* was produced, Palmer, who acted Dr. Viper, imitated Dr. Jackson's manner, and observed the peculiarity of his dress, which was the wearing of black frogs upon his coat. Mr. Snake also was identified as "the editor of a morning paper" and in a line now deleted from the play, he was described specifically as "a writer and critic." *The London Magazine* said that "beside the general satire which will hold good as long as the English language is read or understood, the particular application of it to a certain modern daily publication, is logically true throughout, and ought to crimson with blushes every cheek which has encouraged such butchery of male and female reputations." This seems to denounce *The Public Ledger*, and fits Snake's cap to Jackson's head: it is just possible, however, that the newspaper in question was *The Morning Post*, also attacked in *An Ode to the Genius of Scandal*, which is supposed to have been written by Sheridan in 1772:

> "Intrigues by the score,
> Never heard of before,
> Shall the paragraphs daily augment,
> And by each *Morning Post*
> Some favourite toast,
> A victim to thee shall be sent."

When this Ode was first published in 1781, however, Parson Bate had been succeeded by Parson Jackson as editor of *The Morning Post*, so the satire may again refer to him. The tradition of dressing Snake in black is a legacy of his clerical occupation.

The scandal was not confined to the daily and weekly newspapers, but flourished as the chief "department" of the *Town and Country Magazine*, which contained a series of memoirs or histories of some prominent man and his latest mistress, or some prominent woman and her latest lover, accompanied by the *tête-à-tête*, which was a plate showing their portraits in vignette. In January 1777, four months before the performance of *The School for Scandal*, the *tête-à-tête* represented "Malgrida and Thalia"; "Malgrida," scholar, orator and politician, was Lord Shelburne, afterwards Marquis of Lansdowne, and his mistress, "Thalia, wife of Mr. A——n, musician," was Mrs. Abington, the original Lady Teazle. Although Sheridan insinuated that in some of these *tête-à-tête* memoirs, "the parties perhaps had never seen each other's faces before in the course of their lives," many of these scandalous chronicles were authentic. After the play was performed, the editor of the *Town and Country Magazine* said that Mr. Sheridan had thought proper "to honour these memoirs with his particular, attention, and that, therefore, he could not help thanking him for the peculiar distinction he had paid to the *tête-à-tête*, since the comedy would have a very great run and the author of this department would thereby be immortalized upon the stage." He added that Sheridan seemed to hint that some of the characters, though printed in a *tête-à-tête* have never seen each other before, but entreated him before he pronounced sentence upon the present, to make use of his own recollections, as to the intrigue "between the Amorous Justice, and Mrs. L——m." The actress in this case was Mrs. Lessingham of Covent Garden, and the Amorous Justice was Major Addington, afterwards Sir William. The satire had no effect for *The Town and Country Magazine*, founded in 1769, flourished for nearly a quarter of a century.

6

On the night before his comedy was to be performed, Sheridan received a message that the licence had been refused. In a debate on the Treason Bill, in the House of Commons in 1795, he narrated the circumstances: When the play was in rehearsal there was the famous contest for the office of Chamberlain of the City of London, between Wilkes and Benjamin Hopkins who had been charged with some practices similar to those of *Moses* the Jew, in lending money to young men under age; and the Reader of Plays supposed that the character was levelled at him, in order to injure his contest, in which he was supported by the ministerial interest. In the warmth of a contested election the piece was represented as a factious and seditious opposition to a court candidate. Sheridan, however, went to Lord Hertford, then Lord Chamberlain, who laughed at the affair, and gave the licence.[1]

[1]Speeches, III, 19.

Benjamin Hopkins was duly elected to the office of Chamberlain of the City of London, and it is difficult to see how his prospects could have been injured by the allusions to the Annuity Bill—the "Bill for registering the grants of annuities, and the better protections of infants against such grants." The character of Moses, however, is scarcely to be deduced from the printed page. It gives no hint that, like Isaac Mendoza, he speaks a dialect which was then called "the Jewish cant." When he introduces Mr. Premium as "a gentleman of the strictest honour and secrecy" he is using one of the stock phrases of a money-lender's advertisement, made ludicrous by his foreign accent. Sir Peter's introduction "Here comes the honest Israelite" is, of course, ironical, and Moses has indeed his pound of flesh. When Charles, holding the banker's draft for eight hundred pounds, says "two-thirds of this is mine by right—five hundred and thirty odd pounds," the obvious implication is that the third belongs to somebody else—that is, to the honest Israelite who made the introduction.

7

John Watkins accused Sheridan with stealing *The School for Scandal*:

"Others again had no scruple in hazarding an opinion that the comedy was not the performance of Sheridan, and what was at first merely suspicion, gathered into the substantial form of positive assertion. By some it was attributed to the pen of [the elder] Mrs. Sheridan; and there were persons who roundly asserted that the play was written by a young lady, the daughter of a merchant in Thames Street; that, at the beginning of the season, when Mr. Sheridan commenced his management, the manuscript was put into his hands for his judgment, soon after which, the fair writer, who was then in a state of decline, went to Bristol Hot-Wells, where she died. Such was the rumour, which so far obtained credit, that Mr. Isaac Reed, a man extremely cautious of giving publicity to loose reports, thought it proper to insert this story in the account which he gave of the play in his edition of the *Biographia Dramatica*."

Isaac Reed did certainly mention the rumour, but added that it was probably the product of envy founded on the success of the piece. Nevertheless, there were some people who could "name the father and the farm-house where the babies were put out to nurse." It remained for John Galt to give the names of the authoress and the custodian of the corroborative evidence. She was Miss Richardson, who was present at the theatre on the first performance, and fainted with excess of emotion. In his *Lives of the Players* Galt cited a letter from an old friend who said: "I was assured by a gentleman, John Oswald, who among other literary engagements reported at that time for *The Oracle*, that Mrs. Phillips, the mother of that celebrated vocalist Mrs. Crouch, had in her possession the rough draught of Miss Richardson's comedy which he had seen, and which, if his testimony may be confided in, established the plagiarism beyond a doubt."[1]

8

Sheridan wrote *The School for Scandal* expressly for the King's Company at the Theatre Royal, Drury Lane. He modelled his dialogue on Congreve, but since his company possessed "every variety of elocution," while composing, he meditated upon the peculiar graces of each player—in James Boaden's words, upon "the lingered sentiment of Palmer" in Surface, "the jovial sentiment of Smith" in Charles, "the caustic shyness of King" in Sir Peter, "the brilliant loquacity of Mrs. Abington" in Lady Teazle. There was a large infusion of the players in their parts. Smith, of Eton and King's College, Cambridge, had retired from the University through a frolic which was brought about by "an unlucky elevation caused by liquor," accompanied by "a little extravagance which deranged his finances," though he left behind him a reputation "for good

[1]Salt Library MSS., Stafford.

talents and a laudable disposition." He was the "Smith, the genteel, the airy, and the smart" of Churchill's *Rosciad*, and though in 1777 he lacked the fire of youth, he was still the mirror of fashion—"his gentlemanly manners," wrote Mrs. Robinson, "and enlightened conversation rendered him an ornament to the profession." Mrs. Abington herself, once a flower-girl in the streets, was a very fine lady, who led the *beau monde* in its modes, and, though her youth was in the past, she had all the airs of good breeding. Palmer was Joseph Surface, at least in his polished and plausible manners, of which there were so many stories, and his winning way of making insincere apologies.

King, too, was Sheridan's collaborator :

> "But with the bard the faithful actor moves,
> And the best comment on the author proves,
> The wayward testiness of ancient life,
> The froward jealousy, and peevish strife,
> How well he marks his Teazle shall proclaim,
> Where bard and actor share a mingled fame."[1]

Dodd, "unrivalled in genteel fops," as Sir Benjamin Backbite; bluff old Yates as Sir Oliver Surface; Miss Pope, who in the Green-Room was Mrs. Candour—all of them were perfectly served by their author, down to the inimitable footman, Trip of La Mash, "the most elegantly made man I ever saw," said John Bernard—"La Mash was naturally a fop, though not a polished one: he could not assume the gentleman, but the gentleman's gentleman fitted him like his clothes: one would have thought his mother had been waiting-maid to the Duchess of Kingston, and his father the duster of Lord Chesterfield's clothes."

Only one part was not distributed as Sheridan would have wished, for Maria was played by Priscilla Hopkins, who afterwards married John Kemble; he intended it for another girl of nineteen, Mary Robinson, who, as she wrote in her *Memoirs*, "acquainted me that he wished me to perform a part in *The*

---

[1] *European Magazine*, 1791.

School for Scandal. I was now so unshaped by my increasing size that I made my excuses, informing Mr. Sheridan that I should probably be confined to my chamber when his since celebrated play would firſt make its appearance. He accepted the apology, and in a short time I gave to the world my second child, Sophia."

Perhaps "he accepted the apology" gives a better key to the ceremonial manners of the age than any other. It connotes the modish ritual, and the elaborate and decorative clothes; all the ladies and gentlemen of the play appeared in the full court-dress, which was to disappear from all but court ceremonies within a little more than a decade, when the French Revolution imposed its sumptuary laws upon the fashions of wealth and extravagance. In a few years court-dress was no longer to be seen at the opera, nor were noble lords in their blue and green ribbons. Forty years later Hazlitt was to caſt a longing lingering look behind at the departed *toupées* and sword-knots of the age of Louis Quatorze—to recall how alone in his age Farren as Sir Peter preserved "the *chevaux de frise* of dress, the trellis-work of lace and ruffles, the portcullises of formal speech, the whole artillery of sighs and ogling, with all the appendages and proper coſtume of the *ancien régime* and paraphernalia of the *preux chevalier*." Sheridan's comedy, was not written to be aćted only by his men and women: it was to be aćted by their clothes also, by the purple and fine raiment of the age of chivalry, so soon to be eclipsed by 'the age of sophiſters and calculators.'

9

There are two curious anecdotes of May 5th, 1777. A newspaper notice of *The School for Scandal* said: "Yeſterday morning Mrs. Sheridan was delivered of a son. The mother and child are likely to do well. In the evening of the same day, Mr. Sheridan's muse was delivered of a bantling which is likely to live for ever."[1] Long afterward, Sheridan told Lord Byron that on the night after the firſt performance, "he was so drunk in the ſtreet that he was nearly taken up by the watch."

[1] W. T. Parke, *Musical Memories*, I, 9.

CHAPTER THE SEVENTH

The Creator of Mr. Puff

I

IN spite of the success of *The School for Scandal*, which came late in the season, the affairs of Drury Lane were the reverse of prosperous. "Poor Old Drury!" sighed David Garrick in a letter of July 17th, 1777, to Thomas King, "It will be, I fear, very soon in the hands of the Philistines." And on March 22nd, 1778, Kitty Clive wrote to Garrick, "Everybody is raving against Mr. Sheridan for his supineness: there never was in nature such a contrast as Garrick and Sheridan. What, have you given him up, that he creeps so?" This season of 1777–1778, to which Sheridan contributed nothing as an author, terminated disastrously.

On May 6th the treasurer, Benjamin Victor, notified Garrick curtly: "I am directed by the proprietors to inform you that it will not be in their power for the future to pay the interest on Mr. Lacy's mortgage until the debts and expenses of the theatre are discharged." Garrick replied that he imagined his mortgage was as just a debt as any upon the theatre, and gave them formal notice that he expected it to be paid off in the time mentioned by the deeds. This was a reminder that unless they satisfied his claim, and discharged the mortgage of £22,000 and interest on demand, they were in penalty of £44,000—"a thumper!" as Garrick endorsed their bond, which they had signed on January 3rd, 1777. On May 15th, however, Garrick wrote Lacy that he might depend upon not doing anything which would give him distress, but before the letter reached him "Mr. Lacy had bargained to sell to Mr. Sheridan at an enormous price." For this moiety, Sheridan paid over £45,000

78

which was £10,000 more than they had paid Garrick for his share. By dividing his own former holding between them, Linley and Ford owned one-fourth each, while he retained one-half.

2

In September 1778, Thomas Sheridan, at the earnest request of the proprietors, entered into office as manager of Drury Lane Theatre. This was a position of authority and responsibility which included the selection of plays and the engagement of performers. When the purchase of the theatre was in negotiation in January 1776, Sheridan had told Linley that his father had promised to assist them, but this plan did not mature, for Thomas Sheridan left England for Ireland, and in July of that year he was playing Hamlet in Dublin.[1]

It is unlikely that Garrick urged the engagement of his old rival, "Tom O'Bedlam" as he called him to Tighe, "Old Bubble-and-Squeak," as Tighe named him in return. Sheridan himself, thirty years afterwards, told Michael Kelly he had been reading Davies's *Life of Garrick*, which he pronounced as "well worth the attention of every actor." In the conversation he dwelt particularly on his father's acting in *King John*—"without partiality," he said, "his scene with Hubert was a masterpiece of the art; and no actor could reach its excellence." He also commended his father's Cato as a masterly performance, as well as his Brutus in *Julius Caesar*.[2] But this was a very belated tribute, for he never permitted his father to perform King John or Cato or Brutus, or any other part—indeed, he expressly prohibited him from acting when he appointed him as acting-manager at Drury Lane in 1778—a condition which his father bitterly resented, and which appears to have been the cause of their previous quarrel in 1776. Thomas Sheridan expressed his own views in a letter written in April 1783, to his son Charles:

"At length a scene opened which promised better days. Garrick's retiring, whose jealousy had long shut the London

[1]Moore, 139. [2]Kelly, II, 351.

theatres against me, such an open[ing] was made for me both
as manager and actor as might soon have retrieved my affairs,
and in no long space of time have placed me in easy circumstances. But here a son of mine steps into possession, whose
first step was to exclude me wholly from having any share
in it. Afterwards, when by extreme ill conduct they were
threatened with ruin, he agreed to put the management into
my hands upon condition that I should not appear as a performer, and in this he got his brother managers to join him
with such earnestness, that merely to gratify him I ac-
quiesced . . . I desire to know whether if the theatre of
Drury Lane had fallen into the hands of the worst enemy
I had in the world, determined upon ruining me and my
family, he could have taken more effectual means of doing
it, than those which have been pursued by my own son?"[1]

3

John O'Keeffe says that Garrick was present at Drury Lane
for the last time at a night-rehearsal of the scenery for Sheridan's *The Camp*, at which he caught the cold that resulted in
his death. This entertainment was brought out on November
15th, 1778.

In the June, a French invasion had been expected and several
large military encampments were formed, the most notable of
which was Coxheath in Kent. The militia were assembled from
all parts of the country and the camp became a great show-
place; the military rage swept over the country and it became
the fashion for ladies to dress *à la militaire*. One of the leaders
in this fashion was the Duchess of Devonshire, whose husband,
the Duke, commanded the Derbyshire regiment of militia.
It was said that Sheridan wrote *The Camp* in compliment to the
Duchess, but it is not easy to see exactly where the compliment
came in. When it was played, *The Town and Country Magazine*
declared: "The chief merit of this performance is due to M. de
Loutherbourg, whose fine representation of Cox-heath Camp

[1]Rae, II, 4.

does great honour to him as an artist. Indeed the whole performance seems chiefly designed to introduce the happy effects
of that great master's pencil, as the dialogue, tho' written
by Mr. Sheridan, can only be considered as a temporary *jeu
d'esprit*."

The Camp did, indeed, ridicule the fashionable camp followers, but it also satirized the sutlers and contractors who
infested the camps. Otherwise, it was actually an incitement to
enlist rather than a deterrent; it displayed on the stage of
Drury Lane a series of military evolutions, which, as was said
at the time, afforded much entertainment as well on account of
their novelty as the dexterity with which they were performed.

It has been disputed that Sheridan was the author of *The
Camp*, but this denial was first made many years afterwards by
Tate Wilkinson in *The Wandering Patentee*. Moore declared
that the author was Richard Tickell, because he discovered a
draft in his handwriting. But such evidence would attribute
many scenes in Sheridan's plays to his wife, in whose handwriting the drafts exist. It is possible, however, that in *The
Camp* Sheridan had a collaborator. O'Daub, the painter, is a
character from *The Maid of the Oaks or The Fête Champêtre*, a
musical entertainment by Lieut.-Gen. John Burgoyne. In a
topical military satire of this type, it is most likely that Sheridan would have consulted Burgoyne, who had returned to England after his defeat by the Americans at Saratoga. As he was
awaiting the Court of Enquiry as to his surrender, it would
have been very unwise for Burgoyne's assistance in a military
satire, however lightly written, to have been revealed. If it
was desired to keep his authorship secret, the employment of
Tickell, instead of one of the copyists in the prompter's room,
would be explained.

Several of the songs, however—five out of nine—were not
written by Sheridan, but by Thomas Hull. In the music, an
oblong folio published by C. & A. Thompson, an advertisement declares, "The Words of the following Airs, Trios, &c,
introduced in the entertainment of the Camp, are many of them
taken from the Comic Opera of the Royal Merchant, set by the

G

same Composer, some of the Musick of which was found particularly applicable to the Subject of this Piece." *The Royal Merchant*, "founded on Beaumont and Fletcher," was adapted from *The Beggar's Bush* by Hull, and the songs had been set to music by Thomas Linley in 1767. It was perhaps the presence of so many songs by Hull which gave rise to the rumour that the author was not Sheridan.[1]

4

Thomas Sheridan entered into office with the same determination that his son had manifested two years before, and resolved to bring discipline into the company, and in particular to check the caprices of the actresses. Unfortunately, his temper was soured by age and disappointment, and his drastic methods brought the performers into a state bordering upon mutiny. The proprietors were impelled to intervene, and his powers were restricted; so, "disdaining to continue in his post under such ignominious terms, he relinquished it after three seasons."[2] He blamed Richard continuously, complaining to his elder son Charles of "the behaviour of that wretch." But towards the end of his life, he realized that the fault had not been entirely his son's. His daughter Betsy wrote from Bath in 1786 to her sister in Dublin that: "In speaking of Dick he is the first to say what you or I or any of his friends last year would have wished to insinuate, but in vain. He acknowledges his neglect of him; and that even in the theatrical business, which so severely hurt him, he did not wonder at his conduct, when he reflected that it was all done with a view to serve him and the other patentees, yet still he so thwarted Dick's schemes and wishes that he was not surprised he opposed him."[3]

Thomas Sheridan was manager for three seasons, holding office, it appears, till June 1781. There is not much to be said of his management; while Richard Sheridan had no objection

---

[1]Mr. F. W. Bateson, who called my attention to this advertisement suggests that Hull, instead of Burgoyne or Tickell, may have been the collaborator.

[2]*European Magazine*, December 1789.　　　[3]Lefanu MSS., 110, July 11th, 1786.

to his father being a manager, he was not ready to revive the taunt which rankled so deeply that he was "a player's son."

5

The Critic was performed for the first time on October 30th, 1779.

According to the gossip of the Greenroom, it was "originally intended as an interlude, and only the first act meant to be performed, but at the instigation of that valuable comedian, Mr. Parsons, he changed his design, and added another act, the major part of which he wrote while at Harrow School."[1] Behind this fable was the fact that while at Bath, Sheridan had collaborated with Halhed, his schoolfellow, in the burletta of *Ixion*; he had converted it into "a rehearsal," and created Simile, the author, in whom in Moore's words, "Mr. Puff had a sort of dim and shadowy pre-existence." Yet in *The Critic* Mr. Puff's tragedy of *The Spanish Armada* was an afterthought.

In June 1779, the Spanish Ambassador delivered a declaration of war at the Court of St. James's, and the country was filled with expectation of a Spanish Invasion. As Mr. Puff explains, it is not merely actors but plays that should be the abstract and brief chronicles of the times—"Therefore when history, and particularly the history of our country, furnishes anything like a case in point to the time in which an author writes, if he knows his own interest, he will take advantage of it." Accordingly, at Sadler's Wells Theatre, the manager found in the history of our own country, "a case in point," and he responded with a piece called *The Prophecy; or, Queen Elizabeth at Tilbury*. This concluded with "a perspective of the destruction of the Spanish Armada." It was described in a contemporary periodical: "The curtain rises. The scene discovers a part of the country near Tilbury; an excellent representation of the important fort, the part adjoining the river terminating the perspective." After sundry songs, during which the populace gather, the Queen at length approaches, "riding on a fine

[1]Pasquin, *Life of Edwin*, 1791.

palfrey, richly caparisoned." She is saluted by her people, who express their loyalty in songs to which she duly replies in a song that ends:

> "To herself let England be true,
>   In spite of each threat and bravado,
> Protected by Heaven and you,
>   I laugh at the Spanish Armada."

Thereupon, to slow music, a cloud descends upon earth, out of which steps the Genius of Britain, telling Elizabeth she has nothing to fear from the perfidious House of Bourbon, and promising to present her with a view, "in an airy mirror," of what shall happen in the reign of Great George our King. The genius waves his sceptre, the cloud rejoins the sky, and "a striking spectacle is exhibited in which the Navy of England appears riding triumphant on the seas, and the Fleets of Spain and France, broken, dismasted and vanquished." The "Prophecy"—a contemporary account in *The Gazetteer* gravely concludes—"is that England will ever be victorious if Britons are true to themselves."

The general similarity of *The Prophecy* to *The Spanish Armada or Queen Elizabeth at Tilbury*, is obvious. Tilburina's prophecy of the destruction of the new Armada is finally disposed of by her father's immortal words:

> "The Spanish Fleet thou canst not see—because
> It is not yet in sight."

The manager who produced *The Prophecy*, and who must have planned it, was Thomas King, the original Mr. Puff.

Sheridan did not, of course, find the whole world in favour of *The Critic*. The adverse opinion may be represented by *The British Review*, in an article of 1783, which was written with a political bias against him. It denounced *The Critic* as "the offspring of a pen that had in vain tried to write a tragedy, and felt a malicious pleasure in decrying a form in which it had failed. The models, *The Rehearsal* and *Tom Thumb the Great*, were written by authors who confined their sarcasms to the real defects of tragedy, and not the imaginary ones, as was testified by the Key which accompanied the one, and the Explanatory Notes which accompanied the other." The most cursory examiner "must be disgusted at his *outré* representation of such incidents as must necessarily occur in the best tragedies." Sheridan told Michael Kelly that he valued the first act of *The Critic* more than anything he ever wrote.

6

For the annual pantomime of 1779, Sheridan decided to revive *Harlequin Fortunatus or The Wishing Cap*, and invented an Interlude for it called *The Storming and Taking of Fort Omoa*. It was prepared with great rapidity. On December 18th, 1779, *The London Gazette* contained the despatch narrating the capture of Port Omoa, in the Bay of Honduras. In a fortnight, Loutherbourg had painted three scenes of the Fort, with its defences, and Sheridan had dramatized, or "pantomimed," the despatch, from the scaling by the sailors and the surrender of the Spanish Governor. The despatch applauded "an instance of the elevated mind in a British tar" who scaled the walls with two cutlasses; encountering a Spanish officer who had been roused out of his sleep without arms, he scorned to take advantage, but gave him one of the cutlasses, fought him, disarmed him, and spared his life. This incident was incorporated into the action.

At one of the last rehearsals, when the scenery had been painted, Sheridan found everything in confusion because no time had been allowed for the carpenters to get a scene. It was suggested that another song should be introduced, so there and then he sat down at the prompter's table on the stage, and wrote the ballad of "The Midnight Watch." This was set to music by Thomas Linley, his father-in-law, in a style, says Michael Kelly, which "established it as one of the most beautiful specimens of pure English melody." The first verse ran:

"When 'tis night, and the mid-watch is come,
    And chilling mists hang o'er the darken'd main,

Then sailors think of their far diſtant home,
 And of those friends they ne'er may see again:
  But when the fight's begun,
  Each serving at his gun,
 Should any thought of them come o'er our mind,
 We think but, should the day be won,
 How 'twill chear their hearts to hear
 That their old companion he was one."[1]

This was lofty, this was Ercles' vein, and the Mr. Puff who was within Sheridan was so delighted with it, that he revived it in his two other patriotic interludes of the next decade—*The Glorious Firſt of June*, in 1794, and *Cape St. Vincent or British Valour Triumphant*, in 1797.

7

Robinson Crusoe, a pantomime, produced at Drury Lane on January 21ſt, 1781, was the laſt of Sheridan's attempts at writing pieces for the business of the theatre.

When Horace Walpole found Sheridan's *Robinson Crusoe* incoherent, he added, "how unlike the pantomimes of Rich, which are full of wit, and carried in a ſtory." Sheridan had entered into rivalry with the pantomimiſt of Covent Garden Messink, which moved *The European Magazine* to say that *The Critic* was followed by *Robinson Crusoe*, "the laſt inferior to the worſt performance of Mr. Messink, and a proof that even the greateſt genius will sink beneath contempt when he contends with a mechanic in his own profession." However, this is suspiciously like a general condemnation of pantomime as such, though there was no reason that the author of *The School for Scandal* should be denied the office of inventing a harlequinade. But it happens that of the three parts into which it is divided, only the firſt is founded upon Daniel Defoe's *Robinson Crusoe*— a subjeƈt new to the English ſtage. The aƈtion was summarized in a pamphlet published by Becket under the title of "A Short Account of the Situations and Incidents in the pantomime of

<hr>

[1] *Plays and Poems*, III, 238.

Robinson Crusoe at the Theatre Royal, Drury Lane, 1781,"
which consists largely of extracts from Defoe.

In *The History of the British Theatres*, by Walley C. Oulton, is
the incredible note:

> "*Robinson Crusoe*. It is said that the present Mr. Sheridan
> performed the part of Harlequin Friday the first evening of
> its representation."

CHAPTER THE EIGHTH
Mr. Sheridan, M.P.

I

SHERIDAN'S first appearance in the character of a politician was made at Westminster Hall on February 2nd, 1780, in support of Charles Fox, who on that occasion presented his resolutions in favour of annual parliaments and universal suffrage, together with a report on the question signed by Sheridan as Chairman of the Sub-Committee of the Westminster Reform Association. He was at once ridiculed and attacked in the first squib of his political career, "An Epistle from Joseph Surface, Esq., to Richard Brinsley Sheridan, Esq., of Great Queen Street."

When Parliament was dissolved in 1780, Sheridan determined to enter the House of Commons. He made a tour of the West Country, in search of "free and independent boroughs" where the votes were not entirely controlled by some nobleman or other landowner. His hopes fell upon Honiton in Devonshire, and he requested Ozias Humphrey the painter, a native of the borough, to write two letters on his behalf—the first to tell the burgesses that "before the election, yet a good man and true may offer, and pay them too, and that they should act accordingly"; the second, a letter of introduction, to "notify that I am the person, and puff me, too." Humphrey therefore wrote a letter to "a leading burgess," recommending Sheridan, as "a particular friend of Mr. Charles Fox, Mr. Fitzpatrick, and all the first and most considerable characters in this kingdom," as a person of "the most shining talents and independent principles,"—"Either ministry or opposition would be happy to engage him," he continued, "but he will be independent—If you should chuse to interest yourself, and should have any of your voters unengaged, you could never bestow them on one who has more ability to be generally useful, or who can be more particularly serviceable to the inhabitants of Honiton, as he is beloved and almost adored by all parties."[1]

This panegyric was unavailing, for the "damned fellows of Honiton" as Sheridan wrote to Humphrey on September 3rd, chose "a Scotsman—and a Mac too," one Alexander Macleod, whose election, however was afterwards declared void, on a petition of bribery.

2

But as one door shuts, another opens. On the very day of this disappointment, it seems, Charles Fox carried Sheridan to Devonshire House, where he met Colonel Edward Monckton, a son of Viscount Galway, who was to contest Stafford, where Earl Spencer, the Duchess's father, had considerable influence and property. It was settled that Sheridan should ally himself with Monckton and contest the second seat in opposition to the two ministerial candidates, Whitworth and Drummond. At the borough of Stafford, in the words of Edward Quin in *Public Characters of* 1799, he experienced "uncommon disinterestedness and great liberality of conduct": nevertheless, he could not avoid a certain degree of expense, "which has, for a long time, blended itself with the purest proceedings of the elective system in this country." He soon found "that the moderate sum of one thousand pounds was a *sine qua non* which alone could bring the negotiation between the new champion of liberty and the independent electors to a successful conclusion."

His resources were small, but he succeeded in raising the money, rewarding the largest subscriber with a share in the Opera House. The contest was brief. On September 12th the Mayor. of Stafford declared the poll, and Colonel Edward Monckton and Mr. Richard Brinsley Sheridan contemplated with rapture the figures at the close :

[1]Watkins, I, 252–3.

"*Monckton* 258, *Sheridan* 247, *Whitworth* 168, *Drummond* 46.*"

They indited this letter of thanks to the Free and Worthy Burgesses of Stafford:

"We have found you men of your words—we will deserve the continuing of your friendship. You may truthfully say you have served us. If we deceive you, you will have no difficulty in turning us out again, as we shall deserve. Independent candidates will be no more afraid to offer themselves, for you will have made it appear that you are the *masters of your own rights*, and that you are determined to hold them in your own hands, and to keep your borough *free*."

Five-and-twenty years later, when he was staying with the Prince of Wales at Brighton, he told Thomas Creevey that when, after dinner that day, "he stole away by himself to speculate upon those prospects of distinguishing himself which had been opened to him," it was then "the happiest moment of his life."[1]

Sheridan expressed his gratitude to the Duchess of Devonshire with a stately formality which shows that their intimacy was as yet distant. "Madam," he wrote seven days after the election, "I am entirely at a loss how to thank Your Grace for the Honor and Service which Your Grace's condescending to interest yourself in my election at Stafford has been to me."[2]

Richard Whitworth, who had represented Stafford for three Parliaments, complained of an undue election, alleging bribery and corruption against the new members. Sheridan's first speech in the House of Commons replied to this charge, describing it as frivolous and malicious. It was, he declared, "a most serious hardship, that upon the accusation of a few of the lowest and most unprincipled voters in any borough, a numerous and respectable body should remain traduced and stigmatized in the eyes of this House, for the space of a year, in a petition which should at last be proved a gross and groundless

[1] *The Creevey Papers*, I, 57.   [2] *Anglo-Saxon Review*, September 1899, 46.

libel."[1] Although the contemporary reports state that he was "heard with particular attention, the House being uncommonly still while he was speaking," after the speech, Sheridan went up to the gallery, and asked William Woodfall, the great parliamentary reporter, with much anxiety what he thought of his success. Woodfall answered, "I think this is not your line. No, Sheridan; you had much better stick to those pursuits you are so much more fitted for." Sheridan bowed his forehead upon his hand for a few seconds, and then, looking up, exclaimed, "It is in me; and, by God, it shall come out."[2]

The petition, thus threatened by Whitworth was never completed, though it was not until the statutory lapse of a whole year that he was safe: his wife wrote his sister, Alicia Lefanu, on December 20th, 1781: "You will no doubt rejoice with us on Dick's triumph over the Ministry. All their efforts to procure a petition against him have been overthrown by his spirited exertions and he had the satisfaction of bringing himself the intelligence of their ill success to the House of Commons on the last day of receiving petitions, when they were all waiting in expectation of its coming—so that is one cloud removed which has for some time hung over his head."[3] Sheridan's virtuous indignation is a little curious. How he expended his thousand pounds in 1780 is not recorded; but ten years later a statement was prepared of his annual expenditure as Member for Stafford.

But at the head of the statement is this entry:

"Expenses at the Borough of Stafford for election anno 1784. 248 burgesses paid £5 5s. each . . . £1,302. 0. 0."

There is nothing to indicate the reason for this, yet it continued the custom for the two members for the borough to pay every burgess the sum of five guineas until after the Parliamentary Reform Act of the nineteenth century, at which time it was alleged that the system was initiated by Sheridan in 1780. Upon what legal pretext it was justified, and removed beyond the charge of bribery, is not to be ascertained.

[1]*Speeches*, I, 2.　　　　[2]Rae, I, 359.　　　　[3]Sichel, II, 391.

3

Sheridan was, for the next thirty years, to be regarded by the House of Commons as one of its most delightful speakers. At first he was inclined to take himself very solemnly, and rebuked others for their levity. He was pained by the speeches of Henry Courtenay, who was one of those men whose intervention in debate the House has always regarded with delight. He exercised his raillery upon a bill of Burke's in February 1781, when Sheridan had been only a few months a member.

"Mr. Sheridan then reprehended Mr. Courtenay for turning everything that passed into ridicule; and for having introduced into the house a style of reasoning, in his opinion, every way unsuitable to the gravity and importance of the subjects that came under their discussion. If they could not act with dignity, he thought they might at least debate with decency." How the House must have groaned inwardly at this rebuke! Then the author of *The School for Scandal* proceeded "to indict a trope": saying that Courtenay had "favoured them with a simile which insinuated that Opposition was envious of those who basked in court sunshine, being desirous merely to get in their places. He begged leave to remind the honourable member that though the sun afforded a genial warmth, it also occasioned an intemperate heat that tainted everything it reflected on; that this excessive heat tended to corrupt as well as to cherish—to putrify as well as to animate—to dry and soak up the wholesome juices of the body politic, and to turn the whole of it into one mass of corruption."

After another florid excursion in the same vein, he added that he should not deign to offer any reply to the honourable gentleman, merely observing that the most serious part of his argument seemed to him the most ludicrous. To this ponderous protest, Courtenay instantly observed that "the honourable gentleman seemed to be inimical to mirth and wit in any house but his own."

He soon found the accusation he had made against Courtenay repeated against himself. The famous occasion was during a debate of 1783, concerning the draft Treaty of Peace with

France, Spain, and the United States. William Pitt, Chancellor of the Exchequer, complained that the procedure adopted, was unprecedented, preposterous, and inconsistent with the established usage of the House. Sheridan sneered, "The Right Honourable Gentleman is more a practical politician than an experienced one; his years and his very early political exaltation, have not permitted him to look where there have been precedents, or to acquire a knowledge of the Journals of the House. Had his youth permitted him to acquire such knowledge, his discretion would not have suffered his abilities, which I greatly admire, to be carried away by his heat and precipitancy; he would not have resented with so much indignation the asking of questions, which it was the duty of ministers to satisfy."[1]

At the conclusion of this speech, Pitt, not unjustifiably, returned sneer for sneer: "no man admires more than I do the abilities of the honourable gentleman, the elegant sallies of his thought, the gay effusions of his fancy, his dramatic turns, and his epigrammatic points; and if they were reserved for a proper stage, they would, no doubt, receive what the honourable gentleman's abilities always did receive, the plaudits of the audience; and it would be my fortune *sui plausu gaudere theatri*. But this is not the proper scene for the exhibition of these elegancies; and I, therefore, must beg leave to call the attention of the House to the serious consideration of the very important question then before it." Sheridan then rose to say that he noticed the personality and made no comment upon it; its propriety, taste and gentlemanly point must have been obvious to the House. "But," he added, "let me assure the right honourable gentleman, that I do now, and will at any time when he chooses to repeat this sort of allusion, meet it with the most sincere good humour. Nay, I will say more; flattered and encouraged by the right honourable gentleman's panegyric on my talents, if ever I again engage in the compositions he alludes to, I may be tempted to an act of presumption, to attempt an improvement on one of Ben Jonson's best characters, the character of the *Angry Boy* in the *Alchymist*."[2]

[1] *Speeches*, I, 32–3.   [2] *Speeches*, II, 38.

Sheridan treasured the memory of this rebuke, and twenty years later Michael Kelly restored him from despondency by an allusion to his famous retort. In 1794, however, George Rose mocked him in the same vein in a demand that taxes should be levied on all incomes derived from places or pensions; Sheridan chose to instance the places enjoyed by Rose of which he had received a list, but being too long, he declined to read it. "Read, read," was the cry, so he began: "Clerk to the House of Lords, Surveyor of the Green Wax; Secretary to the Treasury; Master of the Pleas"—here he hesitated, and the cry "Read" being repeated, he enquired whether the House was not satisfied after having heard four enumerated; there were, in fact, two more on the paper, but as they were written in pencil, he could not make them out. George Rose, in reply, assured the House that the statement was untrue; he did not hold six places, but only three: "*Tax Placemen and Pensioners*, is, I admit, a popular cry; yet," he added, "I do not perceive why they should be more taxed than the honourable gentleman as manager of his Theatre, or a man who travels the country with a puppet-show on his back." Sheridan, with considerable indignation, protested against being once more a subject "of the same joke respecting his theatrical property."

4

In livening a debate, no man had ever excelled and few ever equalled Sheridan, who was always alert to entertain the Members by the exercise of good-humour and the graces of a happy imagination. One instance occurred in his speech on the Perfume Tax. "In the recent administration," he said, "acts for taxation have multiplied so excessively that the Justices of the Peace who had to administer them must often have puzzled their wise heads, especially as the bills had been drafted so carelessly, that session after session they came up for amendment and explanation. The preamble of the final act, which repealed the others, reminds me of the ingenious moral tale that had often afforded me amusement in my early days, under the title of 'The House that Jack Built.' First there comes the act imposing the tax; next comes an act to amend the act for imposing the tax; then comes an act to explain the act that amended the act, and next an act to remedy the defects of the act for explaining the act that amended the act; and so on, *ad infinitum*. A tax-bill is like a ship built in a dockyard, which put to sea on the first voyage before it was discovered that they had forgotten the rudder. After every voyage, it revealed some new defect that had to be remedied; it had to be caulked, then to be new-planked, then to be new-rigged, then to be careened, and after all these expensive alterations, the vessel was obliged to be broken up and rebuilt. In fact, every recent bill has gone through as many transformations as a butterfly's egg before it emerges as a butterfly." The tax under consideration being one on perfumery, he concluded an "extremely erratic but entertaining speech" by applying to the House of Commons these lines from Pope's *Rape of the Lock*:

> "Our humble province is to tend the fair,
> Not a less pleasing, though less glorious care;
> To save the powder from too rude a gale,
> Nor let the 'imprison'd' essences exhale."

5

With his entry into Parliament, Sheridan began even more to neglect the theatre, Edmund Burke wrote to Dr. Andrew Halliday of Belfast on July 28th, 1781:

"Mr. Sheridan has at length got disengaged from his attendance at the Parliament house and the playhouse, and has found time to take his pleasure, and having the choice of the pleasures he should take, has read your play. He told me he is extremely struck with it as original in its manner, or at least as differing from the usual style, and highly affecting in several scenes. But he proposes to suggest some alterations to you, from his theatrical experience, which he thinks you will not disapprove, and which he conceives will contribute to the success of the piece. He proposes to bring it on next winter. This I have no doubt he will do. As to the alterations, it may take some time before I shall be able to transmit to you his ideas on that head. For with a thousand good qualities, he has the faults common to men of great genius, as well as of no genius—I mean laziness and procrastination—the faults, however, which have kept back pieces of his own as well as of other people, and have been (as indeed such faults usually are) more prejudicial to himself than anyone else."

Dr. Halliday checked his impatience for two or three years, and then enquired what had happened to his tragedy. The only satisfaction that he received, as he wrote the Earl of Charlemont in 1791, was a message that it had been mislaid, and a search for it had been made in vain.

The most striking evidence of Sheridan's severance from the theatre is to be found in his prologues and epilogues. During their management of Drury Lane and Covent Garden, David Garrick and George Colman wrote dozens of these *pièces d'occasion*. Yet in spite of a talent in which he equalled such masters as John Dryden, Sheridan's output was meagre, and he wrote only nine prologues or epilogues, and all of them in six years. After 1781, during almost thirty years of "management" he wrote no other "head or tail"; when he required a prologue for his own *Pizarro*, he contented himself by taking the first thirty lines of the prologue to *The Miniature Picture*, and added this solitary couplet:

> "Should our play please, and you're indulgent ever,
> Kindly decree 'Tis better late than never!' "

6

Sheridan had been in Parliament for a little more than a year when Lord Rockingham became Prime Minister, with Shelburne and Fox as Secretaries of State. In March 1782, therefore, he was given office as under-secretary for the northern department [for foreign affairs] and he at once decided to relinquish his management of Drury Lane in order to devote his life to politics. His intention was stated in a letter to the Earl of Surrey, the heir to the Dukedom of Norfolk, who had asked him

BURKE, FOX, SHERIDAN　　THE PRINCE OF WALES,　PITT, 1789

for the privilege known as "the freedom of the greenroom." He wrote:

"April 4th, '82.

"The Truth is that what you desire (tho in my opinion it is a compliment from you to ask it) is a matter that does not rest wholly with me, and it is a point about which I have had some bickering with my Partners, who talk of *general rules* being broken, Partialities &c. &c.—however I hope I am settling it to your satisfaction, the Ctee. have never given any formal leave but to those who claim a right, others drop in as private friends and your L'ship will do me honor to use that claim: and when I abandon my Power there I will do my best to leave it as a priviledge.—I shall certainly be obliged to give up my Theatrical administration, and I am even at present only holding it, like Ld. North on the day of your L'ship motion, till a new and I hope a better government is fixed.

"For my own Part I have taken a resolution, which I have confidence enough in myself to know I can help, to give myself up thoroughly and diligently to a Business and a Pursuit which wether I am right or not is more to my fancy and Feelings—

"I have the honour to be

"my Dr. Lord,

"Yours sincerely

"R. B. Sheridan."[1]

But four months later, on the death of Rockingham, the King appointed Lord Shelburne as Prime Minister instead of the Duke of Portland; the party divided into two sections, Fox, Burke and Sheridan being among those who resigned office. He was a minister again as Secretary to the Treasury, in the Coalition government under Lord North and Fox from April 2nd to December 18th, 1783.

But with his preoccupation with the cares of office, it must be deduced that, while the close of the theatrical seasons of 1782

[1]Norfolk MSS., Catholic Record Society.

H

and 1783 did not tax his attention very severely, it was in the September of 1783 that Thomas Linley formally took Sheridan's place in the management of the theatre. For the next five years he was deeply engrossed in his political pursuits.

7

The affairs of the East India Company first engaged Sheridan's attention during this period of office. In the course of time, the Company had been transformed from a trading corporation to a body which exercised sovereign power over the dominions. Its agents had gone to India as poor men, and returned as "nabobs," whose great fortunes were held up to the execrations of their fellows. During the transition, administrative abuses had crept in, and Charles Fox determined that they should be reformed. He founded his case, however, upon an assertion that the East India Company was a bankrupt concern; while its accounts showed a balance of three million pounds, Fox declared that a large number of its assets were quite illusionary, and that actually its liabilities exceeded them by no less than nine million pounds.

His East India Bill of 1783 proposed, in effect, to confiscate the properties of the Company, and vest its affairs in a commission, nominated at first by Parliament, and afterwards by the Crown. The seven commissioners, whose names were suggested, were all supporters of the Ministry and his bill was construed as an attempt to vest the extensive powers into his own hands, and constitute himself a supreme India Dictator. James Sayer, a barrister, who was one of Pitt's supporters, dubbed Charles Fox "Carlo Khan," and caricatured him, in Indian costume, riding on an elephant whose face is Lord North's, preceded by Edmund Burke as a trumpeter, making a triumphant entry into Leadenhall Street, where the East India offices were. This caricature had a tremendous sale, and, as Fox admitted, gave his East India Bill its severest blow in popular estimation. But it passed the House of Commons by a large majority. When, however, it came before the Lords, the King intervened, though he never expressed any disapproval to his ministers. He was fearful that it should destroy his power and alienate India from the Crown. He let it be said that the peers who voted for the bill were not the King's friends, but his enemies, and commanded the Lords of the Bedchamber to vote against it. Accordingly, the bill was thrown out and the King dismissed his ministers. Sheridan was once again in opposition.

8

Sheridan was one of the several members of the opposition who were caustically criticized in *The Royal Register*, a series of 'characters" of 1784 which purported to be written by the King. He was pilloried as:

"The Political Adventurer

"It could not happen in any country but England:

"That a young man, the son of a player, who had exhibited with his father as an oratorical lecturer,[1] and afterwards married the daughter of a musician, should refuse though in very distressed circumstances, to let his wife sing at a royal concert, and at an enormous salary, because it would degrade his character as a *gentleman*:

"That this *gentleman*, after having written a successful piece or two at one theatre, should find the means of raising sufficient sums of money to become the purchaser of a considerable share in another, and afterwards the chief proprietor of a third:

"That this *author* and *manager*, having, by the success and merit of his productions, established his character as a man of wit, and by his wife's concerts made an acquaintance with the fashionable world, should live in a style of elegance and expense, that would soon beggar a large fortune:

"That this *man of fashion*, being so embarrassed as not to find the most common credit, and apprehensive even of fatal inconveniency to his public property, should desert the

---

[1]This appears to have been in confusion with his brother. "Charles Francis Sheridan never recited in public but once, and that was when he was a boy. [On February 26th— cf. Whyte, *Miscellanea Nova*, 105]. Richard was never brought forward in that way.' — Lefanu, 351.

comic muse for politics; contrive, with the laſt guinea of borrowed purse, to get elected into parliament, and set up, at
once, for an active politician, exclaiming againſt placemen
and miniſters, and boaſting the loudeſt zeal for patriot integrity and public virtue:

"That this *upright senator*, after having been very generally black-balled at some of the fashionable clubs, having no
money to lose, and being the object of real dislike to some
very respectable members of one of those societies, should be
able to prevail on men of rank and fashion to concern themselves in a very pitiful and dirty artifice, to secure a clandestine admission for him:[1]

"That this *worthy member of Brookes's*, by his utility as an
active member of parliament, and other little qualifications
useful in the runner of a faction, should, in a change of public men, be at length appointed to a place of real oſtensibil-
ity, and, living in defiance of all economy himself, become an
economiſt for the nation.

" Such a little progressive biographical hiſtory is peculiar to
Old England; a country favourable beyond all others to The
Political Adventurer."[2]

9

The orator had little time for the theatre. Thomas King
entered upon his duties as acting-manager—or producer—in
place of Thomas Sheridan on September 17th, 1782. Six years
afterward, when he resigned, and the critics wished to know
why, he replied with "Mr. King's Address to the Public." He
explained that his powers had been severely reſtricted, and he
had been censured for faults which were not his:—he had been
called to account by authors for breach of promise in not performing plays that he had never heard of; he had been ar-
raigned for rejecting actors and actresses with whom he had no

---

[1]Sheridan was elected to Brookes's on November 2nd, 1780 (Rae, I, 355). George
Selwyn and Lord Bessborough intended to blackball him, but were tricked into absence
from the ballot by false messages (Wraxall, *Posthumous Memoirs*, III, 275–6). The
story is doubtful, but persistent.

[2]Watkins, I, 308–10.

power to negotiate; he had been censured for not providing new plays, which was not his province.

"Should anyone ask," he continued, "the further question, 'If I was not manager, who was?'—I should be forced to answer, like friend Atall, in the comedy—to the first, *I don't know*; and to the last, *I can't tell*. I can only once more positively assert, *I was not Manager*; for I had not the power by my agreement, nor indeed had I the wish to approve or reject any dramatic work, the liberty of engaging, encouraging, or discharging any one performer, nor sufficient authority to command the cleaning a coat, or adding, by way of decoration, a yard of copper lace; both which, it must be allowed, were often much wanted."[1]

Sheridan provided neither new tragedies for Mrs. Siddons, nor new comedies for Mrs. Jordan; and never encouraged authors—"the theatre," as Boaden said, "was never really and truly thrown open to such talent as there was among us." Sheridan would undertake everything, and do nothing. There was "a Committee of Proprietors," who, however, were concerned only with the wardrobe, and their consent for the smallest outlay was not given without the concurrence of Sheridan, who was always too busy either to give it or refuse it.[2]

In the House of Commons in March 1788, when opposing the bill to license the performance at Sadler's Wells, Sheridan alluded to the time "when he knew more of what was going on with respect to the theatres than he did at present, having long since entrusted his interest in them to the management of others."

10

Sheridan wrote nothing himself. Various plays have been suggested as his; for instance, *King Arthur*, *A Fairy Opera*, one of the plays presented to the British Museum by Coventry Patmore. It is argued that this was the play he persuaded Mrs. Crewe, who was departing for Crewe Hall, to attend in Mrs.

[1] *European Magazine*, 1788, 303.　　　[2] Boaden, *Jordan*, 110.

Garrick's box on the first night, at Drury Lane on November 22nd, 1784. But this was printed in 1786 as "*Arthur and Emmeline*, abridg'd from the masque of King Arthur, as alter'd from Dryden by David Garrick."

Sheridan was not acting as director of the theatre at that time; he had left it to his father-in-law, Thomas Linley. His wife, who was a rigid economist, protested strongly against the expense of producing *Arthur and Emmeline*. Mrs. Sheridan was then on a visit to Mrs. Bouverie at Delaprè Abbey, and her sister sent an account of the production in an amusing letter which gives, in a few words, an admirable picture of her mother: she reports Mrs. Linley's conversation to her:

"Oh Tickell, I'm fretted to death. These Devils! but it's all Mr. King's fault." "Why, what's the matter, ma'am?" "Why, do you know they've hired a whole Regiment of Guards a'most for Arthur, and for what? as I said—for you know, there's plenty of common men about our house; that always comes on for sailors and why should they not make as good soldiers?" "Why, because, forsooth, they can't march in time, ma'am."

"But my husband is such a fool."[1]

I I

During Linley's absence, while King was deputy-manager, Mrs. Sheridan continued her interest in the operas and musical entertainments. Writing her father on September 5th, 1785, before the opening of the season, she was glad to hear that he had decided to leave Bath for Brighthelmstone, and cheered him by saying that there was no doubt this would be a better season than they had ever had.

"By Sheridan's desire, too, Mr. Cobb has been some time engaged in writing an Opera, which is finished and which Mr. King thinks very highly of. Sheridan has promised to correct and improve it, and proposes that you should take it

[1]Clementina Black, *The Linley's of Bath*, 165.

with you to the sea-side, where the setting it will, I trust, be no unprofitable amusement to you. Sheridan has a great opinion of Cobb as a comic writer, and means to give him every assistance in his power, but he has been particularly anxious to have this Opera finished on your account, as he thinks (with me) that such an employment will occupy your thoughts, and assist the sea air to dissipate all your glooms and bring you back to us as well and happy as we wish you to be."[1]

The opera was *The Strangers at Home*, acted at Drury Lane on December 8th, 1785, but Sheridan's "corrections and improvements," if they were ever made, are not apparent. Linley wrote the music.

In the same letter to her father, Mrs. Sheridan spoke of a new play by General Burgoyne, about which her sister wrote shortly afterwards: "I must scribble my critique on *The Heiress* (which perhaps is a name you may not know the new comedy by). I think your applause much too cold for it, and I'm sure I can find the hand of the *Master* in several tints—eh? Is it not so ? "[2]

"In the very middle of the night" after the production on January 14th, 1786, Mrs. Tickell wrote her sister at Delaprè Abbey, where they were staying with Mrs. Bouverie: "The play went off with the most brilliant and satisfactory applause, epilogue and all, which poor Burgoyne had prepared in a hurry, in case of an emergency. They have had a meeting at King's to-day, (or I believe rather yesterday) to make a few necessary curtailments which the whole house was of opinion was the only thing to be done to it, to render it the most finished performance since the comedy *The School for Scandal*."[3]

"The epilogue" had been promised by Sheridan, but when the cover which was supposed to contain it was opened, there was no enclosure. There are some fragments of an epilogue to be spoken by "a Woman of Fashion" which appear to belong to it[4] but as for "the hand of the Master" in the comedy, they

[1]Rae, II, 19.   [2]Rae, II, 22.   [3]Rae, II, 22–3.   [4]*Plays*, III, 286.

cannot be detected. Yet it is curious to find that, with Sheridan's tenacity to an idea, he may have revised it. In *The Slanderers*, the first sheet of jottings that he made for *The School for Scandal*, Sheridan wrote:

"Lud, Ma'am, the match is certainly broke—no creature knows the cause—some say a flaw in the lady's character, and others in the gentleman's fortune."

In *The Heiress* this occurs:

Alscrip. That cursed, cursed flaw.
Miss Alscrip. Flaw! who has dared to talk of one? not in my reputation Sir?
Alscrip. No, but in my estate, which is a damn'd deal worse.

12

Mrs. Sheridan assisted her father in many ways at the theatre. In 1787 when Kelly arrived in London, he went to the Linleys' house in Norfolk Street, Strand, where he found Mrs. Tickell, and Mrs. Sheridan, who asked him to go to Drury Lane to see *Richard Cœur de Lion*, for which Grètry's music had been adapted by her father, as she was most anxious to learn the relative merits of the French and English pieces. "General Burgoyne," he explained, "had translated it, and Mrs. Sheridan had adapted it to the English stage." When Kelly joined the company, in April 1787, he made his first appearance in *Lionel and Clarissa*, being coached in the acting by Thomas King and in the music by Thomas Linley, while a new air by Sarti was introduced for him, the words being written by Richard Tickell. His second piece was *Love in a Village*, to which there was added a new song; Mrs. Sheridan writing to an aria of Gluck's the song "Love thou maddening power."

Mrs. Sheridan herself wrote an entertainment called *The Haunted Village*, which she gave her husband "to add some touches to," but could never get it from him again. William Linley, her brother, "seemed to think he suppressed it from jealousy."[1] But surmises of this kind are dangerous, for after all, Sheridan may probably have "suppressed" it for the simple reason that it was not of a suitable nature. She was planning what muſt have been this piece at Dibden in October 1788, when her father was ill, and her mother deprived of her favourite amusement, for Betsy Sheridan wrote Mrs. Lefanu that "Mrs. S. has been telling her Mother the ſtory of the piece that she may make out some amusement for herself out of it to console her for her loss of cards."[2]

From the same correspondence it is learned that Linley was suffering from a kind of paralytic ſtroke in the head; "Her attentions to him are unremitting. She is now working hard at some music they are preparing at Drury Lane, to save him as much labour as possible." Betsy Sheridan added three days later, "She will write soon—at present her father and her music leave her scarce a minute to herself."[3]

As no piece with music by Thomas Linley was performed for several months, she appears to have engaged upon the new orcheſtration of Purcell's music to *The Tempeſt*, which was produced by Kemble "with accompaniments by Mr. Linley" in the autumn of 1789.[4]

[1]Moore, *Journal*, II, 180. [2]Lefanu MSS., 150. [3]Lefanu MSS., 150-6.

[4]Mrs. Sheridan was said by Watkins to have composed the music for the pantomime of *Robinson Crusoe*, and also for her husband's song, "The Mid Watch." The overture to the pantomime was composed by William Shield, and Kelly gives the song to Thomas Linley.

CHAPTER THE NINTH
The Orator

I

THE greatest oratorical achievement—for speech is too simple a word—of Sheridan was that which he delivered in the House of Commons in 1787 against Warren Hastings on the charge of extortion, perfidy and cruelty to the Begums of Oude. Byron placed it in his catalogue of "the best things in their kind" that had been done by Sheridan, and declared in his monody of 1816:

"When the loud cry of trampled Hindustan
Arose to Heaven in her appeal from man,
His was the thunder—his the avenging rod,
The wrath, the delegated voice of God!
Which shook the nations through his lips, and blazed
Till vanquished senates trembled as they praised."

On the day after its delivery, Sir Gilbert Elliott wrote his wife: "It was by many degrees the most excellent and astonishing performance I ever heard, and surpasses all I ever imagined possible in eloquence and ability. This is the *universal* sense of all who heard it. You will conceive how admirable it was when I tell you that he surpassed, I think, Pitt, Fox and even Burke in his finest and most brilliant orations." The House, he added, was "worked up into such a paroxysm of passionate enthusiasm on the subject, and of admiration for him that the moment he sat down there was a universal shout, nay even clapping for half a second."

For that half second, then, the members thought they were an audience at a play. Charles Fox asserted the next day in the

House of Commons that "all that he had ever heard, all that he had ever read, when compared with it dwindled into nothing and vanished like vapour before the sun,"—but "Pitt never gave the least sign of life or feeling during the speech."

It is, of course, impossible to summarize the Begum speech, but at the risk of being unjust to the whole, some idea of his invective against Hastings may be given.

"I profess to God I feel in my own bosom the strongest personal conviction of the facts charged against Mr. Hastings towards the Begums of Oude. I affirm without apprehension of contradiction, that the public capacity of Mr. Hastings exhibits no proof that he has any just claim to either the one or the other species of greatness. We see nothing solid or penetrating, nothing noble or magnanimous, nothing open, direct, liberal, manly, or superior, in his measures or his mind. All is dark, insidious, sordid and insincere. Wherever he has option in the choice of his objects, or his instruments, he instinctively settles on the worst. His course is one invariable deviation from rectitude. And the only trace or vestige of system discernible in the whole of a dozen years' administration is that of 'acting without any.' The serpent may as well abandon the characteristic obliquity of his motion for the direct flight of an arrow, as he can excuse his purposes with honesty and fairness. He is all shuffling, twisting, cold and little. There is nothing in him open or upright, simple or unmixed. There is by some strange, mysterious predominance in his vice, such a prominence as totally shades and conceals his virtues. There is, by some foul, unfathomable, physical cause in his mind, a conjunction merely of whatever is calculated to make human nature hang its head with a sorrow or shame. His crimes are the only great thing about him, and these are contrasted by the littleness of his motives. He is at once a tyrant, a trickster, a visionary, and a deceiver. He affects to be a conqueror and law-giver, an Alexander and a Cæsar; but he is no more than a Dionysius and a Scapin. His very

writings, though here he wants not for admirers, discover
the same intrinsic poverty of intellect, are marked with the
same mixture of littleness and pride. All his letters and
minutes are dry, obscure, inflated and uninteresting, without point, spirit, simplicity or intelligence. He reasons in
bombast, prevaricates in metaphor, and quibbles in heroics.
So that in composition he hurts the mind's taste, as much as
in conduct he offends every feeling of the heart."

2

On February 13th, 1788, the trial of Warren Hastings began. Among the numerous accounts and commentaries, the
most amusing is "The Letters of Simpkin the Second, Poetic
Recorder, of all the proceedings upon the Trial of Warren Hastings, Esq. in Westminster Hall," which were collected in
1789 after having appeared in Topham's newspaper, *The
World*. Captain Ralph Broom, the author, thus introduced the
Managers:

" now I'll describe
The procession of Burke and *his eloquent tribe.*
First Edmund walks in at the head of the groupe,
The powerful *chief* of that powerful *troop*;
What awful *solemnity's* seen in his gait!
While the nod of his *head*, beats the time to his *feet*.
Charles Fox is the second, and close to his right,
Whose waddle declares he will never go straight.
The rubicund Sheridan follows, the third,
The opposer of Pitt and the Treasury Board;
His attention, 'tis said, *has so long been directed*
To the National *Debts*, that his *own* are neglected,
And on public affairs, *where such management's shewn*,
No wonder a man *cannot think of his own*."

On the last speech of the year Gibbon wrote to Lord Sheffield:

"Yesterday the august scene was closed for this year.

Sheridan surpassed himself; and though I am far from considering him as a perfect orator, there were many beautiful passages in his speech, on justice, filial love, etc.; one of the closest chains of argument I ever heard, to prove that Hastings was responsible for the acts of Middleton; and a compliment, much admired, to a certain Historian of your acquaintance. Sheridan at the close of his speech sank into Burke's arms;—a good actor; but I called this morning, he is perfectly well."

The reception of this speech Simpkin described with this gibe:

"The gallery folk, who, misled by the sport,
Conceived 'twas a Play-House, instead of a Court;
And thinking the Actor uncommonly good,
They clapp'd, and cry'd 'Bravo!' as loud as they could
Then Edmund gave Sherry a hearty embrace,
And cry'd, as he splutter'd all over his face,
'At Supper this night thou shalt have the First Place!' "

The close of Sheridan's most famous oration was burlesqued with fine deftness, by "Simpkin," who caught the points in this manner:

"Ye Guardians of Justice, to you I appeal—
Shall Private give way to the General Weal?
Ye Prelates, to whom our Religion belongs,
Our Country to save, may we do private wrongs?
To decide on this Question, my Lords, is your lot,
Whether Hastings's conduct was useful or not?
Let the truth but appear, and the Battle is won,
The Verdict is ours!—Now, my Lords, I have done!"

3

The Speech in Westminster Hall before the House of Lords on the Begum Charge was prepared with great labour, not only by himself, but also by Mrs. Sheridan. The industry, indeed, of all around him was put in requisition for this great occasion—

some, busy with the pen and scissors, making extracts—some, pasting and stitching his scattered memorandums in their places. Hardly a single member of the household could not boast of having contributed his share, to the mechanical construction of this speech. The pride of its success was, of course, equally participated; and George Edwards, a favourite servant of Sheridan, who lived with him many years, was long celebrated for his professed imitation of the manner in which his master delivered his closing words, "My Lords, I have done!"[1]

William Thompson, his father's old manservant, was equally impressed. When Betsy Sheridan arrived in London on July 25th, 1788, with her father, she wrote her sister:

"Thompson sup'd with us, & as my father retir'd early he staid with me to indulge in talking of his dear Master Richard. I should tell you he praised him most warmly to my father, saying, 'Sir, your Son is the first man in England —You will find everyone of that opinion', I thought my father seem'd rather pleas'd. When we were left alone, he began his praise again, & got up to give me some idea of his concluding words & bad as the attempt must have been, yet it convey'd some idea of the manner in which he spoke words, 'My Lords, I have done' which so haunted you."

Having delivered the speech, Sheridan took the manuscript with him to Dibden, the country house which was lent him by the Duke of Norfolk. He left it there, and it was over a quarter of a century later that he recovered it, and read it again, a few weeks before his death.

4

Betsy Sheridan herself went to Westminster Hall for one of the later days, for on "Thursday 21st" [May, 1789]—she wrote Mrs. Lefanu:

"This morning I went with Mrs. Dixon to the Trial—We sat in the King's Box—which directly fronts the Managers

[1]Moore, 378

& the place where Mr. Hastings stands—With the help of
my glass I could see him very well & could perceive him a
good deal agitated at times—Mr. Burke spoke first—His
manner is so much against him that it must require time to
grow in any degree reconciled to it—But that once done it is
impossible not to admire his flow of language & force of
imagination—Next Mr. Fox—his voice I don't like but his
manner is so clear & [,] that a child must at once comprehend
his meaning, & at the same time so earnest as to force conviction—last our Brother—I felt a thousand pulses beat as he
rose, & gulp'd down the tears that were almost choaking
that I might not appear too nervous; (the fashionable expression for feeling of any kind)—It recall'd too the remem-
brance of my Poor Father who had ever so blindly driven
from him the pleasure he might have derived from that
quarter—I was also reminded of him, by his manner which
is certainly very like my Father's tho' not an imitation—
There is a calm dignity in it, yet animated to the greatest
degree where the subject admits of it—His voice is uncommonly fine, & his utterance is distinct that I did not lose a
syllable, which is surprising as you know his general way of
speaking is rather slovenly—The sight in itself is certainly
fine & from accessory ideas must strike the imagination of
any Person—I thought of you & wish'd my poor Neighbour
Mrs. Dixon quietly at home & you in her place—When
they adjourn'd we stroll'd about in some of the outward
courts & met several of the Managers Mr. Burke came up to
take care of Mrs. Dixon, & Irishman like, insisted on the
young Lady as he stiled me, taking his other arm & so under
the care of this Friend of the Begums I got thro' the croud."[1]

The letters of Simpkin the Second concluded with a model for
a Speech of Address to the House of Lords. It burlesques the
irrelevancies of Sheridan with amusing discernment, and it is
no unfair summary of the general want of substance in the case
against Hastings:

[1] Lefanu MSS., 191–2.

"Most Noble Court,

"We are really in a particular situation. We have accused the Prisoner of *Rapine, Fraud, Plunder, Perjury*, Forgery, and Murder! But we cannot get the Witnesses to say a word of this, they know it all, but 'the Devil go with them,' I speak it solemnly, they will not utter a syllable on these matters. O miserable State of Evidence! O infernal Witnesses! O double and trebly ――!!!

"But we will not waste time. We wish your assistance, *Most Noble Court!* Yet have a care! If there be among ye, who cannot construe—'Lex et Consuetudo Parliament!' If there be a man—O abominable State of Blackness! If there be a man, whose gown is nothing in point of colour—or as the Irish Song has it, 'and Kitty cried—*look in my Face*,' If there be any thing more—I mean—*more civil*, than what we have said; all that we can say, is, we certainly want to learn it.

"Most Noble Court—*we have done!*"[1]

After a trial which dragged over eight years, Warren Hastings was acquitted on all the charges brought against him, on April 23rd, 1795. Ten years later Sheridan met him at Brighton, when he was a guest of the Prince of Wales. The position was one of difficulty, and Thomas Creevey recorded the incident with a malicious smile:

"Among other persons who came to pay their respects to the Prince during the Autumn of 1805 was Mr. Hastings, whom I had never seen before excepting at his trial in Westminster Hall. He and Mrs. Hastings came to the Pavilion, and I was present when the Prince introduced Sheridan to him, which was curious, considering that Sheridan's parliamentary fame had been built upon his celebrated speech against Hastings. However, he lost no time in attempting to cajole old Hastings, begging him to believe that any part he had ever taken against him was purely political, and that no one had a greater respect for him than himself, &c, &c, upon which old Hastings said with great

[1] *The Creevey Papers*, 223-4.

gravity that 'it would be a great consolation to him in his declining days if Mr. Sheridan would make that sentence more publick;' but Sheridan was obliged to mutter and get out of such engagements as well as he could."[1]

[1]*The Creevey Papers*, I, 59–60.

CHAPTER THE TENTH

The Phantom Ministry

Hope told a flattering tale.
Bickerstaff, *The Maid of the Mill.*

I

ON November 5th, 1788, while the Constitutional Club were listening to a letter from the Whig Club, containing resolutions moved by Richard Brinsley Sheridan, Esq., on the centenary of the great and glorious revolution of 1688, the King, the third party in a well-balanced government, dining at his own table, burst into delirium, a palpable lunatic. At once arose a constitutional problem without precedent—despite the supposed instances of "Henry ye 6, &c, &c,"—in the history of Great Britain. Was the heir-apparent *de jure* Regent during the King's incapacity? If so, in what law-book or statute was the office of Regent defined? How far did his powers extend in the exercise of the Royal prerogative?

The friends of the Prince of Wales were eager to establish the principle that during his father's insanity he should exert the same rights as if he had succeeded to the throne on his father's death. The Prince, in his turn, was anxious to deprive the ministry of their offices, and replace William Pitt by Charles Fox. Therefore, what should have been merely a constitutional problem was deflected by party politics, and the Opposition created among themselves a phantom ministry, and quarrelled over the spoils before they had won the victory. For three months Sheridan was the Prince's "confidential friend," his right-hand man in all the negotiations, his intermediary with the Lord Chancellor, Lord Thurlowe, and with the Whig Party.

SHERIDAN, BURKE, FOX, 1791

To face page 114

In the summer of 1788 the King had visited Cheltenham to take the waters, but he was still unwell, and though the consequences of his death must often have been discussed in the Prince's circle, there was no feeling of imminent danger. There were rumours, however: on October 22nd Sheridan had been expected to call at Dibden with the Prince on their way to Brighton. As they did not arrive Betsy Lefanu wrote in her Journal, "By the papers you have no doubt seen that the King has been ill—It is perfectly true, & he still continues very ill— We have heard nothing from London yet, but it is not unlikely that the King's indisposition may have been the cause of putting off the Brighton Party." But on the next day she added that "He gave us a flying call to-day on his way to Brighton, where he was engaged to dine with the Prince—" and concluded by mentioning that "on Saturday Mr. & Mrs. Sheridan were due to set out for Stafford." The Sheridans seem to have gone there, though, on November 4th, he was again in London addressing the Whig Club.

2

When the Prince was told of the King's illness, he journeyed with all speed to Windsor Castle, with his brother, the Duke of York. The possibilities were, it seemed, that either his father's death would make him king, or his insanity would necessitate his appointment as Regent. In either case it was certain he would employ against Pitt the full extent of his power. Although at first he avoided any meeting with the leaders of the Opposition, he at once treated the party as if at the conclusion of the formalities they would enter into office as his ministers. Charles Fox was travelling on the Continent in indifferent health, and, although it was supposed to be a secret, it was known in Brookes's Club on November 7th that the Prince had desired him to be recalled. He set out at once when the message reached him at Bologna, but it was not until Monday, November 24th, that he arrived in London, fatigued and harassed by eight days' travel. Meanwhile, for eighteen days of excitement and intrigue, Sheridan was the "confidential friend" of the Prince of Wales. From the outset the Prince was anxious to secure the alliance of Lord Chancellor Thurlowe, the strongest and ablest lawyer of the age. For although there was to be a great searching for precedents—it was clear that the situation was unprecedented. As to this, the Prince had no doubt; he had written to the Chancellor on the day of his arrival at Windsor Castle, and on the following day Captain Payne wrote Sheridan, on the Prince's behalf, that if Pitt proposed restrictions of power, "it might give the Chancellor a good opportunity to break with his colleagues."

The Prince, of his own initiative, at once grasped the constitutional problem: if Thurlowe could be persuaded to declare that, as Fox later argued in debate, it was "in accordance with the spirit of the Constitution for the Heir Apparent to become Regent *de jure* during the continuance of the King's incapacity," his opinion would carry the very greatest weight with parliament, with the city, and with the country at large. In order to secure Lord Thurlowe's support, the Prince was prepared to continue him in his office of Lord Chancellor, which, at the King's express desire, he had formerly retained in the Rockingham administration. It has always been assumed that as an attempt to bribe his support, the Prince approached Thurlowe with this crude proposal. This supposition is a legacy of Holland House, transmitted by Moore, yet it is evident that the Prince was not so utterly devoid of diplomatic sagacity, and his conversations with Thurlowe were confined to an attempt to ascertain the Lord Chancellor's opinion upon the constitutional position. The suggestion that he might be detached from his colleagues was based on the assumption that their proposal of limitations was dictated entirely by the party-spirit, and on such grounds the Lord Chancellor might reasonably be expected to declare against them. It is absurd to suggest that the Prince was so stupid as to avow his intention of dismissing Pitt to Thurlowe, a member of his own administration. No doubt there were delicate innuendoes, but the offer of the retention as Lord Chancellor was not made until December 13th, some three weeks after Fox's return to England, and nearly six weeks after the Prince's first letter to Lord Thurlowe.

3

Sheridan, in seeing the Lord Chancellor, was in the position of the Prince's friend, but it is not to be supposed that Lord Thurlowe acted as if he did not know that the Prince would place the Whigs in office. Yet there are other factors. As Sheridan was the Prince's friend, so Thurlowe was the King's, and he did not regard himself as a party-man. The Chancellor's affection for King George the Third was very deep; he went into hysterics at Kew on November 29th, when the King, while he was being held by force, nevertheless said to him, "You shall dine with me, but perhaps I shall not give you a very good dinner—I have not so much power as I used to have." It was Sheridan himself who brought this story from Carlton House to Devonshire House, where on December 7th, the Prince told the Duke of Devonshire "as a great secret" that Sheridan had been to the Chancellor, who had told him, "Mr. Sheridan, I am of no Party, which to a man of your discernment, that is saying enough." They obviously interpreted this as a kind of Machiavellian promise to accept the highest bid, but Sheridan had mistaken his man. At all events, at the next meeting of the House of Lords, only four days later, when Lord Loughborough asserted the right of the Prince to become Regent, Lord Thurlowe said that the doctrine was a new one to him, and false. By that time, Fox had decided that Lord Loughborough should be appointed Chancellor, and Sheridan was out of spirits because he thought that Thurlowe had not been "courted enough," which means, that although they had used flattery and innuendo, they had made no definite offer. Indeed it was not until December 13th that any offer to him was decided upon. On that day Fox wrote Sheridan:

"DEAR SHERIDAN,
"I have swallowed the pill,—a most bitter one it was,—and have written to Lord Loughborough, whose answer of course must be consent. What is to be done next? Should the Prince himself, you or I, or Warren, be the person to speak to the Chancellor? The objection to the last is, that he must

probably wait for an opportunity, and that no time is to be lost. Pray tell me what is to be done: I am convinced, after all, the negotiation will not succeed, and am not sure that I am sorry for it. I do not remember ever feeling so uneasy about any political thing I ever did in my life. Call if you can.

"Yours ever,

"*Sat. past* 12."   "C.J.F."[1]

4

The Duchess of Devonshire entered in her diary of Sunday, December 14th, her account of this interview:

"I saw Sheridan—he was with the Chancellor till 3 from 10 last night. He carry'd with him a written proposal from Charles to the Chancellor, but he thinks the application late rather as the Chancellor has pledged himself to support ye limitations.—he however at last promis'd to speak for the previous question on Monday. Sheridan says he left him with the impression of his being a great rogue—he try'd to sound Sheridan on the plan of his undermining Fox.—he told Sheridan one limitation wd be the household to be continued under ye Queen for Six months; nor could this, he said, signify, ye Queen and Prince being so well together. He own'd the Qu was a termagant: he sd if the P refus'd ye Regency they must have Lords Justices. Sheridan sd, But what may become of yr head, when he is King: he sd, you may hang the Chancellor, but you can't alter the Law— he however came over at last. Sheridan is rather now for the Prince's accepting, with the limitations of peerages and Lds of ye Bedchamber remaining for 6 months. Charles Fox very much agst it—great embarrassment."[2]

A few weeks later in debate Sheridan was "humorously" to describe the Lord Chancellor as possessing "a natural ferocity and sturdiness of temper" and "brutal bluffness." He was however no match for Thurlowe, who contented himself with saying as little as possible, except to show that he was in support of

[1]Moore, 407-8.   [2]Sichel, II, 416.

the limitations of prerogative. Sheridan's threat about his execution was answered by Thurlowe in the only possible way. If Thurlowe had been a party man, asking his price for deserting Pitt, Sheridan's threat would have been an unfortunate mistake in tactics, but as he regarded himself as "of no party" it was fatal. "He came over at last," said Sheridan, whatever that may have meant, yet two days later in the House of Lords, the Chancellor declared that it was inevitable to discuss the Prince's right to the Regency, but if in the measures proposed, he found any tendency to pursue crooked paths of conduct he would be the first to expose them and abandon them. He was sensible of the honour that the Sovereign had conferred upon him, and, he added, "if ever I forget my King, may God forget me." The fury of men like Wilkes, who exclaimed "He'll see you damned first" and Burke, who added "The sooner the better" is no evidence as to Thurlowe's rascality.

It is curious that, on account of a failure to ascertain the dates of letters, it is not realized that Thurlowe made his attitude clear in Parliament at the earliest possible moment. He ignored Fox's letter, Sheridan on December 18th was again to be sent to him, but instead of going he wrote a letter from Devonshire House, which he sent to Lord Thurlowe by Dr. Warren, who told the Duchess next day that the Chancellor would not make a decision. In fact, Thurlowe remained silent until December 26th when in the House of Lords he "spoke civilly of the Prince, but abused his advisers." Still the Prince hoped for his alliance, but on December 29th they gave up hope, and the Prince sent a message to Lord Loughborough, offering him the great seals of the Lord Chancellor in the Regency administration. Moore, long afterward, from the gossip of Holland House, declared that it was not easy to ascertain the motives that induced Lord Thurlowe to "break off so suddenly in his negotiation with the Prince's party and declare with such vehemence on the side of the King and Mr. Pitt. Possibly, from his opportunities of visiting the Royal Patient, he had been led to conceive sufficient hopes of his recovery to incline the balance of his speculation that way." But it is evident, that whatever consultations the Prince and Sheridan may have had with Thurlowe on constitutional questions, the "negotiations" over his retention of office were very one-sided. It is even possible that the Prince held the view that the office of Lord Chancellor, following the recent precedent, should not belong to any party.

5

It would be tedious to enumerate all the intrigues for place in this phantom ministry, which so strongly recalls one of the fables of the Wise Men of Gotham. The day before Fox's arrival in London, the Duchess wrote to her mother, the Countess Spencer, that "Sheridan might certainly be Chancellor of the Exchequer if he chose, but prefers reaching it by degrees, and when he has proved his capability to the public." The minor appointment which was allotted to him in the schemes was that of Treasurer to the Navy. Perhaps he was content under pressure: The Archbishop of Canterbury writing to Eden, declared that "Sheridan is on all hands understood to be the prime favourite, and to be so sensible of it as modestly to pretend to a Cabinet place, which is hitherto firmly resisted by the Duke of Portland, who says they cannot both be in the same Cabinet. He would willingly submit to be Chancellor of the Exchequer, but it is thought that things are not ripe enough for the manager of Drury Lane to be the manager of the House of Commons." But this rumour was soon replaced by another which expressed the settled intention, for on December 2nd, Edmond Malone wrote Lord Charlemont that "I have this moment heard that Lord John Cavendish will accept his former place as Chancellor of the Exchequer and Sheridan be Treasurer of the Navy." Most of the proposals were indeed *secrets de Polichinelle*.

In *A Letter to Mr. Fox on his Party* (1789) there is an appeal "to exclude this person from his cabinet" saying "The appointment of Lord John was in truth ridiculous enough, but the other would have been a lamentable jest, a tragi-farcical burlesque, on revenue and economy—Mr. Sheridan at the head of finances. Why, sir, the streets of Paris would be illuminated, public rejoicings would be made, and thanksgivings offered up to Heaven by all the enemies of Great Britain."

The intrigue for place was not confined to the leaders of the Whig party. It extended to Sheridan's own relations in Ireland, for as a certain Edward Bellingham Swan, a Commissioner of the Stamp Office in Dublin had shot himself through the head, the appointment seemed a very desirable one for Mr. Joseph Lefanu—though it must in fairness be remembered that all places of this kind were allotted by nomination from the Crown on the advice of the Ministry. Betsy Sheridan accordingly wrote her sister on December 12th:

"Still you see nothing is determin'd. Pitt is determin'd to fight every inch of ground & takes time & gives trouble to others, tho' there is not the smallest probability of his holding out long. Dick came home to dinner yesterday at Seven. He seem'd much harrass'd, for added to the trouble that naturally falls on him, every difficult negotiation, every mistake to be rectified, is put upon him. Our brother was with the Prince till 4 this morning, and as usual I have not seen him today, for he never leaves his dressing room till he goes out. I shall take an opportunity of speaking to Mrs S. about what you say of Swan's place, & she may tell Dick, for in the present situation of things I cannot get his ear for a moment, & the sooner he knows the better."

Another of her letters begins:

"Monday [December] 22 Evening.
"Yesterday we were all at home—Mrs. S. really very much indisposed—Dick meant to have the day to himself, to read over Precedents & prepare for this day's business. Before he was up, comes a message from the Prince to beg him to see him immediately: he sent word he was not very well and had taken a medecine that made it necessary for him to keep house. In less than half an hour, the Duke of York was in Bruton St., & shortly after him the Prince himself—

boring him & preventing him reading said papers. And to compleat all, they beg'd him to see another person, who idled him two more hours in the evening. Tickell and Richardson call'd as usual."

6

Pitt sent a letter to the Prince to inform him of the limitations which the Cabinet had decided to recommend Parliament to place upon the powers of the Regent. The Prince replied in a letter, the vexed question of whose authorship has occupied much ingenuity. Moore said that claims had been preferred for three people, Sheridan, Burke, and Elliott. He considered, however, that all doubts were set at rest by what was written by Sir Gilbert Elliott on January 31st, 1789: "There was not a word of the Prince's Letter to Pitt, mine. It was originally Burke's, altered a little, but not improved, by Sheridan and other critics. The answer made by the Prince yesterday to the Adress of the two Houses was entirely mine, and done in a great hurry half-an-hour before it was delivered." Elliott's description of the authorship agrees with what the Prince told Croker, thirty-five years later, when accounting for the quarrel between Sheridan and Burke: "The celebrated letter which Mr. Burke wrote for me, and which I consider one of the most beautiful and noble compositions that ever were penned, but as in the original draft there were some passages of great violence, I showed the draft to Sheridan, who made some alterations in pencil, some of which I adopted, and others I did not, those I adopted I wrote in with my own hand, the others I erased." The Prince added that a discussion of the proposed changes was held during which Burke was zealous for the retention of his own passages, and Sheridan was as zealous in his support of the alterations—a circumstance which led Burke to suspect that he was the author. It was, the Prince told Croker, this suspicion which sowed the seeds of disagreement between Burke and Sheridan.[1]

[1] *The Croker Papers*, I, 289.

The Prince's letter was copied by Mrs. Sheridan. On January 3rd, Betsy Lefanu wrote her sister:

"Yesterday we were at home, but Mrs. S. did not admit many visitors as she was busy writing out a fair Copy of the Prince's answer to the Restrictions, which was to go to the Council that very night. Nothing could be better than it was, for we made her read it to us. Dick (wrapp'd up in a fine Pelisse the Prince had given him) then went off with it to Carlton House."

Mrs. Sheridan herself wrote her friend Mrs. Canning that the Prince had decided to accept the Regency in despite of the Restrictions, if they should be carried, and he had written an answer to Pitt which should soon appear in the Paper:

"It is vastly well done, and I am sure might make all un-prejudiced Persons love the Prince and hate Pitt. I have had a great hand in it, for I copied it twice, and the copy actually sent to the Cabinet was written by me and signed by the Prince. I intend when he is Regent to claim something good for myself for secret service."

Burke's authorship was, however, well known, and when Caroline, Princess of Wales, who delighted in annoying even her own friends, wished to irritate Lord Thurlowe, she used to praise Burke's letter to Pitt.

7

On January 16th, the Chancellor of the Exchequer, Pitt, after the report of the physicians on the King's health, adduced as a conclusion, that "it was more probable that he would recover than that he would not." He called upon the House of Commons to make no other provision than such as was absolutely necessary. He then moved five resolutions:

First. The Prince of Wales shall be empowered under the title of Regent to exercise the whole Royal Authority, during the King's illness, excepting certain limitations.
Second. The Regent's power shall not extend to the creating

of any peer, but of the royal issue having attained the age of twenty-one.

Third. The Regent shall not make any grant, salary or pension, reversion, or annuity for life, or any other term than during His Majesty's pleasure, except such offices as are required by a law to be granted for life.

Fourth. The Regent shall have no power over the real or personal property of the Crown.

Fifth. The guardianship of the King, and the government of the King's household shall be entrusted to the Queen.

In the debate, the resolutions were strongly denounced by Fox, Lord North, and Colonel Fullarton. Sheridan's own contribution was chiefly concerned with the resolution concerning the Royal Household, which was intended to give nearly a third part of the Crown patronage into the hands of the Queen, or in other words, into Pitt's hands. He concluded with one of his customary witticisms: He declared that it "would be a novel sight to see a popular leader of opposition [Pitt] with a guard of court scullions, and a surly patriot, [Thurlowe] attended by the laced liveries of the royal pages. He represented the ex-minister as coming down to the House in state, with the cap of liberty on the end of a white wand, a retinue of black and white sticks attending him, and a guard of beef-eaters marshalled by the Lord Steward, the Lord Chamberlain, and the Master of Horse, clearing his way through the lobby."[1]

Sheridan objected that the restriction sprang from the supposition of the Prince being likely to give his confidence to those persons who were not at present in office, and that they were meant as chastisement to the Prince for his choice. The resolutions were carried, and a fortnight later, in the House of Commons, Michael Angelo Taylor said that rumours were abroad that the Prince, acquainted with the restrictions imposed on the Regency, had refused to accept it, and had intimated such resolution to the Cabinet. He demanded that such other papers as had passed between the Prince and the Cabinet,

[1] *Annual Register,* 1789, 114.

should be laid before the House, but Pitt replied that it would not only be unparliamentary, but improper, to say on what restrictions and in what manner a Regency would be accepted, at the moment the House was deciding on what manner it should be given. Eventually on January 26th, the Lords agreed to the resolutions which had previously been passed by the Commons; on January 27th Pitt's letter to the Prince, and the Prince's reply appeared in the newspapers. On January 30th, a deputation from both Houses waited upon the Prince and received his reply. The Regency Bill which expanded these resolutions was read in the House of Commons for the first time on February 2nd, for the second time on February 3rd, and for the third time on February 12th. The only modification made was limiting the restrictions as to the creation of peers to a period of three years. It was read in the House of Lords for the first time on February 13th, and for the second time on February 16th. The third reading would have speedily followed, but on February 17th, *The London Gazette* announced that there was every symptom of convalescence and recovery; the King's conversation was rational, and his conduct regular, and twelve days had passed without the smallest relapse. Two days later it was announced in the House of Lords that the physician had pronounced him in a state of convalescence; the Duke of York expressed his pleasure in hearing the report from the Lord Chancellor, and added:

"From the knowledge I have of my brother's sentiments, though I can have had no immediate communication with him upon the subject of this motion, I am convinced that he will feel equal, if not greater pleasure than myself at the hopes of his Majesty's recovery, as it must relieve him from the embarrassment of the situation in which the Bill would have placed him, which nothing but a strong sense of his duty to the public would have induced him to undertake."[1]

8

Within the Sheridan circle, this had been partly anticipated,

[1] *Town and Country Magazine*, 1789, 375.

for on February 12th when hope was ebbing slowly, Betsy
Lefanu wrote her sister:

"the King for these three days has certainly been mending
so much to damp the hopes of the most sanguine people of
the party. The Regency Bill must go on & the Prince will be
in power for a short time, but they now all think the period
will be so short that nothing of consequence can be done.
Charles [Sheridan] will certainly be restored to his appointment, if, as report says, it is true that he has resign'd, but if
the Regency proves a short one, I fear he must lose it without any prospect of any compensation. With regard to us,
our hopes stand much where they did, as it will be in the
Prince's Power to dispose of moderate things, & there is
little probability of persons being changed who were ob-
noxious to either party. What I sincerely wish is that Dick
would endeavour to secure for himself any Patent Place the
Regent may have to dispose of in Ireland, as the Restrictions
on that subject relate only to this country. Mrs S & I have
been talking over this matter, but she says that such is our
brother's shyness in applying for any personal favour, that
she knows tho' the Regent may rejoice in the opportunity of
providing for him, she has no hopes of him taking one step in
the business. So at present there is a heavy cloud over us, but
we will keep up our spirits at all events."

In the evening, Tickell had dined there "as dismal as a prospect of dissapointment could make a man possess'd of a good
share of both vanity and ambition. Dick came to us between
twelve and one, & we did not break up till past two. He
confirm'd the news we had heard, but he has a spirit unac-
quainted with despondence, & tho' fatigue was added to the
anxiety he must feel, yet there was something chearing in his
manner that in a great measure conquered the gloom that hung
over us before his return."

Sheridan was a gallant loser; he entered his own house at
dinner-time

"with the news. There were present,—besides Mrs. Sheridan and his sister,—Tickell, who, on the change of administration, was to have been immediately brought into Parliament,—Joseph Richardson, who was to have had Tickell's place of Commissioner of the Stamp-office,—Reid, and some others. Not one of the company but had cherished expectations from the approaching change—not one of them, however, had lost so much as Mr. Sheridan. With his wonted equanimity he announced the sudden turn affairs had taken, and looking round him cheerfully, as he filled a large glass, said,—'Let us all join in drinking His Majesty's speedy recovery.' "[1]

9

The Parliament of the Kingdom of Ireland, however, took an entirely different course. On February 11th, it was moved and carried that the Prince of Wales be prayed to take upon himself the Regency of that realm, without restriction. The Lord Lieutenant, the Marquis of Buckingham, was requested to transmit the resolution to the Prince, but he refused, and on February 20th, a vote of censure was passed upon him in the Irish Commons, and a delegation of both Houses was sent to England to present the address. Headed by the Duke of Leinster and the Earl of Charlemont, they arrived in London on February 25th. They were laughed at as having come to town on the day after the fair—they were spoken of, wrote Betsy Sheridan, "as so many Indian chiefs. At an assembly of Lady Buckamshire's some of the ladies on the other side groan'd and hooted them as they came into the room: what say you to female delicacy?" Dick, she added had dined with the "Irish delagates" at the Prince's, at the Duke of Portland's, at Earl Spencer's, and all the other great houses. Of the festivities at Carlton House the periodicals were full of eulogies—*The Town and Country Magazine* said that "in elegance and convivial pleasure, the entertainment given by the Prince of Wales to the delegates of the Irish Parliament was truly enchanting. It was

[1]Moore, 428.

'the Feaſt of Reason and the Flow of Soul' such as Pythagoras
and his disciples used to enjoy in the palace of Nilo.—Burke
and Sheridan were among the gueſts, each with abilities to
'keep the table in a roar'—not with gross humour, but wit of
Attic polish and Attic point—bright as the champaigne they
drank, and the champaigne was the beſt the world could
afford."

Sheridan was not content merely to be a gueſt with the Irish
delegates: if the Duchess of Devonshire could give a ball at
Devonshire House, he could give a supper-party in Bruton
Street. Betsy Sheridan, in the same letter of March 2nd ended:

"Wednesday they all sup here & there is to be quite a
croud which I cannot escape, so I make a new dyed satting
gown on the occasion—We are to have the Prince, the Duke
of York, Mrs. Fitzherbert—all the fine people, and I should
be very glad to give them the slip if I had any decent pretext.
—Thursday the Dutchess gives them a Ball at Devonshire
House where Mrs. S. very good-naturedly got me invited,
but I have not thoughts of going for various reasons. J[enny]
Linley goes, and Mrs. S. if she is able, as she has a reason
for appearing in Public of a curious nature. Among other
infamous falsehoods propogated againſt our Brother, it is
now said that he locks her up, and uses her in every reſpeĉt
ill, even to beating and starving her. How such rediculous
falsehoods can ever gain credit! & yet the eagerness for
scandal makes them wellcome."

CHAPTER THE ELEVENTH

The Raree Show

Joyful prospects now appear,
Heav'n restores our monarch dear!
Loyal Britains' lyre and lute
At such blessings can't be mute.
Happy then your voices raise,
Peals of gratitude and praise!

Prelude at Drury Lane, April 15th, 1789.

I

THE King's recovery was the signal for festivities which had not been paralleled for a century—galas, masquerades, balls, operas, and plays were the vogue. On March 21st, the Prince of Wales and the Duke of York were among the brilliant audience which attended Drury Lane for the production of *Mary Queen of Scots* by the Hon. John St. John.

The Queen and her daughters, the Princesses Augusta and Elizabeth, attended Covent Garden, showing her displeasure with Sheridan, by not visiting Drury Lane.

Then came a series of magnificent galas; White's Club, attended by two thousand persons of rank and fashion, was held in the Pantheon, on March 31st. Brookes's Club, anxious to remove any impression of disloyalty, followed on April 20th with a gala—"promenade concert, supper, ball and so on," at the Opera House in the Haymarket, which was fitted up "superbly." An occasional Ode was written by Captain Robert Merry, "this furious zealot for liberty," said the Tories, "contrived to infuse into his composition a subtle mixture of the sentiments of the members of Brookes's; for the vehemence of his longing for the preservation of freedom implied that it was considered to be in danger." In congratulation of the King's recovery, he exclaimed:

"Long may he rule a *willing* land,"

but added immediately, as a check to inconsiderate loyalty:

"But Oh! for ever may that land be free!"

Mrs. Siddons, who condescended to be dressed as Britannia, declaimed this Ode with solemn and melodious dignity, and at the end "to the gratified astonishment of the spectators, she sat down in the exact attitude of the figure on a penny piece." (This *coup de theâtre* was, of course, attributed to Sheridan.) In order to gratify a larger public with her performance, she repeated this Ode for her benefit night on May 11th at Drury Lane Theatre.[1]

2

The Gala of Boodle's Club at Ranelagh was held on May 16th. It was attended by the Prince and the Duke of York, who that morning had fought a duel with Lieutenant-Colonel Charles Lenox. It originated with an incident at the mess of the Coldstream Guards where Colonel Lenox, being intoxicated, toasted William Pitt in the Prince's presence, and continued at Daubigny's Club, where the Duke was supposed to have disparaged his second in command, and on the parade ground. When the duel became then inevitable, the Prince of Wales who was greatly perturbed, had told the circumstances to the Queen in the hope that this would be prohibited, but she concealed the matter from the King, although ten days elapsed between the incident on parade which provoked it and the duel on Wimbledon Common. The Duke was accompanied by Lord Rawdon as second, and Colonel Lenox by the Earl of Winchilsea, one of the Lords of the Bedchamber. The seconds issued a statement that the ground was measured

[1]Boaden, *Mrs. Siddons*, 277-9.

at twelve paces, and both parties were to fire upon a
signal agreed upon. Only Colonel Lenox fired, his ball grazing
the Duke's curl, but, undisturbed by this narrow escape, the
Duke declined to fire, saying that he came out only at the
Colonel's desire to give him satisfaction, and that he had no
animosity against him. Lord Winchilsea then said that he supposed the Duke would have no objection to say that he considered his opponent a man of honour and courage. The Duke
replied that he should say nothing, and did not intend to fire,
though if Colonel Lenox was not satisfied, he might fire again.
On this they left the ground. The seconds concluded that "both
parties behaved with the utmost coolness and intrepidity."

Meanwhile, the Prince of Wales was pacing the ground of
Carlton House in a state of great agitation, and the Duke returned to him saying very coolly that he was unharmed, but
could not stay to tell any more, as he must keep an appointment
to play cricket. However, the Prince insisted upon hearing the
full story, and that evening they went together to Boodle's
Gala.

Betsy Sheridan told her sister what happened there:

"Our brother," she wrote, "is much with them all, and
when a head is wanted they have recourse *to his*. He has great
influence and will no doubt rise one day as high as his utmost
ambition could wish. Mrs. Sheridan told me a little circumstance that happened at Bootle's that shews the footing he is
on. The Prince in the fulness of his joy for his brother's
safety had taken rather too many bumpers to his health.
Some one told our brother, that they feared he was setting
in for drinking and desired he would try to get him away. He
accordingly went up to him but finding that he did not
readily yield to persuasion, he pushed the bottle from him,
saying, '*You shall not* drink any more.' The Prince fired at
the idea of control and said, 'Sheridan, I love you better than
any one, but *shall not* is what I can't put up with.'

"However with the help of one of the Conways they got
him away, and no doubt his Royal Highness was thankful

next morning for having been prevented from giving a handle to his enemies for increasing their abuse."[1]

Three days later, continued Betsy Sheridan, the Duke went to see the King:

"I will tell you a *fact* that sets our amiable Queen's character in a true light. Friday laſt the Duke of York went to Kew for the firſt time since his duel. He found the King sitting in an outward room with a door of communication open to that where the Queen was. The minute he saw the Duke he went softly to shut the door, then running to him embraced him moſt affectionately and with tears congratulated him on his safety—in short in his whole manner was quite the father. On the Queen's entering, he drew back and fell into the reserved manner he had assumed latterly. She took no other notice of her son than with a cold and diſtant air asking whether he had been amused at Bootle's Ball, which was the evening of the day he fought. It is no wonder that all her sons are disguſted with a conduct so truly unfeminine. They showed their displeasure by leaving the [Spanish] Ambassador's grand entertainment [on June 2] before supper, and this ſtep of course has given great offence."[2]

On June 1ſt Sheridan went to the Duke of Clarence's Ball and to the King's Birthday Ball on June 4th, at which the Queen, who had received Colonel Lenox so graciously at the French Ambassador's Ball, again showed him great favour, though the Prince of Wales and the Duke of York refused to dance in the minuet with him, and the Queen was reluctantly persuaded to break up the ball after the third dance. The Queen's behaviour greatly incensed the Prince's friends, who were eager that he should show his resentment. She told the Prince of Wales that she thought Colonel Lenox's conduct had been perfectly correct, though this was not the opinion of the officers of the Coldſtream regiment, who, at his own requeſt, met to consider his conduct; their resolution was that "*subsequent*

[1]Lefanu MSS.   [2]Lefanu MSS.

to May 15th"—that is, ignoring the question of the incident at Daubigny's Club—"he had behaved with *courage*, but
not, from the peculiar difficulty of his situation, with *judgment*." This was virtually a censure, and he immediately
exchanged into another regiment.

3

Before the end of May, the King sent a letter to Prince
William, whom he had created Duke of Clarence, blaming him
for his support of his brothers, the Prince of Wales and the
Duke of York, and complaining of their conduct during the
Regency discussions. The Prince summoned a conference at
Carlton House for the purpose of drafting two letters to the
King, one explaining and justifying their actions, and another
protesting against the Queen's conduct, in particular against
her attitude over the duel. Burke, Sheridan, and Elliott, were
present at Carlton House, together with the Duke of Clarence,
who expressed his opinions with simple and sailor-like oaths.
Eventually, the letter of justification was entrusted to Elliott,
and the protest against the Queen to Burke. Neither letter,
however, was sent, for when the Prince summoned a council
of his advisers to consider the drafts, the remonstrance was
found to "out-Burke Burke" in violence. He told Croker, thirty-
five years afterward, that this epistle "took two hours reading;
it was exceedingly eloquent and violent. I have strong in my
mind's eye the effect it made on the audience. The Duke of
Portland looked more stupid than usual—not that he was at all
as stupid as he looked—he had very good sense. He was really
in a *maze*. Lord North kept up a perpetual noise between a
cough and a growl, and Fox kept digging his fingers into the
corner of his eye, a trick he had when anything perplexed him."[1]
Fox and Lord Stormont considered that it was too bitter, and it
was eventually decided that both letters should be withheld.

For some weeks the matter was left in abeyance, but when
the King left on June 25th for Weymouth, where he had been

[1] *The Croker Papers*, I, 289–292.

ordered for sea-bathing, the Prince had not received the summons he expected to attend him before his departure. He sent a letter, regretting the heavy misfortune of the King's displeasure, which was written for him by Sheridan, and its conclusion reduced to one dignified sentence his complaint about the Queen:

> "Anxious for every thing that may contribute to the comfort and satisfaction of Your Majesty's mind, I cannot omit this opportunity of lamenting those appearances of a less gracious disposition in the Queen, towards my brothers and myself, than we were accustomed to experience; and to assure Your Majesty that if by your affectionate interposition these most unpleasant sensations should be happily removed, it would be an event not less grateful to our minds than satisfactory to your Majesty's own benign disposition."[1]

4

The last great gala of the season was at Mrs. Sturt's mansion at Hammersmith which had been famous as La Trappe, the seat of Bubb Doddington, Lord Melcombe. Sir George Elliott, who was present at this masquerade told his wife how it was attended by the three Princes; how Mrs. Fitzherbert was there in the character of chaperon to a pretty young woman, who on unmasking was discovered to be the Prince's secretary, Jack Payne; how Lady Margaret Fordyce—Sheridan's heroine of Clio's Protest—still retained much of "her beauty and her power of pleasing." But he did not record that the Sheridans had with them Miss Elizabeth Sheridan, who was having her closest view of "the raree show of the great world," before she left its precincts for the seclusion which was, as she knew, to follow her marriage with Captain Henry Lefanu. Yet she was there, and she sent an account to her sister in Dublin, Mrs. Joseph Lefanu. On Tuesday, June 9th, she wrote that at breakfast she had met Mrs. Sheridan—"she began talking to me about a masquerade I had promised to accompany them to

[1]Moore, 432–3.

on Thursday next—I said something that shew'd I wish'd to decline the party, & she then hop'd that there was no bad news from Ireland." She could not say there was: "I only said, in general, that I was not now in spirits to enjoy such a party— This she could not understand—Amusement was the way to banish dissagreeable reflections." While they were talking, "the stuffs for our dresses were brought in. Mrs. Bouverie had undertaken to provide them for all the Party that go with us. We are to be a group of Gypsies—the dress very ugly I think, brown stuff jackets, & blue stuff petticoats, straw hats tied under the chin, & scarlet silk cloak hanging behind, in imitation of the red cloak worn by those Ladies. Our party are Mrs. & Miss Bouverie, Lady Julia Howard, Lady Betty D'Eline, a Mrs. Stanhope, a very beautiful woman, Mrs. S. & I. The Masquerade is to be given by Mrs. Sturt (a very fine lady)."

Her picture of the masquerade deserves to be given in full:

"Sunday 14th June [1789]
"I must now my dear love fulfill my promise of an account of our Masquerade—We went to Hammersmith about ten o'clock—Mrs. & Miss Bouverie, Mrs. Stanhope (a very beautiful Woman), Mrs S. & I, all as Gypsies, & our dress, which I thought ugly enough, was however very much admired—Mrs. Sturt's House formerly belong'd to the famous Lord Melcombe—The Hall & Stair case very lofty & ornamented with colour'd Lamps—The Duke of York's Band playing—We Enter'd first a very fine Gallery paved with different sorts of Marble & ornamented with some uncommonly fine pillars, lighted with colour'd Lamps, & ornamented with a transparency representing the Prince's Crest & devices of the professions of the Two Brothers. Natural flowers in abundance. From thence we went through two or three pretty Rooms to the Gallery, so that tho' there was a great deal of company there was no unpleasant croud—I stuck close to Mrs. S. & we unmask'd very soon—She was of course accosted by a great many with abundance of fine things & I came in for Share of civility.

"About one the Princes arrived all dress'd alike as Highland Cheifs; nothing could be more elegant or becoming
than their dress—The Prince came to Mrs. S. to enquire for
Dick & gave such an enquiring Stare at me that she thought
it best to introduce me, for he has his Father's Passion for
knowing who & what every one is; at two the Supper
Rooms were open'd—The Etiquette is always to have a
Room for the Prince who chuzes his company, So that neither Rank nor the Lady of the House decides that point—
He as usual ask'd Mrs. S. & she kept fast hold of me 'till
we got into the Room—The Duke of Clarence took the head
of the Table & the Prince placed himself on one side, Mrs.
S. at his right hand, The Dutchess of Ancaster, (as Hecate)
on his left—I sat next & *le Cher Frère* next to me, who by the
bye is always particularly civil to me in Public unlike a certain sneaking Puppy (of our acquaintance)[1]. Opposite to us
Lady Duncannon as a *Sœur Grise*, casting many tender
looks across the table which to my great joy did not seem
much attended to—a Young Lady with her in the same
dress—Lady Jersey & her Daughter, (very pretty women)
as Black veil'd Nuns—Dutchess of Rutland in a Fancy sort
of Dress without powder & not looking Handsome—then
Duke of Clarence & then Mrs. Fitzherbert in a White
dress & black veil but unlike a Nun's dress—These were all
the Women; There were a good many Gentlemen at table &
several standing behind.

"When Supper was near over Some excellent Catch Singers belonging to the *Je ne scais quoi* Club sang some very
good catches—After a little time the Prince call'd them round
& proposed to Mrs. S. to join him in a Trio, which she did
at once tho' she has not practised any thing of the kind for
many months & was taken quite by surprise—The company, as you may suppose, were all delighted with this unexpected pleasure—The Prince proposed a couple more, &
then gave over for fear of tiring Mrs. S.—He has a good
voice, & being so well supported, seem'd to me to sing very

[1] Her brother Charles.

well. We sat about an hour at table & then return'd to the
Gallery—we intended going home at first; but Dick, who
came in a black domino, put on a disguise after supper &
made a great deal of diversion as he was unknown to everyone but us; having plagued several people sufficiently, he
resumed his Domino, & return'd to the company pretending
he had just left a party at Supper—& at length at a shamefully late, or rather early, hour—we return'd to Town.

"I saw Miss Cholmondeley there in very bad preservation—Time has used her but scurvily & she has unluckily
retain'd all her little affectations—I could not help thinking
while I was Supping with Princes & great people that my
situation was a little like poor Gil Blas at the Court of
Madrid—but mine is only temporary & I look beyond it to
real comfort & happyness—I have had a peep at the Raree
Shew of the great world without trouble or risk & not being
young enough to have my brain turn'd, shall enjoy my broil'd
bone in Cuffe St with as much pleasure as ever—And shall
have the advantage of having a great deal of talk to myself
as I expect to be as much question'd as Linco when I get
among you.

"There was also a Room for the Duke & Dutchess of
Cumberland & a third for the company at large—After we
all unmask'd Dick walk'd about a good deal with us &
several of the masks remark'd that having such a Partner it
was no wonder he kept by her—I think I never saw Mrs. S.
look handsomer—As Mrs. Sturt had given out Domino's
were not to be admitted it enliven'd the scene very much for
those who did not venture to assume a character at least
wore handsome dresses—She admitted Friends however in
Domino's—You see that I could not have been sufficiently
awake to write you all this yesterday & perhaps you dont
thank me for such a long account—the intention however
is good so at least I shall be forgiven— . . .

"Ever most affectionately yours,
"E. SHERIDAN."[1]

[1]Lefanu MSS., 202–4. Not previously published.

CHAPTER THE TWELFTH

The Other Harlequin

I

RICHARD TICKELL was the most intimate of all Sheridan's friends—his alter ego in "wit and want, talent and thoughtlessness." They played their pranks like a pair of Harlequins, and innumerable stories are told of their escapades, for they were boys even in middle age. When they were staying at Lord Palmerston's at Broadlands, in 1786, they used to go every morning in different boats, as Mrs. Sheridan wrote Mrs. Canning, "splashing one another till one confessed himself conquered by running away, after which they used to come puffing to us, like Tritons in a sea piece, dripping from all parts."[1] At Crewe Hall, Mrs. Sheridan and Mrs. Crewe would be out riding in the carriage, with Sheridan and Tickell on their horses before them: suddenly they would see Sheridan stretched upon the ground, in the agonies of death, and Tickell standing over him in a theatrical attitude of despair.[2]

Lord John Townshend, who had known them both from boyhood, told another story which reads like a scene from a Harlequinade, with Tickell as Pantaloon. Sheridan covered the door of a dark passage leading from the drawing-room with all the household plates and dishes, and provoked Tickell to pursue him. He had left a path for his own escape, but Tickell his play-fellow fell full headlong into the ambuscade, and was severely cut. When Lord John visited his bed-side next day, he found him covered with patches, and vowing vengeance for this unjustifiable outrage. In the midst of his anger, however,

<hr/>

[1] Rae, II, 183.   [2] Rogers, *Table Talk*, 65.

he could not help exclaiming, with the true feeling of a connoisseur in this kind of mischief, "But how amazingly well done it was!"

2

Richard Tickell turned dramatist with an opera called *The Carnival of Venice*, which was acted at Drury Lane on October 21st, 1781. He had recently, on April 24th, 1781, been appointed a Commissioner of the Stamp Office, and granted apartments in Hampton Court Palace, through the influence of Lord North's secretary, William Brummell. He had married Mary Linley, Mrs. Sheridan's sister, at Wells Cathedral on July 25th, 1780, and they had been living at Wells for a year in "poverty and happiness." They may have met at Bath, where Tickell was born about 1751; he entered the Middle Temple in 1768, and after being called to the Bar, was appointed a Commissioner of Bankruptcy in 1777, but was removed in 1778 for neglect of duty on petition of the other Commissioners. He was living a life of pleasure, and exercising his talent for light verse in such poems as *The Wreath of Fashion*, and Sheridan persuaded Garrick to intercede for him with Lord Bathurst, the Lord Chancellor, who refused to reinstate him in office; Garrick then pressed his merits upon Lord North, the Premier, and he was eventually granted a pension of £200 a year to write on behalf of the Ministry.

At Sheridan's request, Tickell wrote the prologue for *The Camp*, which was acted in October 1778, but shortly afterward he excused himself from writing a prologue to Fielding's *The Fathers*, on the grounds that he was engaged upon a work which might "make or mar his fortunes"—which was *Anticipation*, a parody upon the speeches at the opening of Parliament. It was a great success, for Burke and Fox, as Gibbon wrote, "were pleased with their speeches, though serious patriots frown that such things should be turned into farce." Garrick then introduced him to Richard Rigby, who appears to have been acting on behalf of Lord North the Premier, and, however that may be, the pension was granted soon afterward, and part of it was settled after his marriage with Mary Linley on his illegitimate family.

His next dramatic excursion, no doubt at Linley's instigation, was to adapt *The Gentle Shepherd*, by Allan Ramsay, which was played at Drury Lane on October 29th, 1781. He restored "the geniune Doric," which Theophilus Cibber had translated into his own vulgar tongue in *Patie and Peggie, or the Fair Foundling*. Boaden said in his *Mrs. Siddons* that "Linley, by skilful accompaniments to the Scottish melodies, showed how usefully science may be occupied on the grounds of genius."

Some of the Songs in *The Carnival of Venice* have been attributed to Sheridan, by Maria Julia Young, who in her *Memoir of Mrs. Crouch* wrote that "many songs in this piece so perfectly resemble the beauty of those which adorn *The Duenna* that they declare themselves to be the offspring of the same Muse." For this guess there is no foundation. Boaden, who saw Tickell's piece, dismissed it summarily—"compared with *The Duenna* it was flat—Lent rather than Carnival." Probably the music was Linley's.

The only other theatrical effort of Tickell's was trivial, and made after the death of Samuel Linley. Maria Young, in her *Memoirs of Mrs. Crouch* wrote:

"Poor Mr. Linley! after the death of one of his sons, when seated at the harpsichord in Drury-Lane theatre, in order to accompany the vocal parts of an interesting little piece taken from Prior's *Henry and Emma* by Mr. Tickell, and excellently represented by Palmer and Miss Farren,—when the tutor of Henry, Mr. Aikin, gave an impressive description of a promising young man, in speaking of his pupil Henry, the feelings of Mr. Linley could not be suppressed. His tears fell fast—nor did he weep alone."

3

Tickell was an incorrigible joker, but he can hardly have hoped for the success which has attended one of his efforts. Sheridan projected the publication of an edition of *The Rivals*, and Tickell determined to anticipate posterity by editing the comedy as he conceived that it would be published in the learned recension of some Porson or Puffendorf of three centuries later. He wrote a Life of the Author, as he conceived that it would be reconstructed from the scanty fragments that would remain. He added, as if written by Sheridan, a "Dedication to Idleness." Lastly, he made a series of marginal notes upon the text. The copy with these jocular additions fell into the hands of Thomas Moore, who took the textual notes *au grand serieux*. He printed the Life and the Dedication, and, though the one has been ignored, the other has been taken as Sheridan's own work by more than one commentator—Percy Fitzgerald even incorporated it in his biography of Sheridan.

The Life of the Author is a warning and a horrible example to all writers of biography. It is full of half-truths, false deductions, and strange perversions. Moore says that Tickell prefixed to *The Rivals* "as coming from Sheridan, the following humorous dedication, which, I take for granted, has never before met the light."

DEDICATION TO IDLENESS.

"My Dear Friend,

"If it were necessary to make any apology for this freedom, I know you would think it a sufficient one, that I shall find it easier to dedicate my play to you than to any other person. There is likewise a propriety in prefixing your name to a work begun entirely at your suggestion, and finished under your auspices; and I should think myself wanting in gratitude to you, if I did not take an early opportunity of acknowledging the obligations which I owe you. There was a time—though it is so long ago that I now scarcely remember it, and cannot mention it without compunction—but there was a time, when the importunity of parents, and the example of a few injudicious young men of my acquaintance, had almost prevailed on me to thwart my genius, and prostitute my abilities by an application to serious pursuits. And if you had not opened my eyes to the absurdity and profligacy of such a perversion of the best gifts of nature, I am by no means clear that I might not have been a wealthy merchant or an eminent lawyer at this very moment. Nor was it only on my first setting out in life that I availed myself of a connection with you, though perhaps I never reaped such signal advantages from it as at that critical period. I have frequently since stood in need of your admonitions, and have always found you ready to assist me—though you were frequently brought by your zeal for me into new and awkward situations, and such as you were at first, naturally enough, unwilling to appear in. Amongst innumerable other instances, I cannot omit two, where you afforded me considerable and unexpected relief, and in fact converted employments usually attended by dry and disgusting business, into scenes of perpetual merriment and recreation. I allude, as you will easily imagine, to those cheerful hours which I spent in the Secretary of State's office and the Treasury, during all which time you were my inseparable companion, and showed me such a preference over the rest of my colleagues, as excited at once their envy and admiration. Indeed, it was very natural for them to repine at your having taught me a way of doing business, which it was impossible for them to follow—it was both original and inimitable.

"If I were to say here all that I think of your excellences, I might be suspected of flattery; but I beg leave to refer you for the test of my sincerity to the constant tenor of my life and actions; and shall conclude with a sentiment of which no one can dispute the truth, nor mistake the application—that those persons usually deserve most of their friends who expect least of them.

"I am, &c. &c. &c.

"R. B. SHERIDAN."[1]

To this, he added marginal notes, of which Moore said, with becoming solemnity:

[1]Moore, 106-8.

"These opinions are generally expressed in two or three words, and are, for the most part, judicious. Upon Mrs. Malaprop's quotation from Shakespeare 'Hesperian curls' &c, he writes 'overdone—fitter for farce than comedy.' Acres's classification of oaths, 'This we call the *oath referential*' &c. he pronounces to be 'very good, but above the speaker's capacity.' Of Julia's speech, 'Oh, woman, how true should be your judgment, when your resolution is so weak!' he remarks 'On the contrary, it seems to be of little consequence whether any person's judgment be weak or not, who wants resolution to act according to it.' "

As Moore considered these "judicious," it would have been very interesting to have perused some of the more "injudicious" comments which this remark presumes. These deliberate attempts at writing a carping commentary without any sense of humour were anticipations of scholastic sagacity and moral judgment. In fact, they are not to be detached from the editorial preface with which Tickell "filled, in very neat handwriting, the first three or four pages of his copy."

4

Mrs. Sheridan wrote her husband from Crewe Hall in 1787:

"I am very glad to hear *The Rivals* is to be got up at Drury Lane. I dare say it will bring very good houses, especially if you alter Lydia Languish for Mrs. Jordan. Is that to be done, or how? But I can't bear you should be wasting your time, and your pretty thoughts, on foolish epilogues when, if you are to write, you might write something that would be of real service to yourself."

Sheridan did not alter Lydia Languish for Mrs. Jordan. He appears to have glanced through the prompt-book, in which the inordinate length of the play had long been curtailed. In one of Julia's speeches, a big cut had been made. In describing Faukland's character she assures Lydia at great length that "he is too proud, too noble to be jealous: if he is captious, it is without dissembling; if fretful, without rudeness. Unus'd to the fopperies of love, he is negligent of the little duties expected from a lover," with much more to the same effect, ending "But I have learn'd to think myself his debtor for those imperfections, which arise from the ardour of his attachment."[1]

John Kemble, in his own copy of the prompt-book noted that "the ladies" very often improperly omitted this passage. Sheridan, in examining the prompt-book, wrote under it:

"The only speech in the play that cannot be omitted. The pruning-knife, Damme, the Axe! the Hatchet!"

Kemble agreed that it is "necessary for the explanation of Faukland's character," but it is interesting to realize that, so far from altering Lydia Languish for Mrs. Jordan, Sheridan was quite indifferent to the general abridgement. The Dedication to Idleness justified itself.

[1]Now in the library of the Garrick Club.

CHAPTER THE THIRTEENTH

Harlequin Don Juan

No man worth having is ever true to his wife, or ever was,
or ever will be so.

A Trip to Scarborough.

I

WHEN Sheridan in 1777 submitted the manuscript of
A Trip to Scarborough to the Lord Chamberlain's office,
the Deputy Licenser of Plays, Edward Capell, placed
brackets round a cynical comment of Berinthia, "No man
worth having is ever true to his wife, or ever was, or ever will be
so." Against it he wrote austerely "This ought to be suppressed."[1] No doubt it was explained to him that this line was
Vanbrugh's, and not Sheridan's, and that for seventy years
it had been spoken in *The Relapse* and was, indeed, still being
spoken by Mrs. Bellamy at Covent Garden. Accordingly, this
pious expression of opinion must have been disregarded, for
the sentence stands unaltered in the printed copy of 1781, and
all the other editions.

Sheridan himself illustrated the truth of Berinthia's cynic-
ism. In his *Memoirs of Sheridan* Moore said little of his *vie
amoureuse*, except that he was "the object of universal admiration, whose vanity and passions too often led him to yield to
the temptations by which he was surrounded." This can only
be construed as a reflection, at least in part, upon the beauties
of the theatre; but whatever may have happened in his middle-
age, his name is not coupled with that of any actress in the
chronique scandaleuse of the eighteenth century, even in such

[1] MS. in Larpent Collection, Huntingdon Library.

assiduous publications as *The Town and Country Magazine.* Perhaps the Mrs. Lyster who wished, as she wrote to Sheridan, that she had escaped the jealousy of his "best-beloved,"[1] was the actress of that name who as Miss Barsanti was the original Lydia Languish in *The Rivals.* Mrs. Robinson was most anxious to show that the attentions which Sheridan paid to her were entirely chivalrous and disinterested, and there is no reason to think otherwise. As for intrigues with minor actresses, such of their colleagues as were aggrieved over the distribution of parts exposed the frailties of managers to the fierce light of publicity. From their silence as to Sheridan, the theatre then, can be expunged from the history.

Moore's *Journal,* however showed that Harlequin's vagaries had a serious side. After Sheridan's death, Susan Ogle, the second Mrs. Sheridan's sister, was engaged in looking through his papers, and pointed out to Moore that it was melancholy to compare the letters of his two wives, both beginning in the same strain of love and worship for him, and both gradually alienated by his selfish and vain-glorious infidelities and extravagance, till they ended by disliking him, the fate which he brought upon himself from both women who adored him. Nevertheless, "Sukey Ogle" was full of enthusiasm for his memory and his fame, and trusted that his biographer would do him "ample justice"—("i.e.," adds Moore, "praise him through thick and thin").[2]

In Sheridan's love affairs there was more play-acting than passion, more affectation than gallantry. In 1789, when Sir Gilbert Elliott told his wife that "many fashionable amours were likely to be made public," he added "Sheridan is a great gallant and intriguer among fine ladies. He appears to me a strange choice, having a red face, and as ill a look as I ever saw. But he employs a great deal of art with a great deal of pains to gratify, not the proper passion in these affairs, but vanity; and he deals in the most intricate plotting and under-plotting, like a Spanish play." After Mrs. Sheridan's death, her best friend, Mrs. Canning, in telling how Richard had alienated his wife's

---

[1]Rae, I. 254.   [2]Moore, *Journal,* II, 299.

heart, showed William Smyth an album of verses in which
there was a poem addressed "To ——." Smyth remembered
only two verses in which Elizabeth had revealed her grief and
anguish at the discovery of her husband's infidelity. The poem
is long, and four stanzas will suffice:

> "Ah! why, when anguish rends the heart,
>   Dost thou avoid with studious art
>   To meet thy Laura's eye?
>   Alas, no angry glance is there,
>   A mute and unreproachful tear
>   Perhaps may claim a sigh.
>
> "When first the cruel truth I found,
>   Nor thou the wish to change disowned
>   Fierce madness seized my brain,
>   But happier now my milder grief
>   Affords a sad, but dear relief.
>   I weep—and can complain. . . .
>
> "Ingrate! that now has fled these arms,
>   Disdaining all those boasted charms
>   That once had power to bless;
>   Are then these sighs, these endless tears,
>   The sad reward for all *her* cares
>   Who gave thee happiness?
>
> "Say! thou inconstant! hast thou found
>   Those joys in dissipations's round,
>   Thy fickleness requires?
>   Hast thou yet seen the happy fair,
>   Designed thy softer hours to share
>   And fix thy wild desires?"[1]

It is customary to assert that the woman in the case was Mrs.

---

[1] Rae, II. The poem is undated: the album, bequeathed to Mrs. Canning by Mrs.
Sheridan .was started at Harrow on "November 27th, 1782." But the clue is valueless as
it contained *The Grotto,* written by Sheridan in 1772.

Crewe, but the poem is obviously not a lament over one infidelity, but over a heart grown cold, and surrendered to fickleness and dissipation.

Mrs. Crewe, whom Sheridan had celebrated in 1777 as the fair Amoret whom no scandal could touch, was indeed one of the fine ladies with whom he was so great a gallant and intriguer. In 1784, Mrs. Crewe turned her chaise back from Crewe Hall to attend the first performance of *Arthur and Emmeline* at Drury Lane. Her sister Mary, assuring her that Sheridan and Mrs. Crewe "mean nothing but pure innocence," added "I saw the veteran Amoret in all her charms. She was in Dr. Ford's with Mrs. Lane and two gentlemen. They did not come till the play was near over, and indeed had been at the box some time before I had any idea who they were, nor, I believe, should I ever have found them out if Sheridan *had not told me*. But the best of the joke was that even then I took Mrs. Lane for her companion, [Mrs. Crewe], and was quite shocked at the amazing alteration in her. Sheridan joined with me most heartily."[1]

No doubt it consoled Mrs. Sheridan to hear her rival described as "the veteran Amoret," and to hear that her beauty was but a fading flower. Instead of being thirty, as is commonly supposed, Mrs. Crewe was about forty, so there was a little point in Mary Tickell's feminine gibe. Nevertheless, it does not look as if Mrs. Sheridan had taken this *amourette* very deeply to heart. She was a woman of the world.

When staying with them at Dibden in 1788, his sister Betsy wrote in her Journal to her sister, Mrs. Lefanu:

"As to your questions concerning Mrs. Crewe and Mrs. Bouverie; I cannot entirely satisfy you, as I do not know the cause of their difference. That Mrs. Crewe hates Mrs. B. is certain—and to such a degree as to be distress'd if they accidentally meet. Mrs. B. neither seeks nor avoids her, &, by what has dropp'd from Mrs. Sheridan, I fancy she is the

[1] Sichel, II, 64. The date given is 1783, but the performance of *Arthur and Emmeline* was on Monday, November 22nd, 1784. Cf. Allardyce Nicoll, *XVIII Century Drama, 1750–1800*, 319.

injur'd person of the two. Some love affair I believe to be the origin of the quarrel. As to Mrs. Crewe's coldness with regard to Mrs. S.; it is partly jealousy of Mrs. B. to whom Mrs. S. certainly gives the preference. You know also that Mrs. Crewe among other lovers (favour'd ones I mean) has had our Brother in her train. As his fame and consequence in life have increas'd, her charms have diminished; & passion no longer the tie between them, his affection, esteem, and attentions return'd to their proper channel, and he has never seem'd, or I believe never was in truth, so much attach'd to his wife as of late, and this her *dear friend* cannot bear. And Mrs. S. tells me that while they were at Crewe Hall, she took little pains to conceal her jealousy. A strange system you will say altogether, and for such people to associate together & disgrace the name of friendship is truly disgusting. Yet such I am told is the universal practice of the great world—or as poor Jenny Linley calls them, the fine people, to whom she has a comfortable dislike."[1]

The society in which the Sheridans moved was renowned for its gallantries, actual or fictitious, and Betsy Sheridan was shocked to learn that the Duke of Devonshire had for his *chère amie* Lady Elizabeth Forster, who was nevertheless his wife's best friend, and that the Duchess herself was believed to be prodigal of her favours. A month later, in 1788, from Dibden she wrote about Mrs. Sheridan's standard of morality:

"Mrs. S., always amiable and obliging, has adopted ideas on many subjects so very different from what mine must be that we can never converse with that freedom that minds in some sort of the same kind indulge in. She told me last night she had converted Mrs. Canning, who was uncommonly rigid in her notions & therefore was not without hopes of bringing me over to her way of thinking. I assured her, her chance was much worse with me than with Mrs. C., for that, so far from being rigid, I was convinced I was indulgent to the utmost verge of propriety,—that therefore I must

[1]Lefanu MSS., 157, November 29th, 1788.

err to expand my latitude in the smallest degree—that my
opinions on some points were as fix'd as my principles, &
that I was too old to change either—that I allow'd others to
indulge their own way of thinking & should no more quarrel with a woman for thinking differently in a point of morals
than I should on religious matters if she happen'd to be
brought up a Mahometan. In this manner I always treat the
subject & we end in good humour."[1]

This prim passage is hardly to be taken as an admission by
Mrs. Sheridan that she had taken a lover, and Mrs. Canning's
"conversion" can have amounted to no more than a certain
concession as to the morals of the "fine folks," such as the
Princes under the restriction of the Royal Marriages Act, and
the Duke of Norfolk with his imbecile wife. But Mrs. Sheridan's "amiable and obliging" attitude was soon to be very
severely tested.

2

Mrs. Sheridan's voice was still of superlative quality, and
she often sang at such houses as the Duke of Portland's and the
Duchess of Devonshire's. In praise of her singing there was the
perpetual epithet of "angelic." Wilberforce hearing her at Bur-
lington House in 1783, wrote that "she sang old English songs
angelically." Elliott, hearing her with her sister, at Mrs.
Crewe's in February 1787, wrote that they "sang like angels,
nothing could be more enchanting." But when Mary Tickell
died in the July of 1787, Mrs. Sheridan ceased for a time to
sing, and Betsy Sheridan was writing of her voice in the past
tense: she had been to Westminster Abbey, for the Handel
Commemoration, where she was greatly impressed by the singing of Madame Mara—"her voice was uncommonly fine, perhaps beyond Mrs. Sheridan's but that something angelic
which was in the sound of hers is wanting, as well as that
beauty and expression which necessarily gave such additional
charms to our sister's singing." But in the October of 1788,

[1]Lefanu MSS., 164, December 22nd, 1788.

Lacy House in Middlesex, the Seat of Richard Brinsley Sheridan Esq.

LACY HOUSE, 1793

To face page 151

while staying at Dibden, at the same time as Jenny Linley, she wrote "in the evening we had music—Miss Linley's voice goes charmingly with her sister's in Duets—Mrs. Sheridan's voice I think as perfect as I ever remember it—that same peculiar tone that I believe is hardly to be equalled in the world, as everyone is struck in the same way."[1]

These were no unsupported partialities; Michael Kelly, who had first heard her in 1787, after he had been singing with the finest singers in Europe, sang a duet with her at Bruton Street, when her "voice, taste, and judgement combined to make her the *rara avis* of her day."

But it is likely that the last time she ever delighted an audience was in the June of 1789, when, after so many months of silence, she sang duets with the Prince of Wales. For within a few weeks she was seriously ill. On August 20th, 1789, Betsy Sheridan, who had just become Mrs. Henry Lefanu, wrote:

"for the last fortnight she has been so ill as to be hardly off the bed—her situation is truly uncomfortable—she has not herself the smallest hope, yet as they tell her there is a chance that she may not miscarry, she is obliged to submit to medecine and confinement. I spent the day with her yesterday: Harry went to town on business about, & she sent the coach for me & sent me home at night—I found her ill when I first went, but she grew rather better towards night: I endeavour'd to encourage her. I am rather inclined to hope, as she tells me Dr. Ford seem'd to think that with very great care she may go on well—at present appearances are against her. Dick was at Brighton to celebrate the Duke of York's birthday, and we spent the day in her bedroom.[2]

Mrs. Sheridan, still a very beautiful woman, had many suitors who wished to console her for her husband's inattentiveness. But in 1787, as Sir Gilbert Elliott testified, her reputation was unsullied. He wrote his wife:

"Mrs. Sheridan is really nearer one's notion of a muse, or

[1]Lefanu MSS., 143   [2]Lefanu MSS.

an angel, or some such preter-natural or semi-divine personage, than anything I have ever seen alive, and it is therefore not surprising that Mr. Mundy should be very much in love with her. Sheridan it seems has taken notice of it: but there has never been the slightest suspicion of Mrs. S. having listened to Mundy, or to anybody else."[1]

Edward Miller Mundy, M.P. for Derby County from 1784 till his death in 1820, was a friend of the Sheridans as early as 1785. But he was by no means the only suitor of Mrs. Sheridan in their circle. Charles Fox had flirted with her openly, and according to Thomas Grenville, his passion for her revived in 1788.[2]

The young Duke of Clarence, weary of the fascination of Polly Finch, was one of Mrs. Sheridan's most persistent admirers, and at one time she seems almost to have been on the point of yielding. In his *Journal*, Moore made a note about some correspondence which has since disappeared: "From some letters of Mrs. Sheridan to Mrs. Lefanu, the Duke of Clarence appears to have been pursuing her at one time, very seriously—she speaks of the necessity of being 'stout' and putting an end to his pursuit at once." The time appears to have been the autumn of 1789, when she wrote to Mrs. Canning, from Richmond,—"the Duke of Clar. lives within a hundred yards of me, and he generally pays me a visit most mornings."[3]

3

After the dissolution of June 12th, 1790, Sheridan went to Stafford, where he and Colonel Monckton expected to be opposed only by George Sloper, but Bond Hopkins also offered himself. As Lady Palmerston wrote, Sheridan had "the ladies on his side, for he was attended into the town by four hundred, headed by the beautiful Miss Furnio." The contest, however, was violent and embittered. During his absence, he expected to receive from his wife a journal of her activities, with the

[1]*Life*, I, 148, April 2nd, 1787.   [2]Moore, *Journal*, IV, 135.
[3]E. M. Butler, *Sheridan*, from Butler MSS., dated September 12th, 1789.

news of the day. She wrote him three letters, which show how admirably she assisted him in his political affairs. The first of them is:

"Monday [June 14th, 1790].

"This letter will find you, my dear Dick, I hope, encircled with honours at Stafford. I take it for granted you entered it triumphantly on Sunday—but I am very impatient to hear the particulars, and of the utter discomfiture of Sloper and his followers. I received your note from Birmingham this morning, and am happy to find that you and my dear cub were well, so far on your journey. You could not be happier than I should be in the proposed alteration for Tom, but we will talk more of this when we meet. I sent you Cartwright yesterday, and to-day I pack you off Perry with the soldiers. I was obliged to give them four guineas for their expenses. I send you likewise, by Perry, the note from Mrs. Crewe, to enable you to speak of your qualification if you should be called upon. So I think I have executed all your commissions, Sir; and if you want any of these doubtful votes,[1] which I mentioned to you, you will have time enough to send for them, for I would not let them go till I hear they can be of any use.

"And, now for my journal, Sir, which I suppose you expect. Saturday, I was at home all day busy for you,—kept Mrs. Reid to dinner—went to the Opera,—afterwards to Mrs. St. John's, where I lost my money sadly, Sir,—eat strawberries and cream for supper,—sat between Lord Salisbury and Mr. Meynell, (hope you approve of that, Sir,) —overheard Lord Salisbury advise Miss Boyle by no means to subscribe to Taylor's Opera, as O'Reilly's would certainly have the patent,—confess I did not come home till past two. Sunday, called on Lady Julia,—father and Mr. Reid to dinner,—in the evening at Lady Hampden's,—lost my money again, Sir, and came home by one o'clock. 'Tis now near one o'clock,—my father is established in my boudoir,

[1] i.e., whose qualifications might be rejected by the Mayor.

and, when I have finished this, I am going with him to hear
Abbe Vogler play on the Stafford organ. I have promised to
dine with Mrs. Crewe, who is to have a female party only,—
no objection to that I suppose, Sir? Whatever the party do,
I shall do of course,—I suppose it will end in Mrs. Hobart's.

"Mr. James told me on Saturday, and I find it is the report of the day, that Bond Hopkins is gone to Stafford. I am
sorry to tell you there is an opposition at York—Mr. Montague opposes Sir William Milner. Mr. Beckford has given
up at Dover, and Lord —— is so provoked at it, that he has
given up too, though they say they were both sure. St. Ives
is gone for want of a candidate. Mr. Barham is beat at
Stockbridge. Charles Lenox has offered for Surry, and they
say Lord Egremont might drive him to the deuce, if he
would set any body up against him. You know, I suppose,
Mr. Crewe has likewise an opponent. I am sorry to tell you
all this bad news, and, to complete it, Mr. Adam is sick in
bed, and there is nobody to do any good left in town.

"I am more than ever convinced we must look to other
resources for wealth and independence, and consider politics merely as an amusement—and in that light 'tis best to be
in Opposition, which I am afraid we are likely to be for
some years again.

"I see the rumours of war still continue—Stocks continue to fall—is that good or bad for the Ministers? The little
boys are come home to me to-day. I could not help showing
in my answer to Mr. T[ickell]'s letter, that I was hurt at his
conduct—so I have got another flummery letter and the
boys, who (as he is pretty sure) will be the best peace-
makers. God bless you, my dear Dick. I am very well, I
assure you; pray don't neglect to write to your ever affectionate

E.S."

Sheridan found this letter cold, so in her next she replied to
him:

"If you were not so worried, I should scold you for the

conclusion of your letter to-day. Might not I as well accuse you of coldness, for not filling your letter with professions, at a time when your head must be full of business? I think of nothing all day long, but how to do good, some how or other, for you. I have given you a regular Journal of my time, and all to please you,—so don't, dear Dick, lay so much stress on words. I should use them oftener, perhaps, but I feel as if it would look like deceit. You know me well enough, to be sure that I can never do what I'm bid, Sir,— but, pray, don't think I meant to send you a cold letter, for indeed nothing was ever farther from my heart."[1]

When the poll was declared at Stafford on June 18th, the figures were:

Monckton 264, *Sheridan* 264, *Sloper* 182, *Hopkins* 145.

4

About the end of 1790 Sheridan's relations with the Duchess of Devonshire's sister, Lady Duncannon, became so notorious that Lord Duncannon was threatening to issue "a writ of enquiry for *crim. con.*," the first process in the long and tedious method of divorce. The Duke, summoned hastily from abroad, succeeded in preventing this public scandal. At the time when this agitation was at its height, the Sheridans were guests at Crewe Hall.

Mrs. Sheridan was deeply distressed, yet—as she wrote to Mrs. Canning—her husband added to her troubles at the time when he was protesting his repentance—"at the moment in which he was swearing and imprecating all sorts of curses on himself, on me, and his child, if ever he was led by any motive to be false to me again, he threw the whole family at Crewe into confusion and distress by playing the fool with Miss Fd. (little Emma's governess) and contriving so awkwardly too, as to be discovered by the whole House, locked up with her in a bedchamber in an unfrequented part of the house."

Exasperated by this stupid and outrageous infidelity, Mrs.

[1]Moore, 463–466.

Sheridan resolved upon separation, but Mrs. Bouverie and Charles Fox succeeded in talking her over, and he was terribly frightened by her behaviour, so that she received him into favour, but even in forgiving him she had "lost all confidence in his professions and promises."[1]

On returning to London she plunged into the gaieties of London with ardour, seeking distraction at the gaming-table. On March 28th, 1791, Mrs. Henry Lefanu, her sister-in-law, wrote from Bath,

> "I see by the *Herald*, Mrs. S. is giving great parties & making up for last year's moderation—I am sorry to see the Pharaoh table always makes a part of the entertainment; as I know her passion for it, & the consequence of a run of ill-luck must be dreadful."

5

Of all the calumnies of the age, the foulest was propagated against Sheridan by the Princess of Wales. In 1809, she told Lord Glenbervie that Miss Hayman, one of her Maids of Honour

> "once passed two months in the same house as the first Mrs. Sheridan—I believe at Wynnstay, Sir Watkin Williams Wynne's. They contracted a great intimacy, and during the time they were together Mrs. Sheridan told her the whole history of her life, and among other things this very extra-ordinary circumstance: that Sheridan had obliged her to grant the last favour to the Prince of Wales, whom she said she detested, in consideration of his receiving £20,000 from the Prince."

Recording this, Lord Glenbervie moralized that Miss Hayman's veracity was unquestionable, he could not imagine what possible motive Mrs. Sheridan could have had in fabricating such a story. So, he added, "it has long been thought unaccountable that Sheridan, who could have inherited nothing from his family, and never had any known accession of fortune but the

[1]Sadleir, 82–84, January, 1791.

£3,000 damages which his wife recovered from Mr. Long a short time before he married her, for breach of promise of marriage, could have lived for many years, before the resources of the treasury in Drury Lane were opened to him, in the manner that he did—a house in town, an equipage, frequent entertainments, and the train of a man possessed of some thousands a year. The £20,000 may serve to explain this enigma."

This story may be dismissed as a lie, whoever was the inventor, and possibly behind the confusion is some account of the Prince's relations with Mrs. Robinson, to whom he gave a bond for £20,000, in the redemption of which Sheridan, like Charles Fox, may have had some concern. But it is not so easy to dismiss the rest of the Princess's story to Lord Glenbervie:

> "When Mrs. Sheridan was in her last illness, though she acknowledged to him that the child she had borne was Lord Edward Fitzgerald's, her husband attended her to Bristol, and till her death, with greatest tenderness, avowing that whatever ill conduct she had been guilty of, he had been the cause of it. He owned, or more properly adopted, the child, which, however, did not long outlive its mother."[1]

It has been the habit of Sheridan's biographers to pretend that the story of Lord Edward Fitzgerald was a fantastic invention of Mme. de Genlis, although it is attested by William Smyth on the authority of Mrs. Sheridan's most intimate friend, Mrs. Canning. His account is decisive:

> "By outraging her feelings by the most unpardonable indulgence of his unlawful passions, Sheridan at last destroyed the patience, and probably alienated the heart of this incomparable woman; and in a fatal hour, brought up as she had been, and living as she still was, in gay and fashionable society, she turned to listen to Lord Edward Fitzgerald, who was a perfect madman about her."

Lord Edward, said Moore, was the only one among the

[1] S. M. Ellis, *Michael Kelly*, 1930.

numerous suitors of Mrs. Sheridan to whom she was supposed
to have listened with anything like a return of feeling, "that
there should be mutual admiration between two such noble
specimens of human nature it is easy, without injury to either
of them, to believe." To this, however, Moore added an anecdote which was, at least, peculiar. Some months before his
wife's death, when Sheridan had been describing to her and
Lord Edward a beautiful French girl, whom he had lately seen,
and added that she put him strongly in mind of what his wife
had been in the first bloom of her youth and beauty, when he
had left the room Mrs. Sheridan turned to Lord Edward and
said with a melancholy smile, "I should like you, when I am
dead, to marry that girl."[1]

The French girl was the celebrated Pamela, then eighteen,
who was visiting England with Mme. de Genlis. She was supposed to be the natural daughter of the Duc d'Orleans and
Mme. de Genlis—who insisted, however, that Pamela was an
English subject, and one of the reasons for their presence in
England was to enable Mme. de Genlis to adopt her by process
of the English Courts of law. It was towards the close of 1791
that Sheridan met them at a dinner-party at the house of
Citizen Stone, the English Jacobin. Samuel Rogers, a guest at
the same time said that it was her striking likeness to his wife
which attracted and excited Sheridan's notice.

Mme. de Genlis was told of this resemblance, and in her
Memoirs she wrote that Mrs. Sheridan "who died young, was
one of the most beautiful and charming ladies in England, and
Pamela had a most striking likeness to her. She lived very
happily with her husband, till she became acquainted with
Lord Edward Fitzgerald, who conceived a most violent passion for her, which she returned. Remorse of conscience
brought her to the grave."

[1]Moore, 515, and preface to 5th Edition. Sichel paraphrases: "It is even said that in
the year of her death she pointed to the fantastic girl, and begged him to marry her
when she was gone. But if it is true that Lord Edward first saw Pamela some six months
later at Paris, this story must also fall to the ground." Pamela was not there to be pointed
at, nor was Sheridan to hear, although by his unlucky omission of the phrase "on his
leaving the room," until the 5th edition, Moore exposed Sheridan to the charge of being
a *mari complaisant* of the most indifferent kind.

CHAPTER THE FOURTEENTH

Death of St. Cecilia

I

ON August 24th, 1791, seven months before the expected birth of her baby, Mrs. Sheridan gathered together the letters of her dead sister Mary. She wrote on their cover:

"In February 1787, my dear sister came to London in a bad state of health. On the 15th of May she returned to Hampton Court without having received any benefit from the various remedies prescribed for her. The three last letters written between the 15th and 25th when she was once more brought to town, dangerously ill of a fever which turned to a hectic that never afterwards left her.

"On the 15th of June she was carried back to Hampton Court, where I remained with her, and on the 19th we went by slow degrees to Clifton Hill near the Hot Wells, with a faint hope that the air and waters might restore her, but after struggling with this most dreadful of all diseases, and bearing with gentlest patience and resignation the various pains and horrors that which mark its fatal progress, on the 27th of July she ceased to suffer, and I for ever lost the friend and companion of my youth, the beloved sister of my heart, whose loss can never be repaired, whose sweet and amiable qualities endeared her to all those who were so happy to know her. She died in the 29th year of her age, universally regretted and lamented, and she was buried in the Cathedral at Wells, where she spent her infancy, and where she enjoyed happiness and poverty the first year of her marriage.

"In less than two years afterwards Mr. Tickell married again, a beautiful young woman of 18!

"The dear children remained with me till that time. The boys were taken home by their father. The girl, the dying legacy of her ever dear and lamented mother, is ſtill mine and conſtitutes all my happiness."[1]

2

Early in 1792 Mrs. Sheridan was ſtaying at Southampton, and on March 3rd Sheridan wrote to the Duchess of Devonshire and the Countess of Bessborough, who were travelling in Italy, that he was taking Dr. Benjamin Moseley, of Chelsea Hospital, " to see E., who is much better, because I want to decide about moving her." Three days later he added that he had juſt returned from a long solitary walk on the beach. It was a sad letter, full of regret and dread, and his mind returned to the voyage to France of twenty years before, in that wild March:

"What times and changes have passed! What has the interval of my life been! and what is left me but misery from memory, and a horror of reflexion?"

Mrs. Sheridan was moved to London, where three weeks later, the child was born; *The Gentleman's Magazine* for April 1792 records: "March 30, at Cromwell House, Brompton, Mrs. Sheridan of a daughter." It was hoped that, with the birth of her child, she would recover her health. Towards the end of April, "every favourable appearance exceeded our moſt sanguine hopes" but on Friday 27th when the baby was chriſtened Mary, in memory of Elizabeth's beloved siſter, there were many symptoms of rapid consumption.

Sheridan, on the next day, wrote a pitiful and desperate letter to Mrs. Canning, for whom Elizabeth muſt have been sadly enquiring, but who had eſtranged herself from her friend—unhappily, there is little doubt, over her affair with Lord Edward. His letter shows that Mrs. Canning had written to Mrs. B.—perhaps Mrs. Bouverie—explaining her reasons for not visiting Elizabeth. Sheridan was apprehensive that her life

[1]Rae, II, 27.

would be endangered by "the coolness, without explanation even, of the friend she loved best in the world":

> "My dear Mrs. Canning, you do not know the state she has been in, and how perilous and critical her state now is, or indeed you would up braid yourself for harbouring one altered thought, or even for abating in the least degree the warmest zeal of Friendship! of such friendship as nothing in Nature could ever have prevented her heart showing you. Pray forgive my writing to you thus; but convinced as I am that there is *no chance of saving her Life* but by tranquillizing her mind, and knowing as I do, and as I did hope you knew, that God never form'd a better heart, and that she has no errors but what are the Faults of those whose conduct has created them in her against her nature, I feel it impossible for me not to own that the idea of unkindness or coldness towards her *from you* smote me most sensibly, as I see it does her to the soul."[1]

Sheridan visited Wanstead the next day, and Mrs. Canning made "some allusion or other"—of course to Lord Edward—which threw Sheridan into a perfect paroxysm of grief and despair. "Oh, not a word of that kind," he cried, "She is an angel if ever there was one. It is all my fault. It is I, I that was the guilty fiend" and he sank into a chair, covering his face with his hands, quite convulsed with the agony of his feelings.[2]

Mrs. Canning, deeply touched, behaved nobly, and five days later they were at Spean Hill, on their way to the Hot Wells at Bristol—"Her friend whom she loves best in the world," Sheridan wrote the Duchess, "I have prevailed on to accompany her, and she is now with her—there never was a more friendly act than her doing so. She has left her daughter and all her children, whom she dotes on, for this office. Poor E. feels such a difference in her conduct from all her worldly friendships." Mrs. Bouverie, Mrs. Crewe, and the others had all deserted her.

On Sunday evening, May 6th, they rode over Kingsdown.

[1]Sichel, II, 215–6.   [2]Smyth, 26.

M

Sheridan stopped his horse as "poor E.'s chaise was going slowly down the hill, and went to the spot where my life was so strangely saved once"—twenty years before. It was marked by a great stone, cut by the man at whose cottage he had taken a drink of water—"and I remember many thoughts which passed my mind, believing, as I did, that I was dying. What an interval has passed since, and scarce one promise that I then made in my own soul I have attempted to fulfil." He looked at the carriage, and it wrung his heart "to think over the interval, the present, and the too probable conclusion."

A young physician named Bain, who had cured himself of consumption, ordered her to drink the waters: "I avoided asking him distinctly what he thinks," wrote Sheridan to the Duchess on their arrival, "but I flatter myself from Mrs. Canning's manner that he does not think her so ill as I feared." They moved into "a charming house, the white-bow windowed one that looks over the Strawberry Garden," from which Elizabeth went on the Downs twice a day in a sedan chair, her husband walking at her side. When they had been there a week, Mrs. Canning wrote her daughter that Dr. Bain said it really was "a lost case, and she could not live for six months."

Ever since the birth of her child Mrs. Sheridan had turned her thoughts almost entirely to religion and put aside all other contemplation: Sheridan read them a sermon each evening, and he kept up his spirits before her. "I am confident," he wrote, "if she can recover, there never was anything on earth more perfect than she will be, and to be different, she says, to me for ever from what she has been, makes her so seriously eager to live."

On Sunday, May 13th, she occupied herself with making her will, which she handed to Mrs. Canning, in the hope that it would never be opened. Then after dinner, as Mrs. Canning wrote her daughter, she sat down at the piano and taught Betty Tickell a little while, and played several slow movements from memory, "with her usual expression, but with a very trembling hand—it was so like the last efforts of an expiring genius and brought such a train of tender and melancholy ideas to my imagination, that I thought my poor heart would have burst in the conflict. It did not strike Mr. S. in the same light; he was pleased to see her able to amuse herself, and augured everything that was good from such favourable appearances. To me it seemed like the warnings of death and I thought, perhaps this is the last time I shall hear that admirable creature play!"[1]

But Sheridan had no such illusions, for his tenderness and buoyancy were assumed only for her comfort, and he wrote to the Duchess how she desired to be placed at the pianoforte. "Looking like a shadow of her own Picture, she played some notes with the tears dropping on her thin arms. Her mind is become heavenly, but her mortal form is fading from my sight, and I look in vain into my own mind for assent to her apparent conviction that all will not perish."[2] "I mean to send for my son," he concluded, "and she wishes for him." On June 1st, Mrs. Canning wrote to Mrs. Henry Lefanu that Elizabeth was "quite given over by the faculty," and added that she had known from the first, but as Sheridan seemed unwilling to know the truth, Dr. Bain had "not been so explicit with him," and only represented her as "being in a very critical condition." He appears to have left her only to meet his son, and his next letter which has survived, of June 13th, said that he had been called up at four in the morning by "George"—his butler, Edwards—to learn that for three hours she had a violent pain in her side, "a shocking sensation such a message is." She was bled and blistered, according to the practice of the time, and on Wednesday, June 16th, he went on a solitary pilgrimage over the Downs:

"while she slept this morning, I rode to a place where I remember she made me drive when poor Mrs. Tickell was dying here. It is a spot on the side of Brandon's Hill, where she and her sister used to play when they were at a boarding school close by. And I remember how bitterly she cried here and lamented her sister's approaching fate."

On June 21st he said, she wrote "a long paper to be given

[1]Rae, II, 148.　　　[2]Sichel, II, 438.

me by Mrs. Canning in case she should not recover. It was a great ease to her mind to have done this."

3

Two days later, it was his intention of starting for London, because she was fretting that he could not attend to his business. He wished to depart late in the evening of the Saturday after she had gone to bed, and, after spending a few hours in town, to return before she rose on Tuesday. But he never made the journey, for she grew worse, and on that day it was necessary to send to Bath, to summon her father and her family, they were introduced one at a time at her bedside, Mrs. Linley and Jenny, and her father—"The interview between him and the dear angel was afflicting and heart-breaking to the greatest degree possible," wrote Mrs. Canning, "I was afraid she would have sunk under the cruel agitation: she said it was indeed too much for her." She parted from them for the last time, and Elizabeth knew that death was at hand.

The day before her death, she extracted a strange oath from her husband. Its tenor was explained to his sister, Mrs. Elizabeth Lefanu, by Mrs. Canning in a letter written from Wanstead in October of the same year:

"Your brother has taken a house in this village very near me, where he means to place his little girl to be as much as possible under my protection. This was the dying request of my beloved friend, and the last effort of her mind and pen was made the day before she expired, to draw up a solemn promise for both of us to sign, to ensure the strict performance of this last awful injunction, so anxious was she to commit this dear treasure to my care."

She added that Mrs. Sheridan had known well "how impossible it would be for a father, situated as your brother is, to pay that constant attention to her which a daughter so particularly requires."[1] But the undertaking still exists in her own handwriting:

[1]Moore, 499–500.

"I here solemnly promise my dear Betsey never to interfere on any account with Mrs. C. in the education or in any other way of my poor child.

"I cannot write all my wish but he knows my Heart.

"Swear or I shall not die in peace."[1]

At night, Sheridan, who had watched at her bedside for several nights, sat up with Mrs. Canning. At four in the morning Dr. Bain was sent for. When he arrived, she asked to be left alone with him: when she knew that this indeed was death, she asked him to give her some laudanum, to enable her to sustain her last interview with those who were dearest to her, her son Tom, her niece Betty, her friend Mrs. Canning, and Richard. She kept her senses to the last, telling her husband of her confidence in God's mercy, and His sustenance in the hour of death. With a breaking heart, he knelt at her side, and held her hand, till her pulse fluttered for the last time, and he knew that the end had come. He withdrew, and Mrs. Canning closed her eyes, and kissed her "cold pale cheek."

4

She was buried at Wells Cathedral, beside her sister Mary. It was, as Sheridan bitterly remembered, a gaudy parade and show from Bristol to Wells Cathedral. They started from the Hot Wells at half-past seven in the morning, rested five hours at a desolate and uncomfortable inn, reaching the Cathedral towards eight at night. The choir chanted the first part of the service, and accompanied the coffin down the great aisle, where the service was read, but the buzz and tumult was so great that the powerful voice of the priest could hardly be heard. All the mob, high and low were in the church, surveying and surrounding the vault, and the priest was so pressed that he almost fell into it. The coffin was lowered, Sheridan who had behaved with great resolution, gave a look of wild agitation. After the crowd had dispersed, he returned to the Cathedral and knelt over the vault in an attitude of prayer, remaining there, alone in his

[1]Sadleir, 85, from Butler MSS.

misery, till the hour of midnight chimed. His memory was haunted by the beautiful face he had looked upon for the last time. He wrote:

"The loss of breath in a beloved object long suffering in pain and certainly to die, is not so great a privation as the loss of her beautiful remains, if they remain so. The victory of the Grave is sharper then the sting of Death."

CHAPTER THE FIFTEENTH

Second Marriage

Love, like a Meteor, shews a short liv'd blaze.
Lansdown, *The Jew of Venice.*

I

BUT within two months of his wife's death, all the world knew that Sheridan was in love with the beautiful Pamela. In October 1792 Lady Malmesbury asked Lady Elliott, "Did I tell you that he is in love with Mme. de Genlis's Pamela?" Mme. de Genlis narrated how in England she was honoured by the kindness of Charles Fox, and Sheridan, who "was naturally of an agreeable disposition, but was still more pleasing to us as he was passionately in love with Pamela, and being a widower, was desirous of marrying her." She was lively, says Rogers, quite radiant with beauty, and Sheridan even tried to compliment her by writing poems in French, though he hardly knew anything about the language—he sat all one evening labouring at a copy of verses to her, every now and then jotting a few words on paper.

He entertained Mme. de Genlis, Pamela, and the Princess, who was then known as Mlle. d'Orleans, at his seat in Isleworth for five or six weeks at the close of 1792, giving a splendid fête in honour of Pamela.

At the end of November Sheridan and Reid accompanied them from Isleworth to Dover; adverse wind detained them for five days at Dover, during which time Sheridan remained with them. Two days before they sailed Sheridan made, in the presence of Mme. de Genlis, a declaration of love to Pamela, who was charmed by "his agreeable manner and high character, and accepted the offer of his hand with pleasure. It was settled that he should marry her on their return from France, which was expected to take place in a fortnight."

At last the wind grew less unfavourable, though it was still violent, and Mme. de Genlis insisted upon embarking. Sheridan attended them to the very packet-boat, and he would have crossed with them, but that some indispensable duty at that moment required his presence in England. He, however, left them Reid as their escort to Paris, and so far as Sheridan was concerned, that was the end of the romance of Pamela. For in June of the next year, at a performance of *Lodoiska* in Paris, Lord Edward Fitzgerald saw Pamela for the first time, and was instantly so struck, says Mme. de Genlis, by her likeness to the "object of his bitter regret" that he fell in love with her, and married her.

2

After Mme. de Genlis had left Isleworth, Sheridan found a tutor for Tom in the person of William Smyth, of Peterhouse, Cambridge, who, nearly fifty years afterwards, when Professor of History in the University of Cambridge, narrated his experience in a *Memoir of Mr. Sheridan*, printed for private circulation. He recalled how on his first arrival at Sheridan's cottage at Wanstead he saw a baby of "the most extraordinary beauty," whose nurse, "a woman of superior class" assured him that she had "all the graces and phantasies of any woman of fashion in Grosvenor Square,"—which at six months, was surely an example of extreme precocity. But Mary the baby, was small and delicate, and "every human expedient was resorted to for its health and nurture" by Mrs. Canning, who visited her charge every day.

Smyth, who knew—or said—nothing of the strange oath which must have given cause for so many rumours, testified how curious it was that Sheridan, who could attend to nothing, was attentive to this baby: he never visited Wanstead without taking her some toy or cap or ribband, and he would stand over her cot for hours together trying to engage her attention. In her he saw the last image of his lost wife, to whose shade, it seemed to Smyth, his affection for her child was an offering. She was not strong, but her appearance was such as to charm "the eye and heart of every beholder."

The house at Wanstead Sheridan had planned to be a nursery for his children—Tom, whom he had taken away from Dr. Parr, Betty Tickell, whom his wife had adopted, and the baby Mary. Mrs. Sheridan had intended to bring up Betty as her own daughter, and her husband proposed to continue to act as her guardian, but her father had different views. Sheridan promised to explain to Tickell a plan for her education which would provide her with "maternal affection" which no doubt he meant that, like his own child, she should be entrusted to Mrs. Canning. Her father, however, preferred to send her to Belvedere House at Bath, which was conducted by Sophia and Harriet Lee, the literary daughters of John Lee the actor—the Lucius O'Trigger of the first night of *The Rivals*. It was a very highly reputed "seminary" but Sheridan was offended, although he had not condescended to explain his intentions, and Richardson expostulated with Tickell, who wrote to him in reply:

"I do not think Sheridan's habits (irregular and uncertain as they are) nor his taste or judgment, on the subject of education, tally with mine. My principles for Betty's education lead not to anything fantastic, nor to the training her up to the chance of a splendid connexion: but more to give her plainness of mind, and simplicity, yet grace in her manner; in one word, to form her on the model of her mother, who (as you know well) could find her greatest happiness in domestic quiet, though instantly ready to appear with ease in the highest circles. Now, I own, I have often regretted that Betty had a French attendant, and that she was imbibing ideas of elegance, from which a few accidents might lower her into unprepared dejection. You will do me an injustice, if you strain this apprehension into one unkind reflection on Mrs. Sheridan, but both she and Sheridan always proceeded in the confidence of realising great expectations."[1]

[1] Watkins, II, 229-30.

3

The new Theatre was opened on April 21st, 1794, the prologue not being written by Sheridan, but by General Fitzpatrick. Thomas Linley was not able to take an active part in the management, and either on or before his death, a share in the patent was purchased by John Grubb, an attorney, who acted as deputy manager for a season. Joseph Richardson also purchased a share, with money found by the Duke of Northumberland and others. Sheridan, drafting terms in 1802 when Kemble was approached to purchase a quarter in the Property of Drury Lane Theatre, wrote that his several purchases of shares

"have undoubtedly answered well; but in the chance of a Third Theatre consisted the risk; and the want of size and accommodation must have produced it, had the theatres continued as they were. But the *great* and *important feature* in the present property, and which is never for a moment to be lost sight of, is, that the Monopoly is, morally speaking, established for ever, at least as well as the Monarchy, Constitution, Public Funds, &c.—as appears by No. 1, being the copy of 'The Final Arangement' signed by the Lord Chamberlain, by authority of His Majesty, the Prince of Wales, the Duke of Bedford, &c.; and the dormant patent of Covent-Garden, that former terror of Drury-Lane, is perpetually annexed to the latter. So that the value of Drury-Lane, at present, and in the former sales, is out of all comparison,—independently of the new building, superior size, raised prices, &c. &c."[1]

The new building was much larger than the old theatre, and it could "hold" seven hundred pound a night, without crowding the audience, at the old prices. James Boaden described it as "the most beautiful and chaste structure that ever bore the name of theatre," while everything that machinery could accomplish was put within the power of the stage; the scenery

[1]Moore, 593-4.

ascended and descended, and the wardrobe "of more than common or oer-dyed materials" did not disgrace this palace of eastern magnificence; "one might have fancied that the eloquent prosecutor of Mr. Hastings had raised his triumphant theatre out of the divided spoils of India."

The danger of such a structure to dramatic art was obvious; it needed no Burke to say that "The dresses, the scenes, the decorations of every kind, are, I am told, in a new style of splendour and magnificence—whether to the advantage of our dramatic taste upon the whole I very much doubt. It is a Shew and a Spectacle, not a play, that is exhibited," and all the successes came under the heading of "a Shew and a Spectacle."[1]

4

Sheridan was married for the second time on April 27th, 1795. In November of that year appeared a satire against him under the title of *The Political Dramatist in November* 1795, in which there was this characteristic passage:

> "The shackles of a wayward bride he wore;
> For since divine Cecilia was no more,
> He deem'd, inclin'd to ogle and to toy,
> Husbands have pains, but bachelors no joy.
> Sunk in his chair, within his troubled soul,
> Strange thoughts in mix'd tumultuous movements roll.
> Of Drury first (which Holland's art could rear
> Fram'd for all uses, but to see and hear)
> And sums receiv'd, but to no reck'ning brought,
> And shares theatric, bought or to be bought."

The first couplets represent the general feeling as to his second marriage, which was universally condemned. Smyth's hostility still remained almost half-a-century later when he condemned it as "one of a many specimens of the silly vanity of this extraordinary man, but the most fatal to him that his life exhibited: it was a better vanity, but vanity still, on the

[1] Boaden, *Mrs. Siddons*, II, 310.

part of the lady." She was the youngest of four daughters of Newton Ogle, Dean of Winchester, and a niece of Admiral Sir Challenor Ogle. They met, at a party at Devonshire House. "Sheridan had lost the good looks of his youth: his forehead was fine, and his eyes brilliant in the extreme, but the lower part of his face was course, and disagreeable: he looked like the 'old lion,' Hector in the Tower of London." He had destroyed his looks by his intemperance. Esther Ogle was a young woman who prided herself upon saying odd things, and whatever she thought proper, and when she saw him walking about behind her chair, she saluted him with exhortations to get away, calling him by such names as "Fright" and "Terrible creature."

"By this silly woman, this silly man was thus unfortunately piqued," said Smyth. In an evil moment he resolved that she should feel his power, and after some little contrivance, she admitted that though a monster he was clever, and though ugly he was agreeable, and then she realized forcibly that he was one of the most celebrated men in the kingdom. Her age was about twenty, while his was forty-three. When she told her father that she wanted to marry Sheridan, the Dean refused his consent unless the bridegroom could settle £15,000 on his bride, which seemed to be an effective bar. Nevertheless, as Richardson told Smyth, to the perfect astonishment of his friends, and the confusion and amazement of the Dean, the money was produced and lodged at a banker's. "The two youngsters, for Sheridan now appeared in this capacity, laughed at the old ones, feeling that they had outwitted them. They forgot that it was themselves they had outwitted."

After his second marriage, and in spite of his financial difficulties, Sheridan determined to be counted among the landed gentry. He purchased an estate at Polesden in Surrey, which belonged to Admiral Sir William Geary. It was commonly said that he never paid for it in full, but John Graham noted "This is not true: he bought it with money that he had previously settled upon her, which he raised by the sale or mortgage of what were called 3000 Renters' Shares of Drury Lane Theatre —having settled £12,000 which it was agreed should accumulate to £40,000 in the 3 p Cents, but part of the money was drawn from the trust for this purpose."[1]

In order to make this purchase, the trustees of his wife's marriage settlement, Whitbread and Grey, advanced £8,000; but about 1802, when William Adam was investigating his affairs, Sheridan noted that he himself had contributed in all a sum of £6,000. The purchase was made in 1798, and the affairs of the theatre suffered in consequence, for on October 14th, when Thomas Holcroft called on James Aickin, the stage-manager, he found him "determined to resign: forebodings of bankruptcy, such things as wood and canvas not to be had, yet three thousand guineas given for an estate."

5

Two of the successes of the new Drury Lane were *The Castle Spectre*, produced on December 14th, 1797, and *Blue Beard*, produced on January 16th, 1798. The former was written by Matthew G. Lewis, M.P., and it had a prodigious run, owing partly to the "sublime effect" of the sinking of the Ghost in a flame of fire, and in "beautiful Gothic scenery." It was acted forty-six times, and Lewis, during an argument with Sheridan, offered to bet him all the money his play had brought into the Treasury. "No," replied Sheridan, "I can't afford to do that, but I'll bet you all it is worth." He did not pay the author his dues, however, and the case was carried into Court, where Sheridan savagely attacked Lewis. Their enmity persisted until the year of Sheridan's death, when Lewis wrote a bitter epigram:

> "For worst abuse of finer parts
>   Was Misophil begotten,
> There might indeed be blacker hearts,
>   But none could be more rotten."[2]

Blue Beard was adapted by George Colman, from the "programme" of a French piece. Kelly wrote the music, and orders were given that the machinists, painters, and decorators, should

---

[1]Note in Graham's copy of Sheridan's *Speeches*, V, xlvi.   [2]Byron, IV, 417.

bring it forward with all possible magnificence and splendour. It had a success as great as *The Castle Spectre*, which was partly due to the effects.

Peake, for forty years treasurer to Drury Lane Theatre, was appointed to that office by Sheridan. Such was the drought in the exchequer at times, that it was considered vexatious in an actor to apply on two consecutive weeks for his salary. In the old, or "Garrick's Theatre," as it was called, there was no retreat from the apartment of the perplexed treasurer, and Peake was often kept a prisoner in his own insolvent territory for hours together, not daring to unbar the door on the rush of his assailants. But in the new theatre of 1794, matters were ordered more wisely; the window of the treasury was constructed to open on the colonnade in Little Russell Street, so that on blank Saturdays, [when there was no money,] the *sine-cure* cashier might make himself scarce, and leave the besiegers to do their worst, on the other side of the double-locked entrance.

When not under parliamentary protection, Sheridan constituted the houses of his treasurer and his solicitor Burgess his sanctuary, where for weeks he remained concealed. Peake, in his official capacity, had almost daily applications for money from Sheridan, whose letters were always for money—very short; and though scarcely legible, yet intelligible enough for that purpose; and (except when very angry) signed with his initials only:

"DEAR PEAKE—Thirty pounds by return of post, and I am with you in seven hours.

R.B.S."

"DEAR PEAKE—Beg, borrow, or steal; let me have thirty pounds, and send them by return of post. Fear nothing, be civil to all claimants. Shut up the office, and write to me directly.

R.B.S."

"DEAR PEAKE—Without fail, and immediately, give the

bearer five guineas to buy hay and corn for my coach-
horses; they have not had a morsel of either since laſt night.
I shall be with you presently.

R.B.S."

"Dear Peake, Give Johnson a little money to go on with
—keep as punⱦual with Kemble as you can—borrow, and
fear not. Put £60 in your pocket, and come to me direⱦly.

R.B.S."[1]

[1]Raymond, *Life of Elliston*, 276–278; 355.

CHAPTER THE SIXTEENTH

My Own Pizarro

Now then for my magnificence! my battle! my
noise! and my procession!

The Critic.

I

SHERIDAN was very proud of *Pizarro*. When he printed it, he explained that as two translations of Kotzebue's *Spaniards in Peru* had already been published, the public were in possession of all the material necessary to form a judgment on the merits and defects of the play performed at Drury Lane Theatre. And he added "To Her, whose approbation of this drama and whose peculiar delight in the applause it has received from the Public, have been to me the highest gratification its success has produced—I dedicate this play." If these were not the declarations of conscious merit, there is no such thing as modesty extant.

The story of this masterpiece is another example, or series of examples, of Sheridan's procrastination. He based his play on a literal translation, telling John Graham that he laboured for months on his "improvements," and even for purposes of meditation sought the seclusion of Hounslow Heath where he "studied for it, writing it principally at the Black Dog at Bedfont."

In the autumn of 1798, a German, apparently Constantine Geiwsweiler, brought him a translation of *Der Spanier in Peru, oder Rolla's Tod*, whose capabilities, despite its execrable English, he perceived at a glance. He purchased it for one hundred pounds, giving notice at once in the playbills that "a grand new drama from the German of Kotzebue is in preparation."

Hold!—Pizarro—hear me!—if not always JUSTLY, at least act always GREATLY.   Pizarro.

Mrs Siddons

MRS. SIDDONS AS ELVIRA, 1799

To face page 176

The title was kept a secret, but about Christmas an ingenious author who frequented the greenroom discovered what it was, and told Sheridan that he was translating *Der Spanier in Peru*, and intended to publish it without delay unless he was paid one hundred pounds. Sheridan submitted to this polite blackmail, stipulating that he should receive a copy of the translation, and after some delay received three acts of it.

Then, on February 25th, as the printed copy shows, Anna Plumtree published *The Virgin of the Sun* in her series of translations from Kotzebue, stating in her preface that it would be followed "as the natural course directs, by *The Spaniards in Peru, or the Death of Rolla*, which will be published some time in the month of March." Greatly alarmed, Sheridan sent a friend to implore her to suspend publication till after the performance; she consented, and wrote Sheridan telling him that she had arranged to publish her translation about six weeks ahead, but if that time was insufficient she would obtain the publisher's consent to delay it. A month passing without any reply from Sheridan, she concluded that he was indifferent, and gave the translation to the printer. Two days before the date announced for its publication, Mrs. Plumtree was surprised by a visit from Sheridan. Full of apologies, he explained that it was his custom to put all the letters he received in a bag for reading at leisure, and he happened for six weeks to have had no leisure. She consented to the postponement, and Sheridan went to the publisher to secure the delay, paying him fifty pounds, and receiving from him, unknown to Mrs. Plumtree, a copy of her printed version.[1]

Even then, it was two months before the play was staged, a few days before the time for closing the theatre for the summer vacation. Michael Kelly, whose name had been announced as the composer of the music, had the utmost difficulty in learning what was expected of him. When the date of the first performance was advertised, every box in the theatre was booked, yet Sheridan had not even started on the last two acts, nor had he given the words of a single song to Kelly; each day the composer

[1]Cf. Watkins, 396-403.

N

remonstrated, and each day the author promised the songs
"to-morrow." At last, one Sunday night at ten o'clock, when
Kelly was giving a party to some distinguished friends, Sheridan went to his house, and insisted upon carrying him to
Drury Lane. The stage and the house were fully lighted as for a
public performance, and Sheridan seated himself in the middle
of the pit with a large bowl of negus before him, and contemplated the scene of the Temple of the Sun. When Kelly remonstrated about being brought out to inspect scenery, which
was the affair of the painters, carpenters, and machinists,
Sheridan replied that it concerned the composer also, for he
wanted him to see the Temple in which the choruses and processions were to "come over the platform."

Once again he promised Kelly to explain "to-morrow," what
was to be done, and to Kelly's surprise, the next evening he
began:" In the Temple of the Sun, I want the Virgins of the
Sun, and their High Priest to chant a solemn invocation to
their deity." He then made a kind of rumbling noise with his
voice, like a gruff bow, wow, wow, for he had no idea of singing
an air, but so clear was his idea of effect that Kelly understood
his intentions perfectly. He then promised to send all the words
in a couple of days, and actually sent the song for Mrs. Jordan
as Cora, which he wrote himself, and a trio "Fly away, Time,"
which was written by Joseph Richardson. Kelly, knowing that
he could expect no more, was forced in desperation, to obtain
the assistance, as he said, of "a literary gentleman whose
poverty, if not his will, consented" and was supplied with such
poetic gems as the hymn of the High Priest of the Sun:

> "Oh Pow'r supreme! in mercy smile
> With favour on thy servants' toil!
> Our hearts from guileful passions free
> Which here we render unto thee?"

Nor was the music the end of the troubles. The last rehearsal
was held on the day of performance, and its fourth act had
ended before three of the performers, Mrs. Siddons, Charles

Kemble, and Barrymore, had received certain additional
speeches for the fifth act, which were then being written out in
the prompter's room by the author, and carried down to them
piece-meal, while the audience was entering the house for the
performance. Yet, Sheridan was, as Kelly says, "careful in his
carelessness," for although they were in an agony of fright, and
had already learned one version, they were all three very quick
of study. The play was so long that on the first night it did not
end till five minutes before midnight, and though in many
scenes the applause was just and genuine, at the end it en-
countered much violent opposition. Sheridan had introduced
for Suett the part of Alonzo's servant, Diego, whom he had
annexed from *The Virgin of the Sun*. His acting was outrage-
ously bad, but when the author remonstrated, he replied "Sir,
this is what comes of putting me into a German play. I warned
you that I did not understand German." So on the second night,
Diego was summarily eliminated.

The play-bill was an imposing document, distributing the
responsibilities with a most uncommon gratitude and liberality:

"The Scenery, Dresses, & Decorations entirely New.
The Music, Airs, Chorusses & Marches, incidental to the Piece,
compos'd by Mr Kelly.
The Symphony preceeding the Play, & those between the Acts,
compos'd for the Occasion by Mr. Dusseck.
The Scenery design'd & executed by Messrs. Marinari, Greenwood,
Demara, Banks, Blackmore, &c.
The Machinery, & Decorations under the direction of Mr. Johnston
And executed by him, Mr Underwood, & Mr Gay.
The Finale Dresses design'd & Executed by Miss Reis."

2

The success of *Pizarro* was largely political. The English
nation, in dread of Revolutionary France, and threatened with
invasion, accepted it as a loyal allegory; every allusion that bore,
however remotely, upon public feeling was seized with the
greatest avidity, and the more direct and palpable appeals were

applauded with patriotic frenzy. Its most celebrated passage,
Rolla's address to the Peruvians, was repeated as an *encore*
night after night, for in applauding it, the auditors felt that they
were defying the might and power of France:

"My brave associates—partners of my toil, my feelings
and my fame!—can Rolla's words add vigour to the virtuous
energies which inspire your hearts?—No—You have judged
as I have, the foulness of the crafty plea by which these bold
invaders would delude you—Your generous spirit has compared, as mine has, the motives which in a war like this can
animate *their* minds, and Ours.—They, by a strange
frenzy driven, fight for power, for plunder, and extended
rule,—We, for our country, our altars, and our homes.
They follow an Adventurer whom they fear—and obey a
power which they hate: We serve a Monarch whom we love
—a God whom we adore. Whene'er they move in anger,
desolation tracks their progress!—Where'er they pause in
amity, affliction mourns their friendship! They boast, they
come but to improve our state, enlarge our thoughts, and
free us from the yoke of error!—Yes—They will give enlightened freedom to *our* minds, who are themselves the
slaves of passion, avarice, and pride.—They offer us their
protection—Yes, such protection as vultures give to lambs
—covering and devouring them!—They call on us to barter
all of good we have inherited and proved, for the desperate
chance of something better which they promise.—Be our
plain answer this: The throne We honour is the People's
Choice—the laws we reverence are our brave Fathers'
legacy—the faith we follow teaches us to live in bonds of
charity with all mankind, and die with hope of bliss beyond
the grave. Tell your invaders this, and tell them too, we seek
no change; and, least of all, such change as they would bring
us."   [*Trumpets sound*]

This celebrated piece of rhetoric is a thing of shreds and
patches. Kotzebue had written only:

Rolla. They fight for base gold—we for our native country.

Alonzo. They follow to the field an adventurer—we are led on by a monarch we love.

Ataliba. And a God whom we adore.

Sheridan had bedecked this skeleton with all the glittering trophies of his denunciation of Warren Haſtings. Its moſt admired simile was annexed from one of his orations at Weſtminſter Hall, where he had fulminated againſt the "protection" that the government of Haſtings had offered the allies of Great Britain:

"They send all their troops to drain the produćts of induſtry, to sieze all the treasures, wealth and prosperity of the country. Like a vulture with her harpy talons grappled into the vitals of the land, they flap away the lesser kites, and they call it proteċtion. It is the proteċtion of the vulture to the lamb."

In 1803, when Bonaparte again threatened England with invasion, and Sheridan became Colonel of the Weſtminſter Volunteers, he was so proud of this speech that he incorporated it into his "Address to the Surrey Volunteers." When Pitt was asked his opinion of *Pizarro*, he replied: "If you mean what Sheridan has written, there is nothing new in it, for I heard it all long ago at Haſtings' trial." It seems to be forgotten that this is not merely a criticism of *Pizarro*: it is Pitt's oblique comment upon the orations againſt Warren Haſtings. For it is a matter of simple truth that the rhetoric in Weſtminſter Hall, and the rhetoric in Drury Lane, were all of a piece.

Sheridan's pride in its literary ſtyle was the pride of paternity. About the third night, Daniel Stuart, one of the proprietors of *The Courier*, went to see him on political business, but he was sitting with Richardson in a box, repeating every syllable after each performer, counting the measure poetically on his fingers, and sounding his voice like a music maſter. With almoſt everything that Mrs. Jordan said, he was in the utmoſt ill-

humour, almost stamping with anger. With some passages that
Mrs. Siddons delivered as Elvira he was charmed, with others
shocked, frequently telling Stuart that this is the way a sentence should have been spoken, and repeating it in his own way.
With everything Kemble uttered he was invariably delighted,
clapping his hands with pleasure like a child.[1]

Sheridan was accused of forgetting that he was the author of
The Critic: and remembering only the rhapsodies of Mr. Puff:
"Now then for my magnificence! my battle! my noise! and my
procession!" The soul of Mr. Puff was transmogrified into the
soul of his creator: *Pizarro* had all the faults of *The Spanish
Armada*, with others of its own. Mrs. Jordan as Cora had to
enter, wild and distracted, in a storm, and sing a lullaby to her
child, during which the thunder, lightning and rain ceased.

The terrific length of the play was necessarily abridged after
the first few nights, as Boaden says, and it was more likely to
have been cut by Kemble than by its author.[2]

Sheridan, however, when he committed it to the Press, followed the indignant example of Mr. Puff, "I'll print it, egad,
I'll print it every word!" Indeed so zealous was he that his pure
gold should be unalloyed, that with singular ingratitude, he
omitted the added choruses from his edition of *Pizarro*, and
the words would have been lost to posterity but for their publication by Michael Kelly in "*The Music of Pizarro*, A Play: as
now performing at the Theatre Royal, Drury Lane, with un-
bounded applause." The "poet" was an Irishman, Walley
Chamberlaine Oulton, whose authorship would have been
consigned to oblivion except for a casual note in *The Thespian
Dictionary* of 1805 on his share in *Pizarro*.

---

[1]Boaden, *Jordan*, II, 3.
Moore advanced a theory that Sheridan contributed only a few short speeches, and
rewrote only a few short scenes—which is absurd. He argued that Sheridan worked upon
an imitation of Kotzebue by some unknown paraphrase, whose florid style he was so
indolent as to adopt without alteration: indeed, his own additions were "written down
to the model he had before him, as if inspired by an emulation of its faults." The manuscript from which Moore deducted this theory was obviously a fair copy of the incomplete revision by Sheridan himself.

[2]The only copy of the play abridged as it was acted at Drury Lane is one in the
Garrick Club, which formerly belonged to Kemble.

3

But the Prologue to the anonymous "Critique on the Tragedy of Pizarro" deserves to be given in full, without mitigation or remorse:

PROLOGUE

To be spoken by any body, in the Character of a puppet-show man.

"Walk in, walk in, pray, gentlemen and ladies;
Though puffing, you may think, a show-man's trade is,
Yet, on my honour, if you will but stay,
You'll see what does not happen every day.
Grown gentlemen and ladies, pray walk in;
Our *puppet*-show's 'just going to begin';
My little *mistresses*, and *masters* too,
Walk in, the entertainment is for you.
Here shall you see how neatly we have spread
Our *English gilt* on *German gingerbread*;
And when you hear our *trumpets* sound for battle,
Shall soon be *wean'd* from *coral-bells* and *rattle.*
Now, gentlefolks, behind the curtain peep;
The lady you see there, is fast asleep;
Sweetly she sleeps, though war and death surround her,
Close to her nose a four-and-twenty pounder.
Next, you the Temple of the Sun behold:
Who says, that 'all which glitters is not gold?'
See through the roof, along a magic wire,
Straight down from Heav'n descends a ball of fire.
Fear not—The Priests to fire are quite enur'd,
And, for the Virgins, see, they're all *insur'd.*
Then you shall have what children take delight in,
Upon the stage, some pretty small-sword fighting;
Anvil on hammer each by turns shall knock,
Fierce as the heroes of St. Dunstan's clock;
Or, if we may compare small *toys* with great,
The *wooden* butcher thumps the ox's pate.

Fine speeches you shall have, both loud and long,
Thunder and lightning, and, between, a song;
Which proves that thunder, and that lightning too,
Have a fine taste for music—just like you;
And you shall have, the more to raise your wonder,
(Pray, let the *novelty* excuse the *blunder*),
Sometimes the *lightning* first, sometimes the *thunder*.

"In short, whilst we your *eye-sight* are commanding,
We shall not much *fatigue* your *understanding*;
And though, like modest men, we can't be sure
None of our *tricks* you may have seen before,
In this at least our pantomime is *new*,
We give you *five* long acts instead of *two*;
Five *ling'ring* acts stuff'd full of stage *devices*,
Five acts of pantomime—at *playhouse prices*!!!"

4

Charles Fox told Rogers that Congreve's *Mourning Bride* was
execrable, but *Pizarro* was the worst thing possible.

CHAPTER THE SEVENTEENTH
Treasurer of the Navy

I

ON May 15th, 1800, the King and Queen, with the four Princesses, went to Drury Lane to see Mrs. Jordan in *She Would and she would not*. The King had just entered the box and was bowing to the usual applause from the audience, when a man in the pit suddenly levelled a horse-pistol and fired it at the royal box. The house was for a few moments struck with panic. The man was seized by his neighbours in the pit and lifted by persons in the orchestra over the spikes and carried into the music-room of the theatre.

The King behaved with great coolness; on hearing the report of the pistol, he retired a pace or two, and seeing the Queen about to enter the box, waved his hand to her to keep back. But to remove all apprehension among the people, he then advanced to the front of the box, put his opera-glass to his eye, and looked round the house, without the smallest degree of alarm or discomposure. When the Queen asked Sheridan what the noise and uproar was about, he replied that some boys had been firing off squibs. "The King was delighted with Sheridan's behaviour to the Princesses. He prevented their going into their box by saying that a pick-pocket was taken in the pit, which made a riot and required his presence, and he begged their Royal Highnesses to wait in the room."

The orchestra played "God Save the King," and the whole entertainments were proceeded with, though all the while the Queen and Princesses were absorbed in tears. At the end of the play "God Save the King" was again demanded by the whole house, and whilst the performers were singing it, Michael Kelly, who tells the story, received a paper from Sheridan containing a new stanza:

"From every latent foe,
From the assassin's blow,
  God save the King.
O'er him thine arm extend,
For Britain's sake, defend
Our father, prince, and friend,
  God save the King."[1]

The stanza was repeated three times with the most rapturous approbation, and Sheridan's conduct gained him the especial goodwill of the King.

Although he was very fond of play-going, it was very rarely indeed that the King at this period attended Drury Lane, and Mrs. Jordan particularly thought it hard that they should so seldom have the honour of acting before the sovereign, on account of Sheridan's opposition to his government.

It appears to have been a little later than this that the King and Queen were again present at Drury Lane theatre, the play, by royal command, being *The School for Scandal*. When Sheridan was in attendance to light their Majesties to their carriage, the King said to him, "I am much pleased with your comedy of *The School for Scandal*; but I am still more so, with your play of *The Rivals;*—that is my favourite, and I will never give it up."

The Queen, at the same time, said, "When, Mr. Sheridan, shall we have another play from your masterly pen?" He replied that he was writing a comedy, which he expected very shortly to finish. This was no doubt either *Affectation* or *The Foresters*, but the next day, walking in Piccadilly, Michael Kelly made his famous prophecy that he would never write another play. The anecdote is always supposed to have appeared first in Kelly's *Reminiscences*, but it was current in 1806, when it was narrated in indifferent verse by William Meyler of Bath in his *Poetical Amusements*:

"When Players and Managers of Drury
Some full of dread, some of fury,

[1]Kelly, II, 175.

Consulted lately to enhance
Their Treasury's close-drained finance,
Ere bounced had Carlo in the water,
Or Cherry shown his *Soldier's Daughter*,
Mongst various schemes to prop the Stage,
Brinsley declared he'd now engage
His long expected play to finish,
And all their cares and fears diminish,
Make creditors and audiences gay,
Nay, actors touch their weekly pay,
'Fair promises!' Mich Kelly cries,
'On which no mortal e'er relies,
Again to write you will not dare
Of one man, Sir you've too much fear,'
'Fear? Whom? I dread no man's control?'
'Yes, yes, you dread him to the soul'
'Name him at once, detractive Vandal!'
'The author of *The School for Scandal*.' "

2

In 1801 *The Morning Post* said "The Principal Proprietor of
the Theatre of Drury Lane has at length made an arrangement
by which Justice shall keep pace with generosity. He retains to
himself an income of £2,000 a year. To his son he allots £500.
The rest of his revenue is appropriated to discharge within four
years the whole of his debts."

A few months later, in February 1802, Drury Lane was in a
very bad way, the actors' salaries greatly in arrear. Hammersley & Co., the bankers, and John Grubb, one of the proprietors, applied to the Lord Chancellor praying that their demands
on the theatre with those of the old and new renters, might be
taken out of the receipts before the performers were paid.
Sheridan resisted this, and the actors one and all threatened to
strike if such an order were granted.

The suit came before the Chancellor, Lord Eldon; Sheridan
pleaded his own cause before the whole Chancery bar, which
was retained on the other side. In a most elaborate and eloquent

speech, he stated the embarrassments of the theatre—the necessity of paying the performers, as no work could go on without the workmen: if they withdrew their services, the doors
must be closed, the property fall to pieces and general ruin
ensue. "From his eloquent tongue, persuasion flowed, and won
the high debate." The performers gained the day, and an order
was granted that they should be the first persons paid.

A passage of the speech survived:

"It is a great disadvantage, relatively speaking, to any
man, and especially to a very careless, and a very sanguine
man, to have possessed an uncertain and fluctuating income.
This disadvantage is greatly increased if the person so cir-
cumstanced has conceived himself to be in some degree entitled to presume that, by the exertion of his own talents, he
may at pleasure increase that income—thereby becoming induced to make promises to himself which he may afterwards
fail to fulfil.

"Occasional excess and frequent unpunctuality will be the
natural consequences of such a situation. But, my Lord, to
exceed an ascertained and limited income, I hold to be a very
different matter. In that situation I have placed myself, (not
since the present unexpected contention arose, for since then
I would have adopted no arrangements,) but months since,
by my Deed of Trust to Mr. Adam, and in that situation I
shall remain until every debt on earth, in which the Theatre
or I am concerned, shall be fully and fairly discharged. Till
then I will live on what remains to me—preserving that
spirit of undaunted independence, which, both as a public
and a private man, I trust, I have hitherto maintained."[1]

Sheridan was not lacking in frankness when he gave during
this case an instance of his own carelessness. The Duke of Bedford, through his attorney, had threatened a distress upon the
theatre for arrears of ground-rent, and this would have entailed
the sale of the chandeliers, scenery, wardrobe, and so on. In
alarm, Sheridan went to see the Duke, who agreed to accept a

[1]Moore, 714-5.

payment of £10 per night from the pit-door money until the claim should be satisfied, but told Sheridan to make the proposal in writing. This he did, and more than a year elapsed, and Sheridan was greatly enraged that no reply had been sent to his letter. Going with Kelly to the attorney's house in Norfolk Street, he complained of the transaction, and was assured that the answer had been sent at the proper time. On hearing this, Sheridan went home, examined the table on which the letters were thrown, and amongst them he found the Duke's reply, unopened, dated more than twelve months before. Kelly was not surprised, for he had seen numbers of letters brought to Sheridan, who threw the greater part of them into the fire without opening them.[1]

The Lord Chancellor, after passing a high eulogium on Sheridan, quoted in addressing him ("as I was told," said Kelly, "for I was not near enough to hear it"), Doctor Johnson's last lines in the life of Savage, "negligence and irregularity, long continued, make knowledge useless, wit ridiculous, and genius contemptible." "I had thought at the time," added Kelly, "that the quotation might have been spared, and that it was perhaps harsh to speak the truth at all times."[2]

Sheridan "entrusted the reins of theatrical government," as Frederick Reynolds puts it, to John Graham, "who was as active in his new character of theatrical director, as in his long established one of magistrate." To him, and to his stage-manager, Bannister, Frederick Reynolds was chiefly indebted for the success of *The Caravan*, which was acted at Drury Lane in December 1803.

"The introduction," said Reynolds, "of real water on the stage, and of a dog to jump into it from a high rock for the purpose of saving a child, were both incidents at that time so entirely unknown in theatrical exhibitions, that their very novelty rendered every body during the production of the piece most sanguine as to its success; provided, (for there is always one, or more provisos, on these occasions,) that the

---

[1]Watkins, II, 426–7; Kelly, II, 244–5. [2]Kelly, II, 190.

two principal performers, the animal and the element, could be brought into action. The water was hired from old father Thames, and the dog from the proprietor of an à-la-mode beef shop. On the first representation of *The Caravan*, after his performance of this extraordinary feat, and after his triumphant *exit* with the supposed drowning child, the effect far exceeded our most sanguine expectations."

Sheridan was present in the house, and made his way into the greenroom to wish the author joy, as was thought. "Where is he? Where is my guardian angel?" he demanded. "The author has just retired," answered the prompter. "Pooh" replied Sheridan, "I mean the dog."[1]

When Richard Wroughton became acting-manager of Drury Lane, in 1804, among the new members of the company were Charles Mathews, and his second wife, who wrote long afterwards in the *Life of Charles Mathews* that Sheridan "was seldom agreeable in the presence of actors, before whom his cheerfulness and mirth never appeared. He entered into the theatre stealthily and unwillingly, and his appearance among the performers never failed to act like a dark cloud casting a shade for the time over the gaiety of the Greenroom." She adds that Sheridan read Sir Peter to Mathews, to give him an idea of the manner in which it should be acted, but it was so totally unlike any practical conception that it was impossible to adopt any of his suggestions. On the night of this performance, Sheridan went there tipsy. After it was all over he went into the greenroom, and asked what play it was. Wroughton gravely told him. "And who was it," he said, "that acted the old fellow, Sir Peter what d'ye call him?" "Mathews, sir." "Never let him play it again : he looks like an old pastry cook." "I'm sorry, Mr. Sheridan," replied Wroughton, "to say that we seldom see you here, and you never come but to find fault."[2]

3

In 1802, added to the many difficulties of management,

---

[1]Reynolds, II, 352.   [2]Moore, *Journal*, II, 160.

Sheridan was confronted by the establishment of a private theatre, of which the chief promoters were Colonel Harry Greville, and that "old meteor of London fashion," Albina Countess of Buckinghamshire, who until 1793, was known as the Hon. Mrs. Hobart. They formed in London a society of private, or as they termed themselves, "dilettanti" actors, and assumed the name of the Pic-Nic Society, from the manner in which they were to contribute their share to the general entertainment: besides the performance of farces and burlettas, there were to be feasts and ridottos, and a variety of other fashionable amusements, each member drawing from a silk bag a ticket which was to decide the portion of entertainment which he was expected to provide. The performances took place in rooms in Tottenham Street. This harmless piece of fashionable amusement produced a great sensation. The populace had been so long accustomed to hear of aristocratic depravity, that they could understand nothing private in the high life without attaching to it ideas of licentiousness, and there was a notion that the Pic-Nic Society implied some way or other an attack upon public morals. Complaints were made against it which led almost to a pamphlet war. The professional theatricals were angry and jealous, because they thought that the aristocratic love of theatrical amusements which had supported them in their exertions, would evaporate in private parties.

"Nearly the whole periodical press attacked the Pic-Nics without mercy, and the daily papers teemed with abuse and scandal. They were ridiculed and caricatured on every side. Gillray produced no less than three caricatures on the Pic-Nics. The first of these, published on the 2nd of April, 1802, soon after the society had been established, is entitled 'Blowing up the Pic-Nics: or Harlequin Quixotte attacking the Puppets—vide, Tottenham Street Pantomime.' The Pic-Nic party are represented as puppets in the midst of their festivities, which are disturbed by the attack of the infuriated actors, among whom we recognize Kemble, Siddons, Billington, and the Ghost of Garrick, led by Sheridan, who, dressed

as Harlequin, rushes to the assault, armed with the pen of the
Post, *Chronicle*, *Herald*, *Evening Courier*, &c., whose at-
tacks he is supposed to have directed against them. By the
end of 1803 the society sank under the load of obloquy and
ridicule to which it was exposed, and the regular theatricals
were relieved from any jealousy that such attempts might
excite."[1]

4

By 1802, Sheridan was no longer on the same terms of trust
and intimacy with his friends like Charles Fox and the Duchess
of Devonshire. In reviewing her diary that she had kept thirteen years before, during the Regency intrigue, the Duchess
wrote that then

"Sheridan gave not only convincing evidence of his talents, but at the same time evinc'd the danger of his character.
I do not mean to accuse him of duplicity: in fact he has
stood even the test of poverty, and I feel convinc'd of the
honour of his political sentiments—he cannot resist playing
a sly game: he cannot resist the pleasure of acting alone, and
added to his natural want of judgment and his dislike of con-
sultation, frequently has made him commit his friends and
himself."[2]

Sheridan's conduct, like Charles Surface's, gave grounds for
great uneasiness to many worthy men. He committed the greatest crime in the calendar of party politics—he would be independent, so in August 1802, Fox was writing to Grey that
"Sheridan is mad with vanity and folly—but what is he driving
at? I do not know, nor, I believe, does he." In December of
that year, when he had made one of the finest speeches of his
career, Fox wrote to his nephew, Lord Holland, "Sheridan
made a foolish speech, if a speech so full of wit can with propriety be so-called, upon the Army Estimates, of which all who
wish him ill are as fond, as I who wish him well, are vexed at it.
He will, however, I have no doubt, still be right in the end."

[1]Wright, *Caricature History of the Georges*, 565–6.   [2]Sichel, II, 400.

Of the same debate Fox wrote to Grey, "Sheridan's speech (O Lord!!!) gave more concern to his friends and more satisfaction to his enemies, than any he ever made."

Fox, Grey, Holland, and others, had only just returned from France, where they had been paying their respects to the First Consul, who had received them with marked attention, and they had been caricatured by Gillray in a very popular print of the "Introduction of Citizen Volpone and his suite at Paris."

Fox persisted in believing in the pacific intentions of Bonaparte, but in March 1803, an official document was issued under the signature of the First Consul, which declared that "England alone cannot now encounter France." The King's message to the Houses of Parliament on March 9th stated that military preparations were being made in the ports of Holland and France, and he had judged it expedient to take precautions for the security of the country. On the debate, Fox suggested that the apprehensions were premature, but Sheridan, in a fiery speech, supported the proclamations for summoning the militia and volunteers, and trusted that if, unhappily, war proved unvoidable, "by the exertions of a loyal, united and patriotic people, we shall look with perfect confidence to the issue, and we are justified in a well-founded hope that we shall be able to convince not only the First Consul of France, but all Europe, of our capability, even single-handed, to meet all and triumph over the dangers, however great and imminent, which threaten us with the renewal of hostilities."

This debate produced one of the most amusing of Gillray's Sheridan caricatures, published under the title of "Physical Aid, or Britannia recovered from a Trance: also the patriotic courage of Sherry Andrew, and a peep through the fog." Fox, with his hat pulled over his eyes, cannot see the French boats which are to carry the French Army to England, but the chief figure is Harlequin Sheridan, who flourishes a cudgel inscribed "Dramatic Loyalty," and blusters out his menace:

"Let 'em all come, damme!—where are the French bugaboos?—Single-handed, I'd beat forty of 'em!! damme, I'll

o

pay 'em off like renter's shares, sconce off their half-crowns, mulct them out of their benefits, & come the Drury Lane slang over them!"[1]

In the midst of it all, on June 9th, 1803, Joseph Richardson died. Sheridan fell into an agony of tears at his loss, and arranged to go to Egham for the funeral. He arrived at the grave, just in time to see the clergyman turning away. The name of Sheridan softened the rector, and the close of the service was repeated in his presence, so that he might say with truth, that he had heard the words of peace breathed over the remains of poor Richardson. After the interment, the mourners dined together at the inn, and "no stinted libation was poured to the memory of the departed."

There are several other versions of this story, but after the dinner at the Black Dog at Bedfont, Sheridan returned to London with John Taylor, who says that "on parting he manifested great emotion, and in the agony of his feelings struck his head against the door of the nearest house exclaiming that he had lost his dearest friend, and there was now nobody who could enter into his domestic cares, and be a confidential agent, when occasion might require, between himself and Mrs. Sheridan."[2]

This is explained by a note of Lady Bessborough to Lord Holland:

"Poor Richardson is dead. Sheridan (if Richardson's death does not sober him) will do the same, for he is never sober for a moment, and his affairs worse than ever. *Pour comble*, he had quarrelled with Mrs. S. A sort of separation took place, but I believe it is partly made up again—at least I believe they live in the same house again, but not very good friends. I am very sorry for it, for she was the only chance there was of stopping his drinking."[3]

His drunken habits were notorious, and so also were his infidelities. One of his escapades—with which the subject

[1]Cf. Wright, *Caricature History of the Georges* (1867) 591–2. The speech of March 9th is not in the collected edition of the Speeches.

[2]Taylor, *Records of My Life*, II, 170.   [3]Sichel, II, 270.

may be left—occurred about this time. Charles Ward, the secretary of Drury Lane, and husband of Jane Linley, told Moore a story which was confirmed by Sheridan's attorney, Burgess. Sheridan was in the habit of carrying a bag of papers with him to the Coffee House, where he used to look over them. One day by mistake he took a bag of love-letters, *gages d'amour*, locks of hair, and so forth, which vanity had induced him to keep. Getting drunk, he left them behind, and they fell into the hands of a fellow who demanded one hundred guineas from Sheridan, or from the woman concerned, for their restoration. Sheridan consulted Ward and Burgess, and they secured the assistance of a Bow Street runner, made a forcible entry with pistols into the man's house, and after gaining the treasure defied him to bring any action.[1]

On June 30th, 1802, however, he wrote to his wife "By my life and soul, if you talk of leaving me now, you will utterly destroy me. I am wholly unwell, and neither sleep nor eat." It was unfortunate for him that he had married a wife who, unlike Elizabeth Linley, was not interested in politics, and regarded the theatre only as a source of income. She had accused him of misrepresenting his affairs before marriage, but he replied that Sir Arthur Pigott reported that he could rely upon a permanent income of £10,000. Then, however, the theatre had been his own, but, after the money for the rebuilding had been found, "the detected villainy of two lawyers and one banker stole £30,000 from the fund" and the architect had grossly exceeded the expenditure beyond the estimate. "You have never known me," he protested, "though I am aware you are confident that you do." They came to some sort of an agreement, and at another debate on the Additional Forces Bill in June 1804, as Elliott wrote "Sheridan made one of his brilliant openings, and came prepared for the purpose, for Mrs. Sheridan came into the gallery in a man's frock coat and trousers, under the care of Lord Lauderdale."

But at this time, Fox was still cold to him, and told Grey that he could place no dependence upon him, adding that he feared

[1]Moore, *Journal*, II, 356; IV, 296.

"many will follow Sheridan *whom* we should be sorry to lose," and, to make sure that there was no possibility of ambiguity, to "whom" he made a foot-note "*quos* not *quem*." Sheridan had to pay the price of independence. As to his political conduct, there is a great need to remember Byron's warning about the "angry lies of the humbug Whigs."

5

On the death of Pitt in 1806, a new administration was formed under the direction of Lord Grenville, who was First Lord of the Treasury, with Charles Fox as Foreign Secretary. Their ministry was known as "All the Talents," with Lord Henry Petty as Chancellor of the Exchequer, Lord Sidmouth as Privy Seal, Lord Erskine as Lord Chancellor, Lord Ellenborough as Lord Chief Justice, Windham at the War Office, Charles Grey, who was now Lord Grey of Howick, at the Admiralty, and Earl Spencer at the Home Office. Fox himself, with many claimants for office, was afraid equally of Sheridan's "independence," and his intemperance. He advised him to accept a patent place of £2,000 per annum, which would have made him independent for life, but which Sheridan had "magnanamity enough, notwithstanding his obvious necessities, to refuse."[1]

Sheridan accepted the office of Treasurer of the Navy, without even a seat in the Cabinet—though it had the compensation of being nearly a sinecure, with a salary of four thousand a year, and apartments in Somerset House. He told Fox that he took the office "without the slightest feeling of obligation to anyone living, I might say more." It was the appointment that had been designed for him seventeen years before, and he contended that either a seat should be found for him, or his expenses of re-election at Stafford paid, and that some provision should be made for his son Tom. The Earl of Moira, who was appointed Master of the Ordnance, found Tom the required position as Muster-Master-General, and took him to Ireland.

[1] Rae, II, 254, from *The Biographical Index to the House of Commons*, 1808. Cf. Watkins, II, 458.

Sheridan was sworn of the Privy Council on February 7th, and his appointment inspired even the directors of the Bank of England with an unprecedented levity—at least, the Earl of Essex wrote Viscount Lowther: "I heard of Sheridan's appearing before the bank directors to open his Navy Office Account. The joke is that they all ran out of the room, carrying away their books and papers."[1]

His colleagues all gave inauguration entertainments, but his own at Somerset House was, as *Le Beau Monde* said, "in so magnificent a style as entirely to eclipse" theirs. He gave a splendid fête, at which not only the ministers, and a long list of nobility were present, but also the Prince of Wales—a ball and supper followed the dinner. Morelli, Rovedino, and the Opera company, appeared in masks, and sang a complimentary address to the Prince, which Pananti wrote, and Kelly composed. The music in *Macbeth* was then performed; and, in short, nothing could surpass the gaiety and splendour of the entertainment.[2]

6

The Rising Sun, "a serio-comical romance, by Cervantes Hogg" was a satire upon the Prince of Wales and his Whig followers, written by one of the political janissaries of the day, an Irishman named Eaton Stannard Barrett. It professed to be a narrative of the life of Farmer Gildrig, who was King George, and his son the young Squire. Charles Fox figured as Charles Brush, and Sheridan as Merryman. Mrs. Fitzherbert, whose obesity was a constant source of vulgar jokes, appears as Mrs. Maria Fitzwaddle, and several chapters in the first volume contain scenes from *The School for Profligacy, or the Land we Live in*, a sort of parody of *The School for Scandal*:

Brush. But come, Squire, you have not given us your real favourite.

Squire. Faith, I have withheld her only in compassion to you, for if I give her, you must toast a round of her peers, and that is impossible on earth.

[1]Lonsdale MSS., March 26th, 1806.   [2]Kelly, II, 254–5.

Brush (Aside). The earth could scarcely support a score of such unwieldy queans. Talk of prize-cattle!

Squire. Come, bumpers,—bumpers all round! Here's Maria!—Maria!

Cutlas. Maria! That's d———d common: What's her surname?

Brush. Never mind; Maria will suit any body.

Squire. Maria,—fair—fat and forty!

All. Maria,—fair—fat and forty!

The same volume (1806) contains also one of those mock-lives of Sheridan, which, unhappily, ended with a gibe that was the sharper for its truth.

"Merryman was of Irish extraction, and the son of a mountebank doctor, from whom (contrary to *strolling* custom) he derived a good education; it was not scattered on barren ground, as he had naturally great talents, and a fine flow of elocution; but excessive indolence prevented him from drinking deep of the Piërian stream, for which, however, he made ample amends another way. His wit was shining and keen, but low, probably the effect of his first mumming kind of life. He was supposed to be possessed of great courage, as he had once received a bloody nose in a contest with a *rival*. Thus accoutred, with wit for his weapon, and the reputation of bravery for his shield, he maintained a front of brass, and carried matters with a high hand in the Lord's stables, where he had sought an asylum from his creditors. For, besides making a practice of *chalking-up* wherever he went, he still hankered after the mimic scenes of life, and had converted an old barn into a sort of theatre, for which he never paid the carpenters. The landlord of whom he had hired the barn—the persons who had advanced the money to have shares in the concern—and even the performers, whom he engaged when they came in his way;—all complained that he *sacked* the receipts, without letting them touch one farthing; and the latter, at length refused to perform any more, till proper persons were appointed to

Uncorking · Old · Sherry ·

...the hon.ble Gent." tho' he does not very often address the House, yet when he does, he always thinks proper to pay off all arrears, & like a Bottle just uncork'd bursts all at once into an explosion of Froth & Air, — then, whatever might for a length of time lie lurking & corked up in his mind, whatever he thinks of himself or hears in conversation, — whatever he takes many days or weeks to sleep upon, the whole common-place-book of the interval is sure to burst out at once, stored with Studied Jokes, Sarcasms, arguments, invectives, & every thing else, which his mind or memory are capable of embracing whether they have any relation or not to the Subject under discussion. — See Mr. Pitts Speech m[?] Defence&ll Mar[?] 6.th 1805

PITT AND SHERIDAN, 1805

To face page 199

receive the money, and pay their salaries. He wrote several pieces for his stage, which went off very well. Every one allowed him wit, but no one could throw one grain of honesty into the scale. The public good was always at his tongue's end, but his fingers longed to be at variance with it. To cover his duplicity in some measure, he followed the example of his archetype Thespis, who—

> '—smear'd with lees and void of art,
> The grateful folly vented from a cart;
> And as his tawdry actors drove about,
> The sight was new, and charm'd the gaping rout.'

But not finding the lees of wine strong enough for his purpose, he resolved to improve upon Thespis, by using a stronger preparation distilled from the lees of wine, called *brandy*. In a word, he was a lineal descendant from the Parthians, of whom it has been said:

> '*quo plus bibunt, eo plus sitiunt:*'

that is—ever drunk, and ever dry."[1]

[1]*The Rising Sun*, I, 58–60.

CHAPTER THE EIGHTEENTH
The Prince of Wales

I

THE Prince's affection for Sheridan remained unaltered over a long period of years, during which his good humour must often have been sorely tried. Kelly gives an instance in 1802, when Sheridan desired an audience with the King on some point connected with the theatre. He mentioned it to the Prince, who, as Kelly says "with the kindness which on every occasion he showed him," offered to take him to Windsor Castle himself and appointed him to be at Carlton House two days later at eleven in the morning. Sheridan begged a bed at Kelly's house in Pall Mall, so that he would only have to cross the way to Carlton House. When Kelly returned home that day at four in the afternoon, he was surprised to find that Sheridan was still upstairs fast asleep, and though the Prince had sent for him several times, nothing would induce him to get up. He had dined the night before at Kelly's with Charles Ward, his brother-in-law, and Joseph Richardson, and he had consumed so many bottles of wine that he could not raise his head from the pillow, and remained there till seven in the evening.

The Prince relied upon Sheridan more than any other man for his counsel, for it was always disinterested, and actuated by a sincere desire to serve him, even when it was contrary to the Prince's own inclinations. During the Addington administration, "he formed," as Moore says, "a kind of connecting link between Carlton House and the Minister," taking a leading part in the negotiations in January 1803, when the King's illness appeared to make a Regency imminent. Moore alluded to a note from Charles Fox to Sheridan, which shows how close was his association with the Prince:

"P.S.," it ends, "I am told the Prince has heard rumours. that the Queen and the Duke of York are to associate with him in the Regency. Both he and Mrs. Fitzherbert are alarmed to the laſt degree. Surely he ought, after what you told him, to be easy about so senseless a report. I think it worth while for you to see *her* at leaſt, if not him, to tran- quillise them."[1]

The legend so assiduously propagated of the Prince's in- sincerity and heartlessness to Sheridan is at no place more perverse than in the comments upon his grant of the office of Receiver-General to the Duchy of Cornwall, which occurred shortly after Sheridan had opposed in Parliament the Prince's. desire for active service in the field.[2]

2

The Prince of Wales had no appointments at his disposal, except those of his own household, which from the duties they required could not have been held by Sheridan. The one "place" that could be discharged largely by deputy was the Receiver-Generalship of the Duchy. In this there had been no vacancy for forty-five years. Edward Elliot had been appointed by Frederick, Prince of Wales, in September 1749, and re- tained the office till his death, as Lord Elliot of St. German's, on February 17th, 1804. When the Prince received the news three days later, he wrote this cordial letter:

"DEAR SHERIDAN,

"You well know that I never forget my old friends. The death of Lord Elliott affords me the opportunity of offering you a trifling proof of that sincere friendship I have always profess'd and felt for you through a long series of years. I wish to God it was better worth your acceptance.

"Ever affectionately yours,
"GEORGE P."

"Carlton House, Monday night, Feb. 20th, 1804."[3]

[1]Sichel, II, 302 from B.M. Add. MS. 29764/73. cf. Moore, 609.
[2]For the records from the archives of the Duchy of Cornwall see Part Two.
[3]Rae, II, 243.

The next day Sheridan wrote to Addington:

"George Street, Tuesday evening.
[February 21st, 1804.]

"DEAR SIR,

Convinced as I am of the sincerity of your good will to-wards me, I do not regard it as an impertinent intrusion to inform you that the Prince has, in the most gracious manner, and wholly unsolicited, been pleased to appoint me to the late Lord Elliot's situation in the Duchy of Cornwall. I feel a desire to communicate this to you myself, because I feel a confidence that you will be glad of it. It has been my pride and pleasure to have exerted my humble efforts to serve the Prince without ever accepting the slightest obligation from him; but, in the present case, and under the present circum-stances I think it would have been really false pride and apparently mischievous affectation to have declined this mark of His Royal Highness's confidence and favour. I will not disguise that, at this peculiar crisis, I am greatly gratified at this event. Had it been the result of a mean and subservient devotion to the Prince's every wish and object I could neither have respected the gift, the giver, or myself; but when I consider how recently it was my misfortune to find myself compelled by a sense of duty, stronger than my attachment to him, wholly to risk the situation I held in his confidence and favour, and that upon a subject on which his feelings were so eager and irritable, I cannot but regard the increased attention, with which he has since honoured me, as a most gratifying demonstration that he had clearness of judgment and firmness of spirit to distinguish the real friends to his true glory and interests from the mean and mercenary sycophants, who fear and abhor that such friends should be near him. It is satisfactory to me, also, that this appointment gives me the title and opportunity of seeing the Prince, on trying occasions, openly and in face of day, and puts aside the mask of mystery and concealment. I trust I need not add, that whatever small portion of fair influence I may at any time possess with the Prince, it shall be uniformly exerted to promote those feelings of duty and affection towards their Majesties, which, though seemingly interrupted by adverse circumstances, I am sure are in his heart warm and unalterable—and, as far as I may presume, that general concord throughout his illustrious family, which must be looked to by every honest subject, as an essential part of the public strength at this momentous period. I have the honour to be, with great respect and esteem.

"Your obedient Servant,

"R. B. SHERIDAN.

"Right Hon. Henry Addington."[1]

On the same day Sheridan replied to the Prince, gratefully accepting the office, and instructions were given to make out the patent. But there was an objection raised. In 1795, during the reconstruction of his Household in consequence of his marriage, the Prince had granted the reversion of the office to one of his equerries, Major-General Gerard Lake, who had afterwards been appointed Commander-in-Chief of the Forces in India. The Prince, who held that the reversion had been invalidated by Lake's absence from the country, was surprised to receive a letter from Warwick Lake, claiming, by power of attorney granted by the General, his brother, the right to receive the income as his deputy. William Adam, the Prince's Attorney-General, confirmed the opinion that the office had essential duties which no Deputy was competent to perform— for instance, the annual audit—and that even for the collection of rents the Deputy could not be appointed except by a principal actually in possession of the office, having been sworn into it before the Prince's Council.

The Prince, who was ill at the time, sent for Sheridan, and told him to state the position to Warwick Lake, and in a letter dated only "Thursday," Sheridan wrote to Colonel Macmahon, the Prince's Secretary:

"Nothing on earth shall make me risk the possibility of

[1]Moore, 605–6.

the Prince's goodness to me furnishing an opportunity for a single scurrilous fool's presuming to hint even that he had, in the slightest manner, departed from the slightest engagement. The Prince's right, in point of law and justice, on the present occasion to recall the appointment given, I hold to be incontestible; but, believe me, I am right in the proposition I took the liberty of submitting to His Royal Highness, and which (so far is he from wishing to hurt General Lake), he graciously approved. But understand me—my meaning is to give up the emoluments of the situation to General Lake, holding the situation at the Prince's pleasure, and abiding by an arbitrated estimate of General Lake's claim, supposing His Royal Highness had appointed him; in other words to value his interest in the appointment *as if he had it*, and to pay for it or resign to him."[1]

The terms of this letter cannot have been final, for Sheridan had as yet to see Warwick Lake, and while the Prince had already agreed to the suggestion that Sheridan should resign on Lake's return to England, he cannot have agreed to the surrender of income which would nullify his intentions. He was, however, seriously ill at the time, and on February 27th, 1804, Sheridan wrote his wife "the Prince, just recovered from an illness in which his life was despaired of for two days, is so nervous and anxious that it is not easy to thwart him, though he runs a great risk of making himself ill again. I now see him openly, but till lately I never saw him till twelve at night, and he has often kept me till four in the morning, not supping or with a drop of wine, but in his bedroom."[2]

At Sheridan's interview with Warwick Lake, the Duke of York was present as the Prince's representative. This was stated by Sheridan in the House of Commons in 1812, when he said that his only income was derived from the bounty of the Prince of Wales:

"I will explain," he added, "on the death of Lord Elliott, when the office of Receiver of the Duchy became vacant, the

[1]Moore, 630.　　　　　[2]Rae, 249.

Attorney-General [to the Prince of Wales, William Adam], and a number of other learned gentlemen, some of whom are now in the House, who were then consulted, agreed in thinking that Lord Lake could not accept the situation when he was absent from this country, and it was then proposed that I should take it. I apprized his brother, [Warwick Lake] in the presence of the Duke of York, that if I took it, I should immediately resign it on Lord Lake's return; and accordingly I did resign it when he returned. When he died, the Prince was pleased to give it me by Letters Patent, for my life, in the same manner as it had been given to Lord Lake."[1]

An "Authentic Statement" on these lines was transmitted at the Prince's command to General Lake in India, but it made no reference to the surrender of income. Sheridan was appointed to the office "during the Prince's pleasure" by letters patent of March 6th, 1804.

But eighteen months later, Sheridan tried to persuade the Prince to transfer the appointment to his son, Tom Sheridan, who had married Charlotte Callander in June 1805. With that purpose he paid a visit to the Prince at Brighton, when Thomas Creevey, who was also a guest, recorded:

"Among other visitors to the Pavilion came Sheridan, with whom I was then pretty intimate, though perhaps not so much so as afterwards. I was curious to see him and the Prince daily in this way, considering the very great intimacy that had been between them for so many years. Nothing, certainly could be more creditable to both parties than their conduct. I never saw Sheridan during the period of three weeks (I think it was) take the least more liberty in the Prince's presence than if it had been the first day he had ever seen him. On the other hand the Prince always showed by his manner that he thought Sheridan a man that any prince might be proud of as his friend.

[1] *Parliamentary Debates*, XXIII, 554-5.

"So much for *manners*; but I was witness to a kind of altercation between them in which Sheridan could make no impression on the Prince. The latter had just given Sheridan the office of Auditor of the Duchy of Cornwall, worth about £1,200 per annum, and Sheridan was most anxious that the Prince should transfer the appointment to his son, Tom Sheridan, who was just then married. What Sheridan's object in this was, cannot be exactly made out; whether it really was affection for Tom or whether it was to keep the profit of the office out of the reach of his creditors, or whether it was to have a young life in the patent instead of his own. Whichever of these objects he had in view, he pursued it with the greatest vehemence; so much so, that I saw him *cry bitterly* one night in making his supplication to the Prince. The latter, however, was not to be shaken . . . he resisted the demand upon the sole ground that Sheridan's reputation was such, that it made it not only justifiable, but most honourable to him, the Prince, to make such a selection for the office. . . ."

For over three years the position was unaltered, and Sheridan continued in office, but he kept his promise of resignation, when Lord Lake returned to England. In 1807, by letters patent of March 12th, Lake was appointed "for life," being made Governor of Plymouth in September, and advanced to the dignity of Viscount Lake of Delhi a few days later. But for some reason, it was not until November 5th that *The London Gazette* announced his appointment by the Prince as "Receiver-General of the revenue of His Royal Highness's Duchy of Cornwall"—"vice Sheridan resigned." His tenure of office, however, lasted only a year, for he died on February 20th, 1808, and on April 20th it was gazetted from Carlton House that Sheridan had been appointed for life, and on May 1st he nominated Thomas Cocks the banker as Deputy Receiver in London and on September 8th, 1809, he appointed Charles Carpenter of Moditonham his Deputy in the Duchy.

There was, however, an interval between Lord Lake's death

and Sheridan's appointment which is difficult to explain. By sign manual warrant, Richard Gray was appointed Receiver-General during pleasure, "until we shall think fit to grant the same by Letters Patent." In the "Receiver's View" from December 12th, 1807, to February 21st, 1808, there is this N.B.:

"No Receiver-General from 21st day of February to 1st April when Mr. Richard Gray was appointed to the Office pro tempore, and who continued to hold it till the appointment of Mr. Sheridan on April 20th, 1808."

It seems strange that Sheridan was not appointed at once, but that after an interval of forty days, Richard Gray, Clerk to the Council, held office for nineteen days. The explanation must be sought elsewhere. Sheridan having been anxious in 1805 to transfer the Receiver-Generalship to his son Thomas, perhaps the request was renewed, though more probably Sheridan was, for reasons of his own, not visiting the Prince.

3

The accounts of the Duchy show that in the year 1809–1810 there was a large increase in the income, the receipts being over £90,000, against sums from £5,000 to £38,000 during the previous years of office. Sheridan's fees were therefore greater in proportion, and Creevey gives a typical illustration of Sheridan's prodigality with money. He was accustomed to visit Cocks's Bank in Charing Cross to obtain advances wherever possible from a favourite clerk. One morning he thought his friend looked particularly smiling upon him, so he said:

"I looked in to see if you could let me have ten pounds."

"Ten pounds!" replied the clerk; "to be sure I can, Mr. Sheridan. You've got my letter, sir, have you not?"

"No," said Sheridan, "what letter?"

("It is literally true," says Creevey, "that at this time and for many years Sheridan never got twopenny-post letters, because there was no money to pay for them, and the postman would not leave them without payment.")

"Why, don't you know what has happened, sir?" asked the clerk. "There is £1,300 paid into your account. There has been a very great fine paid for one of the Duchy estates, and this £1,300 is your percentage as auditor."

"Sheridan," adds Creevey "was of course very much set up with this £1,300, and, on the very next day upon leaving us, he took a house at Barnes Terrace where he spent all his £1,300. At the end of two or three months at most, the tradespeople would no longer supply him without being paid, so he was obliged to remove. What made this folly more striking was that Sheridan had occupied five or six different houses in the neighbourhood at different periods of his life, and on each occasion had been driven away literally by non-payment of his bills and consequent want of food for the house. Yet he was as full of his fun during these two months as ever he could be—gave dinners perpetually and was always on the road between Barnes and London, or Barnes and Oatlands (the Duke of York's), in a large job coach upon which he would have his family arms painted. . . . "[1]

[1] *The Creevey Papers,* 195.

CHAPTER THE NINETEENTH

The Westminster Election

Then fill up your glasses, my lads, while I sing,
The Navy, Hood, Sheridan, and their good King,
May Englishmen never with nonsense be crammed,
And Boney's supporters all die and be damned.

Thomas Dibdin, Election Song, 1806.

I

ON the death of Charles Fox, it was generally anticipated that his successor as member for Westminster would be Sheridan. But unexpectedly the Duke of Northumberland expressed a desire that the candidate should be his son, Lord Percy, who at once received the entire ministerial approval. Nevertheless, when the meeting of electors was held on September 18th at the Crown and Anchor Tavern in the Strand, and Lord Percy's name was proposed by Dennis O'Brien, the show of hands was greatly in favour of Sheridan. His speech in response took the form of a eulogium on the Death of Mr. Fox.[1]

It had been insinuated that he was about to retire from the contest because he was afraid of the disapproval of the government in which he held office:

"To such insinuations I shall scorn to make any other reply than a reference to the whole of my past political life. I consider it as no boast to say that any one who has struggled through such a portion of life as I have, without acquiring an office, is not likely to abandon his principles to retain one when acquired. To be at all capable of acting upon principle,

[1]For the full speech, see Part Two.

it is necessary that a man should be independent: and for independence the best thing to that of being very rich is to have been used to be very poor. Independence however, is not allied to wealth, to birth, to rank, to power, to titles, or to honours. Independence is in the mind of a man, or it is no where. On this ground were I to decline the contest, I should scorn the imputation that should bring the purity of my purpose into doubt. No minister can expect to find in me a servile vassal. No minister can expect from me the abandonment of any principle I have avowed, or any pledge I have given. I know not that I have hitherto shrunk in place from opinions I have maintained while in opposition. Did there exist a minister of different cast from any I know existing, were he to attempt to exact from me a different conduct, my office should be at his service to-morrow. Such a ministry might strip me of a situation, in some respects of considerable emolument, but he could not strip me of the proud conviction that I was right; he could not strip me of my own self-esteem; he could not strip me, I think, of some portion of the confidence and good opinion of the people."

Sheridan ended by declaring that it was his reluctant intention to retire from the contest, because he was bound by gratitude to the electors of Stafford, whom he had represented for over a quarter of a century. Lord Percy was therefore declared to be duly elected. But before he could take his seat Parliament was dissolved. Lord Gardner, the other member, having been promised a peerage of Great Britain, did not seek re-election, and Sheridan declared his intention of contesting the seat, and vacating his candidature at Stafford in favour of his son Tom. The Court-party nominated another Admiral, Sir Samuel Hood, as successor to Gardner. Sheridan was charged with attempting privately to supplant Lord Percy while affecting publicly to support him, and the Duke of Northumberland, with patriarchal solemnity, commanded his son to retire from a contest which would bring him into alliance with such dishonourable company. Hood and Sheridan would therefore have been returned without opposition, when a third candidate appeared in the person of James Paull, who had formerly been an ally of Sheridan in the House of Commons, but was now in league with Sir Frances Burdett, Horne Tooke, and William Cobbett. He was a "Nabob", having made a fortune in the East Indies, but his opponents made great play of his humble origin as the son of a Scots tailor.

2

The Westminster Election of 1806 was second only to Fox's contest of 1784 in its violence and animosity. Its incidents are recorded in a "History of the Westminster and Middlesex Elections in the Month of November 1806," containing the candidates' addresses, reports of their speeches, and a diversity of scurrilous handbills issued by all parties. Actually, it was the most momentous election of Sheridan's life, for not only did it mark his severance from Stafford after a quarter of a century but also it estranged many of his friends.

In his election address he said:

"I make no profession, and I am confident that you do not expect any from me. What I have been I shall continue to be. The maintenance of the principles of Mr. Fox is now more than ever a sacred duty. It is a solemn trust bequeathed especially to those who shared his confidence, gloried in his friendship and followed in his steps while living."

The proceedings were conducted in the old style over fifteen days. Sheridan went to the hustings escorted by "a parcel of men armed with bludgeons," and wearing his colours; and the disturbance was so great that his first audible words were: "Gentlemen, I wish to know whether you really want a riot or an election." Sir Samuel Hood appeared in his full dress naval uniform, with all his medals and orders, and the empty sleeve which reminded his supporters, as they did not fail to reiterate, of "our much lamented hero, Lord Nelson." The polling began at eleven o'clock, and ended at four. Paull, at the close of the second day said that his enemies had represented that he ought not to be chosen for Westminster, "because he possessed no ribbands, and was not descended from noble ancestry: he had only to say that he might have had a ribband as broad as that which was worn by Sir Samuel Hood, if he would have consented to surrender his independence." The version of this retort preserved in *Sheridaniana* was: "envious of the brilliant uniform and more brilliant decorations of Sir Samuel Hood, Paull observed with some spleen that if he had chosen he might have appeared before the electors with such a coat himself." Sheridan is said to have answered—"Yes, and you might have made it, too."

As he left the hustings on the first day, Sheridan was assaulted. A reward of a hundred pounds was offered by a handbill, signed by Peter Moore, chairman of Sheridan's Friends, beginning:

"Whereas, on Monday evening, after the close of the poll, a daring and desperate assault was made on the Right Hon. R. B. Sheridan, immediately as he passed through the door of the Hustings, particularly by three ruffians, who it appears had planted themselves there for that purpose; one of whom, named Davenport, now in custody and committed for trial, aimed a stroke at Mr. Sheridan's head, which by testimony of four respectable witnesses, would probably have killed him on the spot, had not his weapon been arrested."

On the fourth day, a coalition having been formed between the "Friends of Hood," and the "Friends of Sheridan," the Admiral's supporters came up to the hustings in different bodies from various parishes, led on by naval officers, bearing Hood's banners, accompanied by parties of seamen wearing his cockades, and carrying laurel branches in their hands, vociferating, "Hood for ever!" and preceded by fifes and drums, playing "Hearts of Oak," and "Rule Britannia." At the other end of the scene, parties of Mr. Sheridan's friends were preceded by "a posse of Hibernians from the purlieus of St. Giles's," armed with cudgels, roaring "Sheridan for ever!"

and speedily clearing their way through the multitude, who fled on all sides. In tactful allusion to Paull's paternity, they were headed by a banner-bearer, carrying at the top of a long pole a cabbage, surmounted by a tailor's smoothing-iron; next came a man dressed as an ape, borne upon a cutting-board, and adorned with shears and other tailor's tools; and lastly, came a man attired in the revolutionary costume of French democracy, wearing a huge hat, with a great cockade of Paull's colours; bearing in one hand a truncheon, inscribed "Liberty, Protection, and Peace."

From the hustings Paull demanded, "Who introduced the low mummery and pantomimical tricks this day exhibited, to give *stage effect* to the proceedings of those performers? The public have been to-day amused by the first act of *Robin Hood* and the farce of the *Forty Thieves*, brought forward by the manager as an election manœuvre." Viscount Petersham appeared in procession with "a gang of scene-shifters from Drury Lane" who were described by Paull as "one hundred and fifty hired armed bandits and assassins, marching in battle array from the committee-room of one of the candidates, headed by a nobleman, an officer in His Majesty's Service, for the avowed purpose of committing acts of atrocious enormity."

So it went on from day to day, the libels becoming more ferocious as the contest proceeded.

The choicest specimen of invective against Harlequin Sheridan was:

3

"*To the Independent Electors of Westminster.*

"Who is asking to be one of your Representatives? The Son of an obscure Irish Player, a profession formerly proscribed by our laws; and its followers by various statutes stigmatized as *incorrigible rogues and vagabonds.*—Possessed of a considerable portion of Ribaldry, disgusting obscenity, and dissoluteness of manners, this *Harlequin Son* of a *Mountebank Father* was indulged by some few of the depraved Nobility of the age with admission into their society, as a kind of *hired Jester*, whose grossness of conversation was calculated to stimulate their already too luxuriant debauchery.—From these beginnings he moved through all the gradations of *meanness, tricking* and *impudence,* to the station he now fills; his career has been marked with every species of profligacy and extravagance; to support which, he has been compelled to resort to low cunning and vile impostures.

"I will not make any *honest man* blush by the recital of them—my paper shall not be thus stained: The ruin of hundreds of industrious Tradesmen and their innocent families are the evidences, and will rise up in vengeance against such oppressors!—If you look at his political life, you will find it exhibiting equally repulsive traits:—At one time the friend and supporter of principles subversive of the Constitution and of all order; the advocate of the French Revolution and its wildest theories; the defender of an O'Connor; the systematic opposer (whether right or wrong) of all the measures of the Government; yet, when in *place,* pursuing the same measures; inconsistent, tergiversating, unpatriotic, and the Apostate of Public Liberty: Ever regardless of the true interests of his Country, the acquirement of place his *only* object, the love of its advantages *his only* care.

—"And can such a MAN be a fit Representative for the Independent Electors of Westminster? No!! NO!!!—Let it not be said, that the dictates of an imperious Minister shall determine your actions! *Debased, sunk* below the possibility of recovery, *mortified* and stung to the soul by the success of his opponents, this would-be and cannot-be popular Candidate, on his knees, most humbly sues his masters to raise him from the dirt. Yes! and *they will attempt* to raise him, but it will be only to *sink him* the lower, to make him their *tool,* their *dependent,* their *slave.*—And, Gentlemen, will you be represented by a dependent and a slave of the Grenvilles? Forbid it Justice! Forbid it Virtue! Forbid it Freedom!!!

"A Calm Observer."

On November 9th a public subscription was raised so that

"no part of the expenses attending the election should fall upon the Right Hon. R. B. Sheridan," and the Duke of Queensbury contributed a thousand guineas. Sheridan stayed at the bottom of the poll, from the first day until the eleventh, when the figures were:

Hood 4812: Sheridan 4057: Paull 3754.

At this moment Cobbett became exceedingly virulent, and in replying from the hustings, Sheridan said, "that though in the notions of Mr. Cobbett there is much which I abhor, there is something in his character I respect. He has by his own unassisted talents and energy raised himself from a very humble position to a situation of respect, reception and property; and he has the manliness and good sense not to be ashamed of the fact,"—the last sentence being, of course, a back-hander for Paull. The several parties charged one another with "flagitious falsehoods" and "foul and illiberal abuse." The favourite electioneering tune of "Mistress Arne, Mistress Arne" was pressed into service, and the verse applied to Sheridan was:

"Oh, Sherry! red Sherry!
You'd make us all merry.
With your drolls, your stage-tricks, and curvets;
But don't, on old Davy,
Draw drafts for the Navy:
Nor pay 'em as you pay your debts,
Red Sherry;
Nor pay 'em as you pay your debts."

When the poll-books were closed for the last time, on the fifteenth day, the High Sheriff declared:

Hood 5478: *Sheridan* 4758: *Paull* 4481.

Hood and Sheridan being duly elected, they proceeded to the triumphal car which had been constructed in anticipation. It was about twelve feet long, with a gallery for their chief supporters, and a raised platform for themselves, where they sat in state upon two chairs, upholstered in crimson velvet and richly gilt, before an emblematic trophy containing the Royal Arms and the legend "George Rex," and beneath an arch of laurel branches, thickly interwoven. The carriage was drawn by six horses, profusely decorated with ribbons of orange and blue, Sheridan's colours, and each horse was led by a man wearing an orange and blue cockade.

Corbett denounced this tasteful specimen of the scenic art, and the procession that accompanied it through the streets:

"the car," he said, "which had been constructed by the people of Drury Lane, was surrounded by beadles, constables, police-officers, and police-magistrates, and as even their own venal prints inform us, by the numerous officers of the Thames police. 'The People,' of whom they talk as *huzzaers*, consisted of the play-actors, scene-shifters, candle-snuffers, and mutes of the Theatre, aided by a pretty numerous bevy of those unfortunate females who are in some sort inmates of that mansion, so that altogether the procession bore a very strong resemblance to that of *Blue-Beard*."

The Westminster Election was disastrous to Sheridan. He alienated the supporters at Stafford who had been his friends for a quarter of a century. He exposed himself to virulent criticism as being one who had consistently denounced "placemen," and yet had secured sinecures both for himself and his son. Lord Holland, who resented Sheridan's attempt "to assume the mantle of Charles Fox," recollected the circumstances with great bitterness in later years. He declared that Sheridan,

"had seen with emotions of envy the uniform popularity of Fox at Westminster, and tried to entrap him to resign in his favour during the secession. On the General Election and the retirement of Lord Percy, he again stood for Westminster against the advice of his friends and without the concurrence of a government to which he belonged. He, through his inordinate vanity, thought that he might defy the Court, the Aristocracy, and the Reformers, and such was his confidence in his own personal popularity that he not only neglected, but derided and insulted, the clubs and committees through whose agency Mr. Fox's elections had been generally secured. He was bitterly deceived. Our party supported him but feebly. He was absolutely execrated by the people. With great exertion I obtained for him some reluctant assistance from the Ministry and he was elected with much difficulty against the cry of the people, the reluctance of our friends, and the unbiassed wishes of the voters."[1]

4

At Paull's dinner after the election, some curious allegations were made as to Sheridan's relations with Stafford: "It had always been the pride of the electors," said a speaker, "to return the gentleman who had so long and so ably fought against corruption, but their minds had very much changed of late as to the conduct of Mr. Sheridan himself. Some time before the dissolution Mr. Thomas Sheridan, his son, went thither and sent the bellman round to call a meeting of the Corporation, to return thanks to his father. When the meeting took place, although a very numerous one, there was not a person to be found to make the motion." During the Stafford election "Mr. Sheridan and his Friends" made enquiry concerning the circumstances of Maunsel Phillips, one of the candidates. They found that a friend of his had owed a bill of two hundred pounds to his tailor, and Phillips had guaranteed payment and accepted the liability in order to save him from jail. Sheridan's party persuaded the tailor to issue a writ, which they sent from London, and Phillips was arrested upon it. The writ was brought down by Major Downs, and the agent for carrying it into effect was Mr. Burgess, "domestic attorney to Mr. Sheridan." Phillips, however, being bailed by some of his supporters, the friends of Mr. Sheridan found out another demand against him, and caused him to be arrested at the suit of Harvey Combe; the agent employed upon that occasion was "Mr. Cocker, an intimate friend of Mr. Sheridan, and an attorney of

[1]Holland, *Memoirs*.

the Whig Club." The speaker argued that "it might be said that all this was done by the agents or friends of Mr. Sheridan without his knowledge, but he must have had sufficient power and control over them and he must be responsible for their acts. Notwithstanding all these attempts, the party of Mr. Sheridan was unable to succeed. The voters at Stafford were more than six hundred, and out of these Mr. Thomas Sheridan could obtain no more than a hundred and sixty-five." Whereupon with great applause Mr. Paull's friends drank "the health of the electors of Stafford."

In the General Election of 1807, Sheridan was defeated by Lord Cochrane at Westminster, but he had taken the precaution of securing a seat for the borough of Ilchester, where he had for his colleague Michael Angelo Taylor. He was "brought in" for this seat by the Prince of Wales, who perhaps bore the expense of this election. In 1812, when he had decided to relinquish Ilchester in favour of Stafford, which until then he had again hoped to secure for his son Tom, he wrote a letter to him saying in explanation of the change in his intentions:

"Another thing that threw cold water on my wishes as to Stafford was the Prince's confessed dislike to my declining to continue to be brought in by him. This, observe, was months before his decision to bring in his present ministers, but while he continues them arrayed against the Catholic claims, they cannot have a vote in their support from me, and therefore I ought not to continue to owe my support to their master."[1]

[1]Rae, II, 258.

CHAPTER THE TWENTIETH

Downhill

I

ON February 24th, 1809, Sheridan was in the House of Commons during a debate when cries of "Fire!" were heard and the red glare of a burning building was seen through the windows. Sheridan whispered across the table that the theatre was burning, and he drove rapidly to Drury Lane, where he stood for some moments in dreadful agony. Then he retired to the Piazza Coffee House, from which he witnessed the entire destruction of his property. Among the friends who hastened to his side was the Duke of York. As Sheridan sat in the window his fortitude impressed all who saw him; he looked on, taking some refreshment. When a friend remarked upon the philosophical calmness with which he bore his misfortune, Sheridan answered, "A man may surely be allowed to take a glass of wine at his own fireside!"

The calamity was complete. Scarcely a thing was rescued, except an iron chest containing the patent and other documents of the greatest importance, which was saved by Peake the treasurer and three assistants, who dashed into the theatre at the peril of their lives. The building which had been erected only fifteen years before at a cost of three hundred thousand pounds was insured for only thirty-five thousand. Among the possessions which perished were an organ, worth eight hundred pounds, which had belonged to Handel, and a clock which had been Garrick's and in his time had been wound up only once a year, on the day when the accounts were completed. There were other personal properties, including the whole of the "elegant furniture" which on the change of Ministry,

had been removed into the theatre from "Somerset House."
Amongst it were two treasures which Sheridan valued beyond
all price—a bust of the Prince of Wales by Nollekens, which, as
he told John Graham a few weeks before his death, had been a
gift from the Prince himself, and was almost unrecognizable
when it was found among the ruins, and the harpsichord belonging to Elizabeth Linley, at which she had been painted by
Sir Joshua as St. Cecilia. Although this furniture is said to have
been brought from Somerset House, it appears to have been
from the Red House in Pall Mall, adjoining Carlton Palace,
which had been given him by the Prince when he relinquished
the office of Treasurer of the Navy. The wits had commented
that "H.R.H. was on the *face* of the thing compelled to give
Sheridan the Red House in order to keep him in *countenance*."[1]

Sheridan was at once faced by ruin, but he set upon the work
of reconstruction. If, however, he had not applied to Samuel
Whitbread, the brewer, a connection of his second wife, it is
doubtful if the theatre would have been rebuilt so speedily. A
committee was formed, which was joined by Lord Holland,
the Hon. Douglas Kinnaird, Lord Byron and others, and the
first stone being laid in October 1812, the building itself was
completed and opened in twelve months.

Meanwhile, however, his wife complained bitterly of his
neglect and indifference to her comfort and happiness, to
which charge he replied from his country house at Richmond
on April 20th, in a long letter which ascribed his faults not to
this, but to his "negligent, forgetful, and procrastinating state
of mind," united with "a most unfortunately sanguine temper,
and a rash confidence that I am capable of exertions equal to
any difficulty, whenever extremity may call for them." There
was no attempt to hide or diminish his faults, and he added
that "I have broken through the rule of my life, which has
formed its pride also, and have with a broken spirit, stooped
for the first time to solicit and accept the pecuniary assistance
of private friendship." He ended with the information that he
had avoided contracting new debts, for if he should fail to

[1]Watkins, II, 81. Cf. *Sheridaniana*, 202.

obtain a seat in Parliament, "a thing infinitely probable," by losing his immunity for arrest, "you would be sorry to see me dying in jail."

An earlier passage in the same letter shows that the Prince of Wales had behaved very generously to him. For the sake of Tom, and in order to gratify his ambition, he had "incurred the obligation of the expenditure of not less than £8,000" on the part of the Prince in his three attempts to bring Tom into Parliament—"I, who for myself have more than once peremptorily refused the offer of a moderate loan from him when I have been in the greatest distress." Tom Sheridan had been defeated three times—at Liskeard in Cornwall in 1803, and at Stafford in 1806 and 1807.[1]

2

The extreme virulence of party politics is illustrated by the result of certain speeches which were made at a dinner on St. Patrick's Day in March 1812. Sheridan was from the beginning a prominent supporter of the Benevolent Society of St. Patrick, which was established in 1784, for the education of the children of poor natives of Ireland living in London. At the St. Patrick's Day dinner, its chief public function, Sheridan's speech was for thirty years one of the standing dishes. Though these surveys of Irish affairs were always applauded for their wit and wisdom, hardly a trace of them remains. But Sheridan, even when his finances were most distressed, was always particularly anxious that his annual subscription to this Society should be secure. One of the notes he scribbled to Peake, the Drury Lane treasurer, reads:

> "Twenty pounds more will not break our backs. Let them go by nine in the morning to Hammersley's, to answer my draft given to-day to the St. Patrick's Society. R.B.S."

On such occasions the money was sent from the Treasury of the Theatre to Hammersley's Bank, by a man who waited at the

---

[1]Rae, II, 218–9. The Prince did not exaggerate in his statement to Croker that Sheridan had cost him altogether over £20,000.

counter from the opening till the cheque was presented by the
representative of St. Patrick's Society. Then, and not till then,
was the money paid over—otherwise it might have been
applied to reducing the overdraft!

Leigh Hunt in his *Autobiography* gives an account of the
dinner which followed Perceval's retention as Prime Minister:

> "At these annual dinners of the Irish on St. Patrick's
> Day the Prince of Wales's name used to be the reigning
> and rapturous toast, as that of the greatest friend they pos-
> sessed in the United Kingdom. He was held to be the jovial
> advocate of concession to the Catholic claims. But the
> Prince of Wales, now the Prince Regent, had retained the
> Tory ministers of his father; he had broken life-long en-
> gagements; had violated promises, particular as well as
> general, those to the Catholics among them; and led into a
> different political life from what had been expected. The
> name, therefore, which used to be hailed with rapture, was
> now, at the dinner in question, received with hisses."

The chairman, Lord Moira, made not the slightest allusion
to the Prince Regent, and Sheridan, "who manfully stood up
for his royal friend, declared that he still sustained the principles of the Prince Regent, was saluted by angry shouts and
cries of 'Change the subject!' The Whig *Morning Chronicle*
moralized this theme; and *The Morning Post*, which then
affected to be the organ of the Court, in a strain of unqualified
admiration replied to the *Chronicle*, partly in vapid prose ob-
jurgation, and partly in a wretched poem, graced with epithets
intended to be extravagantly flattering to the Prince." To this
reply, Leigh Hunt rejoined in *The Examiner* in a paper of considerable length, in which he claimed to have "translated the
language of adulation into that of truth." This is the passage he
selected for transmission to posterity:

> "What person, unacquainted with the true state of the
> case, would imagine, in reading these astounding eulogies,
> that this 'Glory of the people' was the subject of millions of
> shrugs and reproaches!—that this 'Protector of the arts' had

named a wretched foreigner his historical painter, in disparagement or in ignorance of the merits of his own countrymen!—that this 'Mæcenas of the age' patronized not a single deserving writer!—that this 'Breather of eloquence' could not say a few decent extempore words, if we are to judge, at least, from what he said to his regiment on its embarkation for Portugal!—that this 'Conqueror of hearts' was the disappointer of hopes!—that this 'Exciter of desire' (bravo! Messieurs of the Post!)—this 'Adonis in loveliness,' was a corpulent man of fifty!—in short, this delightful, blissful, wise, pleasurable, honourable, virtuous, true, and immortal prince, was a violator of his word, a libertine over head and ears in disgrace, a despiser of domestic ties, the companion of gamblers and demireps, a man who has just closed half a century without a single claim on the gratitude of his country, or the respect of posterity!"

Hunt was tried for libel, and sent to prison on February 3rd, 1813. The indecencies of political invective could hardly have gone further.

3

After the assassination of Perceval, in 1811, the Prince Regent requested first the Marquis Wellesley, and then the Earl of Moira, to form a new administration, and finally invited Lord Liverpool. Sheridan was involved in these transactions so seriously that he was finally alienated from his party. It is difficult to sift the truth from the mass of allegations and exculpations which survive, but he was accused of secretly influencing the Prince against the interest of his friends. He replied to the charges against him in the House on three days in June, his explanation being twice interrupted by illness. He asserted that "I have only spoken once within the last two months to the Prince. I purposely abstained. I had one audience since my return from Stafford, to explain my visit there."

The Prince, therefore, only learned at this audience of Sheridan's desire to relinquish his seat for Ilchester, and contest Stafford, a resolution that he had formed in November. If a letter from Colonel MacMahon, dated only "Wednesday, May 13th" belongs to this year, Sheridan had been neglecting Carlton House, by reason of illness, for he wrote "I have not failed to make your excuses in your own words to the Prince Regent for your absence at the last Levee, with which H.R.H. was highly pleased, though greatly concerned for the reason of that absence." MacMahon's letter was affectionately worded, saying how he rejoiced to receive Sheridan's kind and welcome letter, "for your long silence to my last, together with your not calling, . . . gave me all the pangs which must be the attendant upon rejected Friendship." This was written, it seems, two days after Perceval's death.[1]

In the House, Sheridan continued that he gave his opinion to the Prince on the "negotiations that were going on, and devoutly wish it could be published," which seems to refer to a letter that he wrote the Prince after the audience. Moore cites some extracts, in which, after praising the "wisdom and magnanimity" displayed by the Prince, in confiding to Lord Wellesley the powers that had just been entrusted to him, he repeated his opinion that any "proscription" of the Noble Earl in question would be "a proceeding equally derogatory to the estimation of His Royal Highness's personal dignity and the security of his political power"—adding, that the advice, which he took the liberty of giving against such a step, did not proceed "from any peculiar partiality to the Noble Earl or to many of those with whom he was allied; but was founded on what he considered to be best for His Royal Highness's honour and interest, and for the general interests of the country."

The "noble Earl" whom the Prince wished to exclude must have been Lord Grey, a point which is important in its later bearings. Sheridan's letter, while fearing that this expression of opinion may have incurred the Prince's displeasure, concluded:

"Junius said in a public letter of his, addressed to Your Royal Father, 'the fate that made you a King forbad your

<hr />

[1]Sichel, II, 357.

SHERIDAN AND MASTER BETTY, 1805

To face page 225

having a friend.' I deny his proposition, as a general maxim
—I am confident that Your Royal Highness possesses
qualities to win and secure to you the attachment and devotion of private friendship, in spite of your being a Sovereign. At least I feel that I am entitled to make this declaration as far as relates to myself—and I do it under the assured
conviction that you will never require from me any proof of
that attachment and devotion inconsistent with the clear and
honourable independence of mind and conduct, which constitute my sole value as a public man, and which have
hitherto been my best recommendation to your gracious
favour, confidence, and protection."[1]

In his explanation in the House, Sheridan declared "I did
know what was going on. How? By no means from Carlton
House, but from the Marquis of Wellesley, who called at my
house in the face of day, the morning he was authorised to form
his administration, and showed me his written terms. In an
hour he came again, offering a situation and received a disinterested denial. I knew more from Lord Moira. Lord Grey desired the Household to resign if certain persons came into
office. This was discharging them." At the end of the next sentence, Sheridan was forced to break off through faintness.

Lord Yarmouth, the Vice-Chamberlain, stated in the Lords
that he had told Sheridan of the intention of the Household to
resign, so that this information might be conveyed to Lord
Grey and Lord Grenville, thus removing the sole ground upon
which they were refusing office. Not only did Sheridan try to
persuade Lord Yarmouth against resignation, but, when ques-
tioned by Tierney about their rumoured decision, he offered,
"to bet five hundred guineas that there was no such stay in
contemplation." Sheridan admitted an offer, but put the
amount as five shillings, his reason for making this reply being
that their resignation was "contingent upon circumstances
more remote from taking place than ever."

This mysterious sentence seems to mean that he knew that

[1]Moore, 676-7.

Q

since Moira had been entrusted with the formation of an administration, instead of Wellesley, Grey and Grenville would not serve under him, quite irrespective of any question of the Household. His conduct he insisted, was not "that of an interested caballer. Lord Moira had authorised what he had done. He believed the two noble lords were honourable: he gave them credit for purity of motive. But he was not the channel of political communication with them." The rest of his explanation does not matter, but he told how he hoped, until the eleventh hour, for the success of the negotiations between Lord Moira, and Grey and Grenville, and it was to his surprise that he learned on June 8th that Lord Liverpool had been appointed Prime Minister.

His defence of his honour is much stronger than was, or has been, allowed, though the members of his Party regarded his conduct, especially in the suppression of what he had been told by Lord Yarmouth, as an act of treachery. It finally terminated his friendship with the Whig leaders and their followers, and, as *The Edinburgh Review* declared, in defending their subsequent neglect of him "Sheridan behaved inexcusably to the most distinguished of his former associates in 1812, and from that period, naturally lived in a state of alienation from their society."

The Morning Chronicle, the chief organ of the Whig Party, attacked him ferociously, making the old charge that he looked upon life as a play:

> "the actors in the plot," it said, "have been various, and those who have played the most prominent parts have been farthest from the real secret of the drama, the manager and contriver of which has hitherto kept himself in the background; and if his vanity would have allowed him to be silent, the piece might have gone off successfully, without any one suspecting who was its author. Sly Boots is a 'notable contriver,' but he has the misfortune to be leaky in his cups, and when overtaken, confirms the old adage *in vino veritas.*"

His conduct was not such as to forfeit him the friendship of Lord Moira, nor was he blamed in any way by the Prince Regent. His vindication contained one actual passage, in which he repudiated any suggestion that he intended to vote with Lord Liverpool's administration:

"My objection to the present Ministry is, that they are avowedly arrayed and embodied against a principle,—that of concession to the Catholics of Ireland,—which I think, and must always think, essential to the safety of this empire. I will never give my vote to any Administration that opposes the question of Catholic Emancipation. I will not consent to receive a furlough upon that particular question, even though a Ministry were carrying every other that I wished. In fine, I think the situation of Ireland a paramount consideration. If they were to be the last words I should ever utter in this House, I should say, 'Be just to Ireland, as you value your own honour;—be just to Ireland, as you value your own peace.' "

His "last words" in the House of Commons were spoken two days later, on June 21st, against the French overtures of Peace, in which he replied to Whitbread, who advocated their acceptance. But it was the question of Catholic Emancipation which decided his political fate.[1]

[1]Moore, 677.

CHAPTER THE TWENTY-FIRST
Defeat at Stafford

October, 1812.
The failure at Stafford completed his ruin. He was now excluded from both the Theatre and Parliament: the two anchors by which he held in life were gone, and he was left a lonely and helpless wreck upon the waters.

Moore, *Life of Sheridan.*

I

THE new theatre of Drury Lane was opened on October 10th, 1812, but Sheridan was not present to hear the prologue by Lord Byron which declared:

Dear are the days which made our annals bright,
Ere Garrick fled, or Brinsley ceased to write.

The new corporation was directed by a committee of twenty-one persons, all nominated by himself, and all his own friends —among them Lord Holland, William Adam, Harvey Combe, John Dent, Richard Ironmonger, Douglas Kinnaird, Colonel John MacMahon, Peter Moore, Charles Ward, and Samuel Whitbread. He had hoped for some share in the management, but his agreement to have "no concern or connexion of any kind whatever with the new undertaking" was made "a *sine qua non* by all who embarked on it." He had hoped that this would not have been enforced, but Whitbread as chairman was adamant.

2

It was Whitbread to whom he attributed his defeat at Stafford for lack of funds, complaining that he had deliberately and unjustly refused an advance of £2,000, which was needed for his election campaign, from the sum due to him as chief proprietor of the old theatre and its two patents. Whitbread was one of the supporters of the Princess of Wales, and Sheridan told the Prince Regent that it was for this reason he wished to prevent him entering Parliament, for fear of his opposition. The motives that Sheridan had in contesting Stafford were entirely honourable, for he desired an independent seat that would leave him free as an advocate of Catholic Emancipation. But it was his own procrastination which lost him the seat to an unexpected opponent, Colonel Wilson.

At the close of November 1811 he decided to relinquish his seat at Ilchester in favour of his old constituency. On November 24th he wrote to one of the leading burgesses,

"Upon mature consideration and reviewing those accounts I have received of the disposition of your borough, I have decided in my own mind to embrace the present opportunity of declaring again for Stafford. I am not only secure of Ilchester for myself, but also of the second seat for my son, yet I pant for my own independent seat. You are a sportsman, and, as all lovers of field sports must be more or less friendly to poetry, I may refer you to Goldsmith for my feelings on the present occasion:
'And as hare whom hounds and horns pursue
Pants to the goal from whence at first she flew,
I still have hopes, my long vexations past,
There to return, and die at home at last.'
Political death, I mean. But even before that I trust that we and the few surviving old friends may yet spend some pleasant days together."[1]

He felt that as the seat at Ilchester was found for him by the Prince Regent, he could not consistently accept it, and yet continue to vote against the Ministry. He addressed a letter to one of the Jerninghams, who had great influence in Stafford:[2]

[1]Rae, II, 259–60.   [2]Salt Library MSS., Stafford.

"Cavendish Square

"Private.   "Monday 25th Nov. 1811.

"MY DEAR SIR,

"In consequence of Sr. Oswald Moseley having publicly declined to ſtand for Stafford at the next general election. I have been ſtrongly solicited by the leading Party in the Town to *return* again to *my old farm* I had promised Sr. Oswald as a Party friend and a *Friend to the Catholic Rights* every Support in my Power, and He now I am sure will do the same by me. many motives *under the present circumſtances* lead me to accede to and pursue this offer—& none so much as my ardent wish to support the catholic claims in an *independent* seat.

"This is the sole political object now near my heart, & that which I wish resolutely to support both in the House of Commons and with whatever humble influence I may possess with the Prince Regent. I am sure of my return again for Ilcheſter and even of the second seat for my Son, yet perhaps you may surmise—and pardon me at the same time for not being more explicit—my motive is to ſtand the master of my own motions in the ensueing session of Parliament, especially on the *Queſtion of the Catholic Claims*—

"The conſtant support which I am indebted for to your family in Stafford, and the kind allacrity with which you offerr'd to accompany me to that Place on a former occasion from Carlton House are remember'd by me with juſt gratitude. I have now only to requeſt you to communicate this letter to your Brother—sanguinely confiding that He will continue on the present occasion the same cordial support which I have so long experienced from your moſt respected family.

"I have the Honour to be
"My Dear Sir,
"Yours moſt sincerely
"R. B. SHERIDAN.

"S. Jernyngham."

Four days later he wrote Sir Oswald Moseley, who was a large landowner in the country, saying:

"I have determined to accept the very cordial invitations I have received from *old friends* in that quarter, and (though entirely secure of my seat at Ilchester, and, indeed, even of the second seat for my son, through the liberality of Sir W. Manners,) to return to the old goal from whence I started thirty-one years since! You will easily see that arrangements at Ilchester may be made towards assisting me, in point of expence, to meet *any opposition*, and, *in that respect*, nothing will be *wanting*. It will, I confess, be very gratifying to me to be again elected by *the sons of those* who chose me in the year *eighty*, and adhered to me so stoutly and so long."

He visited his old constituency a few weeks later, and returned to London with the assurance that he had found once more a safe seat. But when the election came, he procrastinated, perhaps with some idea that he would be invited to stand for Westminster, but he arrived too late to make an effective canvass. In 1826, after the publication of Moore's Life, the account of the first day's polling in a local paper[1] began:

"*Stafford Election*.
"Dec. 13—(first Day's Poll).
"This borough, the well known scene of Sheridan's electioneering contests, has been proverbial for its *hospitable* reception of any strange candidate who chose to present himself for the suffrages of the *independent* burgesses. The borough, as is well known, is a town of shoemakers, a very large portion of the home & foreign demand for that essential necessary of life being supplied from its far famed emporium. The traditions of Sheridan's numerous witticisms and puns on these symbols of the local trade, are highly amusing, and would form 'a new edition,' and saleable 'addition' to Mr. Thomas Moore's life of that distinguished and inconsistent politician. But be it recorded to the honour

[1]Salt Library Collection, Stafford.

of that celebrated individual, 'covered with frailties,' that his memory is nowhere so unsullied or respected as at Stafford. He is everywhere spoken of with respect, the oldest burgesses conceit themselves with the pride of having supported & polled 'Old Sherry.' And it appears that his last election would not have been lost, but for the untoward circumstances & disadvantages which attended his procrastinated & unlucky appearance before them."

After the declaration of the poll, his address to the electors promised an explanation of his failure. It does not appear to have been published, but a draft of it survives, all but the first two paragraphs being in his own handwriting. This explanation is so angry that it is evident that Sheridan was bitterly disappointed by his defeat.[1]

"Borough of Stafford. 1812.

"Many anxious enquiries having been made as to the failure of the election of the Rt Honble R. B. Sheridan for this Borough. A short statement of facts from an eye witness will he hopes illucidate it.

"Several & repeated letters of solitation were adressed to that Rt Honble Gentn from the most reputable electors of the Borough of Stafford requesting him (in case of a dissolution of Parliament) to offer himself again as a candidate for that Seat in which they should feel a pride in replacing him. In consequence of these applications Mr. Sheridan visited the Town of Stafford and canvassed the Burgesses at the latter end of May last upon that Canvass he not only received the promise of support from all the respectable part of the Burgesses but the general support of the Electors as a proof of which the canvass Book of that date can be produced upon that canvass there were not more than twenty of the resident Burgesses refused him their support out of upward of six hundred. In canvassing the Town he found that the

[1]Salt Library MSS., Stafford.

utmost distress prevailed amongst the Tradesmen and
workers, *for want of employ* so much so, that numerous
families were starving for want of bread.

"[1] The Masters in order to serve the work Men as well as
they could nearly exhausted their Capital and created an
unsalable stock both at home and abroad nearly to their
Ruin, one of them to the amount of many thousand Pounds.

"The natural disposition of Mr. S. induced him to dis-
tribute a considerable sum of money amongst those starving,
Passed on his Canvass & after it was finished (as is
usual) he gave them tickets of entertainment 560 of these
were taken by the *free and independent* Burgesses & received
by them with blessings and vociferous sayings that they
never would disert Him and they had the impudence to add
that they admired his political consistency. *These Men
totally devoid of either Honour or Principle* as the sequil will
prove on the disolution of Parliament, Mr. Sheridan refused
a Seat which was offered him in the House of Commons on
the full confidence & faith of the Promises (of these vagabonds).

"Mr. Sheridan arrived at Stafford on Friday the   of
October & was assured that every Man was faithful & no
opposition was intended or could effect Him and the Election was fixed for the Tuesday following.

"On Sunday morning the friends of Mr. Sheridan were informed that a Colonel Wilson had arrived in the Town for
the purpose of offering himself as a Candidate and that he
had been fetched by a number of the Burgesses for that
purpose. He made his Canvass and they went to the Hustings on Tuesday and opened the Poll—on that day & the
following these free & independant wretches to the amount
of nearly 400 disregarding their solemn promises to Mr. S
broke their words turn'd their *coats, and voted against Him* such
Reptiles with the exception of about three hundred con-
scientious honest Men are the Electors of this infamous
borrough of Stafford composed of—a Correct alphabetical

---

[1] Sheridan's handwriting begins here.

List of the Turn Coats is in Preparation and will be distributed through every part of the united Kingdom as a caution to all honest Men to have nothing to do with the rotten Borrough.

"N.B. In order to assist the Tradesmen and Journeymen of this Town Mr. Sheridan had exerted himself for their good and Actually got orders for shoes to a considerable ammount."

3

After his defeat, Sheridan desired to find another seat. According to what the Prince Regent told Croker in 1825,[1] after Moore's *Life of Sheridan* had appeared:

"the Duke of Norfolk had a seat to dispose of for which he expected £4,000, but he consented, as he called it, to subscribe £1,000 towards bringing Sheridan into Parliament: or in other words, to accept £3,000 from Sheridan for the seat.   As even payment of this sum was not to leave Sheridan personally independent, the Duke expecting that he should vote with him, I did not consider the offer quite so noble as the offer of subscribing £1,000 towards bringing Sheridan in seemed to affect to be."

He must therefore have gone to the Prince Regent in the hope of borrowing the rest of the purchase-money. It may be assumed that the Duke, though he and Sheridan were agreed on all political questions, had specified or implied a condition that on any aspect of Catholic disabilities, Sheridan would not develop his erratic "independence." The Prince Regent, who had shown no resentment against Sheridan vacating Ilchester, was nevertheless not agreeable to any such condition, and advised Sheridan to find an independent seat.

The subsequent events, however, involved Sheridan in a calamity, which was his estrangement from the Prince Regent. What purported to be his own version of this affair appeared

---

[1] This account was not published till *The Croker Papers*, 1885.

shortly after his death in several newspapers, but it originated
in *The Sun*, and was therefore almost certainly written by his
friend the editor, John Taylor. The author of this account
said that some few months after the Stafford election he had
waited by invitation upon Sheridan, who told him that for some
time previous to his assassination in May 1812, Spencer Perceval, then Prime Minister, was in the habit of calling frequently
upon him, apparently in the spirit of merely friendly intercourse,
Sheridan however suspected that the civilities had a political
motive, and one day Perceval, with a studied casualness, observed, "Sheridan, you never give us a vote now." "Look at
my political life," said Sheridan, "my poverty carries its excuses with it." (That is to say, if he had chosen to go over to the
administration he could long ago have received office and
wealth.)

"After the General Election Sheridan saw the Prince
Regent, who had up to that period invariably treated him
with the most undisguised kindness and cordiality. He mentioned to the Prince the visit of his late Minister, adding
something to the effect that his life was at the service of his
Prince, but his character was the property of his country.
The Prince, with that well-bred suavity of manner which
never deserted him under any hostility of feeling, replied
that Sheridan might impeach his Ministers on the morrow,
and it should not impair their friendship. The Prince then
turned on his heel, and 'we believe from that moment
the Prince and Mr. Sheridan never exchanged another
word.' "[1]

The implication of this anecdote is that the Prince Regent
deserted Sheridan on account of his refusal to support the
Ministry. Apart from Sheridan's supposition that Perceval had
been acting on the Prince Regent's instructions, there is no
evidence that any attempt was made to fetter him. The Prince
Regent himself said that "just before Moira went to India [in

[1]*The Bath Chronicle*, July 18th, 1816.

April 1813] he came to me and said that it was a pity that poor Sheridan at the close of such a life as his has been, should be out of Parliament. I told him that Sheridan's own indolence and indecision, and his being neither on one side nor the other, were the causes of his being thus left out, but that I had always been ready, and was still, to do all that I could to bring him into Parliament; and *that*, without exacting any dependence on me or any allegiance to the Ministers."[1] Moore, however, declared that the Prince Regent "offered to bring him into Parliament, but the thought of returning to that scene of his triumphs and his freedom, with the Royal owner's mark, as it were, upon him, was more than he could bear, and he declined the offer." This statement was promptly answered by *The Westminster Review*, as part of its exoneration of the Prince Regent from the charges brought against him of treating Sheridan with harshness and ingratitude. It asserted:

"The truth then is, that the Prince Regent did not merely offer to bring Sheridan into Parliament, but about the latter end of 1812, with a view to this object, his Royal Highness conveyed to him, through Lord Moira, four thousand pounds. The money was deposited by his Lordship with Mr. Cocker, the solicitor, who acted as a friend to Mr. Sheridan on this occasion, and a treaty was opened with Mr. Attersol for a seat for Wootton Basset.

"The negociation, indeed, was all but concluded, nothing being wanting but Sheridan's presence on the spot. On three successive evenings Mr. Cocker dined with Sheridan at a hotel in Albemarle-street, a chaise being on each night waiting at the door to convey them down to Wootton Basset; on each night Sheridan, after his wine, postponed the journey to the next day, and on the fourth day he altogether abandoned the project of purchasing a seat in Parliament, received the four thousand pounds, and applied them, as he was warranted to do by the permission of the donor, to his private uses. This transaction certainly delivers the King

[1] *The Croker Papers*, I, 305–6.

from the reproach of never having ministered to the relief of Sheridan—a charge which has been urged against His Majesty in numberless smart satires and lampoons."[1]

Sheridan's son Charles was greatly disturbed by this account, and enquired as to its truth from Moore, who replied that he was convinced that it was an imposture as to the main fact of the Prince's giving four thousand pounds to Sheridan; Lord Holland, he said, had told him that Sheridan would never enter Parliament for a seat purchased by the Prince, yet he would be most happy if the Prince would lend him the four thousand pounds to enable him to purchase a seat for himself, "for then," (said he)"I shall only owe the Prince one thousand pounds." Moore concluded:

"This anecdote, coupled with the certainty that there was no more important or urgent use to which your father would have been impatient to devote such a sum (if he had it) than that of placing himself in Parliament, satisfies me that the *sequel* of this story, which is the only part of it that is new, is *not* true."[2]

These were not, as it has been invariably assumed, Moore's last words upon the subject. In 1827, in the preface to the Fifth Edition of his *Life of Sheridan*, he began by repeating them in substance, while protesting that he did so "not from any doubt of the disposition of the Illustrious Person in question to perform such an act of kindness to Sheridan." Having denied the version in *The Westminster Review*, he was compelled to add a postscript which admitted his conviction, on further evidence, that "the Royal Personage did actually bestow this gift, yet, through the fault of the agent to whom the money was entrusted, Sheridan never received it." It was transmitted, he asserted, through the hands of Lord Hastings, to "Mr. Cockrell, an attorney," who professed to be able to secure the

[1] *Sheridaniana*, 225–6.

[2] Sichel, II, 372. What Sheridan may have meant by "only owing the Prince one thousand pounds" is beyond surmise. Moore's letter to Charles Sheridan was written in January, 1826.

seat. When Sheridan declined to accept a seat on such terms, "the Prince generously ordered that the money intended for the purchase should be given to him," but it was detained "under unwarrantable pretences" by the attorney.

This admission, demolished the whole of Moore's previous assumptions: it was disingenuous, for Moore knew that the other party in the case was not a "Mr. Cockrell, an attorney" but John Cocker, of Cocker and Fonblanque. It was incomplete, because it disregarded Sheridan's delay of three days after the money had been paid over to his agent before he "declined the seat" which he had solicited. It was reluctant, because it professed that Moore's "own original impression and the statement opposed to it," were "in some degree, reconciled;" whereas the whole intention of his attack had been to show that in 1812 the Prince Regent, without cause, abandoned Sheridan. But disingenuous and incomplete and reluctant though it was, it proved beyond all doubt that the Prince Regent provided the money for the purchase of a seat, and it was put to other uses. It vindicated him from the charge of behaving ungenerously to Sheridan after his failure at Stafford.

4

The account in *The Westminster Review*, however, was not nearly so conclusive as the account which King George the Fourth dictated to John Wilson Croker, on November 26th, 1825, when he was astonished at the malice of Moore's *Life of Sheridan*. This left no doubt as to the private reason for Sheridan's alienation from the Prince Regent. In its essentials, it agrees with the story as told by *The Westminster Review*, but in details it is more explicit. The King told Croker that Sheridan had found a young gentleman who had bought a seat with the right of vacating it for another, which could be purchased for £3,000. Lord Moira held this sum as trustee for Mac-Mahon, and it was guaranteed by the Prince Regent, and deposited with Cocker. Sheridan was supposed to be going to Wiltshire, but three days later, when the Prince was riding in Oxford Street, he thought he saw him at a distance, and began to make enquiries. When he discovered that Sheridan had not left London, he sent MacMahon to ask for the money to be returned. Cocker answered that "the question of a seat in Parliament was quite new to him; that Sheridan, when he desired him to receive the money, had not hinted at such an object; that it had been paid him on Sheridan's account; and that he had disposed of it according to Sheridan's directions, viz., to pay certain pressing debts, and partly a debt to himself, [Cocker] which he was obliged to press Sheridan for, and which Sheridan had directed him to take out of the sum he held." Sheridan, on being asked for an explanation, told MacMahon that he had resolved not to accept the seat, as Whitbread had paid him a debt of £2,000 that was owing to him, on condition that he did not enter Parliament, but that the money would not be refunded, as Cocker had chosen to apply it to his own debts.[1]

The Prince said that the mutual recriminations of Sheridan and Cocker were like those of Peachum and Locket in *The Beggar's Opera*.

There is no question as to the period of these events, for the Earl of Moira, who had been appointed Governor-General of Bengal, sailed from Portsmouth to Calcutta on April 14th, 1813. After that date, at the very latest, Sheridan neither saw nor wrote to the Prince Regent, nor did he make any attempt to explain his relations with Whitbread. Of his own accord he ceased to attend Carlton House, though the Prince gave no orders for his exclusion, yet he felt quite naturally that he had been swindled out of £3,000. Since the money had been appropriated to the payment of Sheridan's debts, he made no attempt to recover it. The Prince Regent, Lord Moira, and Colonel MacMahon kept to themselves the facts which reflected upon Sheridan, and no hint of the truth reached the leaders of the Whig Party, for Lord Holland told Moore that he had never been able to understand the Prince's mysterious "desertion" of Sheridan, as "he seemed to be really attached to him."

Indeed, but for the virulent attack in Moore's *Life*, no

[1] *The Croker Papers*, I, 306–9.

explanation would have been made public, and the King, in placing the true facts before Croker, must have instructed him to place Sheridan's conduct in the least unfavourable light while exonerating the Prince. It was only the publication of the original account in 1885 that solved the mystery of the Prince Regent's "desertion" of Sheridan.

As the Prince's investigations must have been made through Colonel MacMahon, there may have been some slight confusion over Whitbread's share in the negotiations. The reason for Sheridan's strange conduct is not however beyond reasonable deduction. He vacillated over accepting a seat which would place him in the same position as he had been in while sitting for Ilchester. He was pledged to Catholic Emancipation, and voting against any administration which did not introduce such a measure, and he felt that this position was inconsistent with holding a seat purchased by the Prince Regent. His conduct, though vacillating, would have been entirely honourable if it had not been for his failure to give proper instructions to Cocker over the purpose and disposal of the money. He may be acquitted of intentional dishonesty, but not of culpable negligence. But the price of his devotion to Catholic Emancipation was the forfeit of a seat in Parliament, with its privilege of immunity from arrest for debt, which he had enjoyed over thirty years.

The Death of Sheridan

I

IN August 1813 the blow which Sheridan had so long feared fell upon him. He was arrested for debt and taken to a spunging-house in Cursitor Street, Chancery Lane. He wrote an angry letter to Whitbread:

"Whitbread, putting all false professions of friendship and feeling out of the question, you have no right to keep me here!—for it is in truth *your* act—if you had not forcibly withheld from me the *twelve thousand pounds*, in consequence of a threatening letter from a miserable swindler, whose claim you in particular knew to *be a lie*, I should at least have been out of the reach of *this* state of miserable insult—for that, and that only lost me my seat in Parliament. And I assert that you cannot find a lawyer in the land, that is not either a natural-born fool or a corrupted scoundrel, who will not declare that your conduct in this respect was neither warrantable or legal—but let that pass *for the present*."

Whitbread was acting on behalf of the committee who were, under Act of Parliament, responsible for paying the creditors and proprietors of the old Drury Lane Theatre. He was about to discharge the claims, including Sheridan's, when John Taylor of the King's Theatre lodged a claim for over £20,000, threatening to file a bill in Chancery to prevent the distribution of funds until his account was discharged. Whitbread was advised by counsel not to pay the proprietors until it had been disposed of, for in the event of it proving genuine, it would fall to his own liability if he made any payment to Sheridan. It was

subsequently ascertained that the claim was impudent and unfounded, and the proprietors, including Sheridan, were accordingly paid.

Moore declared that arrangements for his release from the
spunging-house were made by Whitbread, but *The Quarterly
Review*, in an article written by Lockhart, asserted that his
liberation was effected by the interposition of the Prince
Regent.[1] It is curious that in 1825 he told Croker he gave
Sheridan one thousand pounds on the day of his bankruptcy,
which may refer to some arrest for debt. Moore dated the letter
"1814" on circumstantial evidence, for he said that although
Sheridan afterwards wept at "the profanation of his person,"
Whitbread on his visit to the spunging-house found that he was
"confidently calculating," in the sanguineness of his disposition, "on the representation of Westminster, the proceedings
about Lord Cochrane then promising a vacancy." This would
fix the date of the imprisonment as several months later, for in
February 1814, Lord Cochrane, who had defeated Sheridan in
the General Election of 1807, was convicted of complicity in a
fraud upon the Stock Exchange, of which he was certainly
guiltless, and which he had actually exposed. He was, however,
expelled from the House of Commons on July 5th, 1814. On
that day Sheridan was confident of being elected in his place,
and he had the strong support of the Duke of Norfolk, to
whom he wrote:

"Saville Row,
"Tuesday, July 5th.
"My Dearest Lord,
"On the subject of the Westminster Election I was
compelled to make my decision before I had an opportunity
of again consulting your Grace.—The messages I have re-
cieved from you, the words which you have utter'd in my
behalf, in short your whole conduct in this business, impress
on my mind the deepest sense of unalterable gratitude.—
This crisis and last effort in the winding up of my political

[1] Moore, 5th Ed., xvii.

exertions and perhap's the last gratification remaining to my public or even private Feelings.—I feel very sanguine of success but I protest I think I shall owe that success principally if not solely to *you*.

"Your Grace's

"ever most faithfully,

"R. B. Sheridan.

"His Grace the Duke of Norfolk.

"I will wait on you tomorrow if returned to Town."[1]

Eventually, however, he declined to oppose Lord Cochrane, and in a letter to the High Bailiff of Westminster he wrote for publication "Never will I accept a seat in the House of Commons but on the sole condition of being master of my own vote and voice, the servant of my own conscience."[2]

Lord Cochrane was, however, returned without opposition, as a declaration that the electors believed him to be entirely innocent. Sheridan's retirement appears to have been determined as much by discretion as by magnanimity.

2

In the summer of 1815, he stayed for a few days at Leatherhead, taking with him his nephew Nathaniel Ogle, who wrote Moore that "during the few days we remained there, he rose early, and, after breakfast, proceeded in his barouche to his estate, over a portion of which he walked each day, making minute inquiries relating to his affairs, over which he seemed very anxious."

The estate was Polesden, which Sheridan visited from time to time from Leatherhead, although the house was no longer in his occupation. It was in that neighbourhood that the Prince Regent saw him for the last time on August 17th, 1815, but Sheridan, no doubt visiting one of his farms turned aside into a lane. The Prince was returning from Oatlands, the seat of his brother the Duke of York, whose birthday he had just been

<hr>

[1] Norfolk MSS., Catholic Record Society.   [2] Rae, II, 233.

celebrating. He appears to have made enquiries, for he told Croker that Sheridan "now took to live in a very low and obscure way, and all he looked for in the company he kept was brandy and water. He lived a good deal with some low acquaintance—a harness-maker, I forget his name, but he had a house near Leatherhead."

Sheridan's former associates were by no means so devoid of generosity. He was indebted to the bounty of friends, for about this time the Duke of Bedford, who in 1811 had very generously relinquished all claims for arrears of rent due to him from the proprietors of Drury Lane, lent him £200; George Canning also lent him £100. Lord Wellesley lent him the house in Savile Row. Of course they knew that such loans were in fact gifts. His salary as Receiver-General of the Duchy of Cornwall still continued, except for the audit, and he was appointed a Commissioner of Assessionable Manors for the Duchy in 1815, though his duties at the Courts in Cornwall were probably discharged by deputy.

At some period previous to this, Tom Sheridan had been appointed Treasurer to the Cape of Good Hope, where it was hoped that the climate would enable him to regain his health. He was already in a "decline," having inherited consumption from his mother. Before his departure Sheridan took Tom and his wife to a private performance at the Priory, the seat of the Marquis of Abercorn, writing to Mrs. Sheridan:

"They played *The Rivals* really extremely well indeed. Lady Cahir very good and a Mrs. Haseltine, a great Priory personage, and a very pretty woman, admirable . . . I don't know when I have sat out a play before; it made me very nervous. I don't mean the writing or sentiments of the play, but the recollection of the days when, just twenty-one I wrote it, many years before I knew some *dear friends*! who sat on the bench with me, or their world or their system."[1]

[1]Rae, II, 225. There is some uncertainty as to when Tom Sheridan went to the Cape of Good Hope. Rae says vaguely (II, 286) that it was "not many years before Sheridan's death." Tom was at Cadiz in June 1812 (Rae, II, 260). He appears to have been in England for the production of his own play *The Russian* (May 1813).

In the autumn of 1815, after the death of Samuel Whitbread, there were changes in the direction of Drury Lane, Thomas Dibdin and Rae being appointed joint acting-managers, and at the very beginning of the season—on September 14th—they revived *The Duenna*, with Cooke as Don Carlos. One of the first notes Dibdin received was:

"DEAR SIR,

"This is the first application I make to your new Directory: I am very earnest in urging it: it is in favour of Robert Fairbrother an old and true servant to me and the theatre, though latterly discountenanced. I will pledge my life for his zeal, integrity, and ability in whatever he may be employed. What the line is in which he may be made most useful, Mr. Ward is most competent to explain. I say nothing of his large family, many of whom are qualified to give fair assistance at the theatre. I have only to add that your kind attention to this will oblige me more than I can express.
"Yours,
"R. B. SHERIDAN."[1]

Fairbrother was permitted by the committee to reside in the house in Drury Lane which was formerly the treasury of the old theatre, and it was there that Michael Kelly saw him for the last time, when they sat chatting till four in the morning.

Whitbread's death changed Sheridan's attitude towards the theatre, which, although it had been three years built, he had never entered. But one of the committee, his old friend the Earl of Essex—the Lord Maldon of forty years before—persuaded him to dine with him, and visit the scenes from which he had so long absented himself, in order to see Edmund Kean. Between the acts, he was missing from the box, and Lord Essex, who feared that he had left the house, was delighted to find that he was seated in the Greenroom, where he was cordially welcomed by the players, who all joined in drinking a bumper to his health, and in the wish that he would often appear among them. He was exhilarated by his reception, and

---

[1] *The Reminiscences of Thomas Dibdin* (1827), II, 84.

as he parted from Lord Essex that night in Savile Row, he declared in triumph that the world would soon hear of him again, for the Duke of Norfolk had promised to find him a seat in Parliament.[1]

It muſt therefore have been within a day or so that he wrote to his wife that his friend

"the Duke of Norfolk is I fear in a very bad way, indeed, likely to die. He had juſt settled a plan to give me a seat without expense, and he is the only one I would accept one from, because he knows my condition of being my own absolute maſter, and in politics no difference exiſted between us."[2]

The Duke of Norfolk died on December 16th, and was succeeded by his third cousin. Sheridan recalled that at Dibden, a quarter of a century before, he had left certain papers of which the Duke had taken charge, and he wrote to his executor and relation, Thomas Howard of Corby Caſtle:

"Saville Row,
"Monday, Jany. 22, 1816.

"My Dear Sir,
"I sincerely condole with you on the death of our noble friend!—After an indisposition which had confined me for more than six weeks I went out for the firſt time on Saturday when I did myself the pleasure of calling on you. the particular subjeꝗt I wish'd to mention relates to some private papers and MSS of mine which I left in the Dukes care ever since he lent me his house at Dibden and I know he preserved them safely for me—having the honor only of a slieght aquaintance with the present Duke I take the liberty of applying to you and I will take my chance again of finding

---

[1]Moore. The date of this visit might perhaps be fixed with precision. Lord Essex was absent from London in the early part of the season, and Thomas Dibdin sent him a regular "Journal." He was at his seat at Cassiobury as late as 12th November. (*Reminiscences*, Dibdin, II, 74.)

[2]Rae, II, 231–2.

you at home in the course of the morning or I will attend
any appointment convenient to you—

"Yours truly

"R. B. SHERIDAN."[1]

Among the documents which he duly recovered was his
speech in Westminster Hall, which he read after five-and-
twenty years with a melancholy pride. It happens that he was
visited by John Graham, who, in a volume of Sheridan's
Speeches, wrote against the speech of June 31st, 1788, a note
which needs no comment:

"While reading one of the 12 Quarto volumes containing
this Speech about 6 weeks previous to his decease, he said
to me taking a few steps across the Drawing room in Saville
Row—'There are certain periods of a Man's life when the
horizon looks clear and beautiful, and the grass beneath him
assumes a brighter green: at such a time I made use of five
words which I will show you.' Then, turning to the last
volume, he put his finger to the concluding sentence, 'My
Lords, I have done.' J.G."

3

This conversation was, according to Graham's dating, about
the middle of June, but it was probably earlier. Three months
before, Sheridan had been compelled to cancel his promise to
attend the dinner of the Society of St. Patrick on March 17th.
The Duke of Kent, as President, sent him an affectionate
letter.

"Kensington Palace,
"March 27, 1816.

"MY DEAR SHERIDAN,

"I have been so hurried ever since St. Patrick's day, as to
be unable earlier to thank you for your kind letter, which I
received while presiding at the festive board; but I can
assure you, I was not unmindful of it *then*, but announced the

[1] Norfolk MSS., Catholic Record Society.

afflicting cause of your absence to the company, who expressed, in a manner that could not be *misunderstood*, their continued affection for the writer of it. It now only remains for me to assure you, that I appreciate as I ought the sentiments it contains for me, and which will ever be most cordially returned by him, who is with the most friendly regard, my dear Sheridan,

"Yours faithfully,

"EDWARD."[1]

Writs and executions, however, came to Savile Row in rapid succession, and bailiffs entered into possession. About the beginning of May, Samuel Rogers, who had visited him in his illness, took Lord Holland to see him, and they promised their assistance. On Wednesday, May 15th, Rogers received this affecting note:

"Saville-Row.

"I find things settled so that £150 will remove all difficulty. I am absolutely undone and broken-hearted. I shall negotiate for the Plays successfully in the course of a week, when all shall be returned. I have desired Fairbrother to get back the Gurarantee for thirty. They are going to put the carpets out of window, and break into Mrs. S.'s room and *take me*—for God's sake let me see you.

"R.B.S."[2]

The next morning, Moore took a draft for £150 from Rogers to Sheridan, who was sanguine of receiving a large price for the publication of his plays. But this relief was only temporary; as he lay in his bed, a sheriff's officer arrested him, and, after staying in the house for some days, was about to carry him in his blankets to a spunging-house, when his friend and physician Dr. Bain interfered. He told the bailiff that such a step would be fatal, and in that case he would institute a prosecution against him for murder. While this removal was averted, the sheriff's officer remained in possession until Sheridan's death.

[1]Moore, 690-91.   [2]Moore, 692-3.

Two or three days before he died, Mrs. Sheridan summoned her friend, Dr. Howley, the Bishop of London, to pray for him, and he journeyed instantly from Oxfordshire. William Smyth, who had heard that Sheridan was dangerously ill, was told this from Mrs. Sheridan, when he called at the house in Savile Row. "Nothing," he said, "could be more deplorable than the appearance of every thing, wherever I turned my eyes. There were strange-looking people in the hall"—the bailiffs. "The parlour seemed dismantled into which I was shewn. On the table lay a bit of paper, thrown carelessly and neglected: I took it up and it was a prescription—if I recollect, from Sir Henry Halford—but it was only, I saw, a strong cordial." Mrs. Sheridan was displaying a "dignity and calmness that I had not expected from her," and had "evidently become inured to the calamities, not to say horrors, of her situation."[1]

It may have been known that Sheridan had bailiffs in the house for that was no new experience; but it was not known outside that he was enduring privations. Lord Holland and Rogers can hardly have suspected the state of affairs, for two months elapsed between their visit and his death. John Taylor Vaughan, however, chanced to hear a distressing account of the poverty and distress in which Sheridan lay dying, and his compassion was so strongly excited that he went to Carlton House. He saw Colonel MacMahon, who went instantly to the apartments of the Prince Regent and told him, that Sheridan and his wife were both dying, "with hardly a servant left" in the house. The Prince, however, was deeply moved and greatly shocked, and at once empowered Vaughan to place £500 at the disposal of Sheridan's family as a present relief.

MacMahon gave this authority to Vaughan, who said that so large a sum was unnecessary, and could only be prevailed upon to take £200, promising to ask for the remainder when it was wanted.   He left a draft at Dr. Bain's house, with a letter saying that he was "a mere agent," but that a friend of his, hearing of Sheridan's "forlorn situation, and that he has neither money nor credit for a few comforts, has employed me

[1] Smyth, 67–8.

to convey a small sum for his use," though he suggested that it was not intended for "the purpose of satisfying troublesome people." When he saw Dr. Bain on the next day, Vaughan told him that he was authorized to provide a sum of £200.

The proposition said Moore, "being submitted to Mrs. Sheridan, that lady, after consulting some of her relatives returned for answer that, as there was a sufficiency of means to provide all that was necessary for her husband's comfort as well as her own, she begged leave to decline the offer." Moore added a scathing comment that while Vaughan always declared that "this donation, thus meant to be doled out came from a Royal hand," he denied utterly that "so scanty and reluctant a benefaction" was "the sole mark of attention accorded by a gracious Prince and Master" to the death-bed wants of an accomplished and faithful servant. He said this, in spite of the fact that Vaughan had assured him that the Prince Regent was the donor, and that "a further supply was intended."

4

King George the Fourth read this calumny with great indignation, and on November 19th, 1825, *The New Times*, probably on the information of Colonel MacMahon, denied it, saying that part of the sum was applied to furnish Sheridan with all that could contribute to his comfort,

"Shortly afterwards, however, Mr. Vaughan again repaired to Carlton House, and to the amazement of Colonel MacMahon, returned to him the whole of the money that had been paid out of the Prince's privy purse, stating that Mr. Sheridan's friends had insisted on restoring it to the donor, as they were not willing that, under the circumstances, Mr. Sheridan should lay himself under obligations to the Prince Regent."[1]

Sheridan himself was not consulted in the matter, and he must therefore have died in ignorance of the Prince Regent's kindness. It was denied by his family that Sheridan was ever in

[1]*Sheridaniana*, 247.

such poverty, but it seems to be more likely that Mrs. Sheridan's relations, who were in ignorance of the cause of Sheridan's alienation from the Prince, were roused to a sense of their responsibilities by this offer. Perhaps the most curious aspect of the story is one which has entirely escaped comment. While the Sheridans were in debt, the trustees of Mrs. Sheridan's estate, among them Earl Grey, were administering a considerable estate, for when she died twelve months after her husband, it amounted to £40,000, including the estate at Polesden all of which passed to their son, Charles Brinsley Sheridan. No doubt the provisions of the trust, in extremity, might have been varied by legal process, at least so far as to provide for necessities. But in any case, Moore's indignation against the Prince Regent, which has become incorporated in the Sheridan legend, was unjustified and unjust.

Moore was indignant with the Whigs as well as with the Prince Regent. Lord Holland, however, explained that it was useless to give a sum which would secure a temporary immunity, to be followed immediately by another execution. He considered that Moore's castigation was entirely unmerited. "I *whom he almost inaccurately exempts from his censure*, am bound to say that it is unjust. To my knowledge, some aid of that nature was offered, and more was possibly accepted than the biographer relates, or than his benefactors ever wished to have recorded."[1]

Moore believed that Lord Holland insisted upon taking his share of Rogers' benevolence, but the Prince Regent commented that all that went from Holland House was "some ice and currant water," which he dismissed, not unjustly, as "an odd contribution."

5

About the middle of June, Moore added, an article appeared in *The Morning Post*, supposed to have been written by Sheridan's old opponent, Denis O'Brien, which exposed his desolate

[1] *Holland*, Further Memoirs, 237.

situation, and was full of indignation against those who had deserted him.

"Oh, delay not," it said, "delay not to draw aside the curtain within which that proud spirit hides its sufferings." "Prefer ministering in the chamber of sickness to mustering at 'the splendid sorrows that adorn the hearse.' I say, Life and Succour against a Westminster Abbey and a Funeral."

This article created consternation, and among the callers was Michael Kelly, who commented that "it was malignantly and industriously circulated through the kingdom that in his latter moments, he was in want of the common necessities of life, and that when he called for a lemon, when exhausted with thirst, there was no money in the house to buy one." Kelly, however, had sent for Sheridan's man-servant a few days before his death, and entreated him to say if his master was in want of any comforts, and offered that anything his means could afford should furnish him. He was told that Sheridan wanted for nothing, and the tales were the falsest of calumnies.

Similarly, Charles Sheridan wrote to his brother Tom, "You will be soothed by learning that our father's death was unaccompanied by suffering, and that the reports which you may have seen in the newspapers of the privations and the want of comforts which he endured are unfounded; he had every attention and comfort that could make a death-bed easy."[1]

Kelly declared that the reports were "fabricated for the most atrocious purposes of scandal"—that is, no doubt, for reasons of party and faction. Allowing for exaggeration in the account which was transmitted to the Prince Regent, there must have been a time when Sheridan was suffering the consequences of abject poverty, although the appearance of O'Brien's article must have been belated. But the death-bed arrest, which was testified by Dr. Bain, was no fabrication, though Sheridan was otherwise quite accustomed to the presence of bailiffs in possession, and executions had no more terrors for him than they had for Charles Surface. When a bailiff was in possession at

[1] Rae, II, 286.

Lord Byron's, he assured him: "But, my Lord, I have been in Mr. Sheridan's twelve month at a time—a civil gentleman—knows how to deal with us."

O'Brien's article, says Moore, "produced a strong and general sensation," and it was the first intimation to most of his former friends that his illness was serious, and his distress extreme. Among the numerous enquirers who hastened to the house was the Duke of York. "But it was now too late—the spirit that these unavailing tributes might once have comforted was now losing fast the consciousness of anything earthly but pain."[1]

On July 7th, he died.

6

Although he was buried in Westminster Abbey the obsequies of Sheridan were conducted with the simplicity that he himself had often desired. His body was taken to Peter Moore's house in Great George Street, Westminster, so that it could be followed to the Abbey on foot, without the customary long procession of coaches, draped in black, led by footmen in mourning, and drawn by horses with waving plumes. The mourners, though they were dressed in black, did not display the conventional additions of the period, the full-length mourning cloaks, the long scarves, the hat-bands. Seldom, said Moore sarcastically, "has there been seen such an array of rank as graced this funeral." The mourners, however, among whom were many of his alienated friends, "were expressly written to, and requested to attend, by Mrs. Sheridan," which converts "what otherwise might appear to be mere selfish ostentation into an act of kindness and propriety."[2]

At Charles Fox's funeral, none of the Princes had been present, and it was explained, in a communication which appears to have emanated from Carlton House, that their appearance "at a private funeral was prohibited by the imperious rules of Court etiquette." Sheridan's obsequies were not

---

[1]Moore, 696–97.   [2]*The Edinburgh Review*, quoted by Moore, 5th Ed., xix.

"public," which meant conducted by direction of Parliament at the expense of the Realm, but nevertheless, the Duke of York and the Duke of Sussex attended—of course with the Prince Regent's sanction. The Duke of Sussex arrived at Peter Moore's very early, and refused to allow an apartment to be opened expressly for him as etiquette demanded, but waited upon the stairs. The pall-bearers were the Duke of Bedford, the Earl of Lauderdale, Earl Mulgrave, Earl Spencer, the Lord Bishop of London, and Lord Holland. The chief mourner was Charles Brinsley Sheridan, who was followed by others who were connected with Sheridan by marriage; William Linley, Charles Ward, Henry Ogle, Sir Charles Asgill, and the Hon. Edward Bouverie. Among other mourners, following, of course, in their order of precedence, were the Princes, the Lord Chamberlain (the Earl of Yarmouth),[1] the Earl of Bessborough, the Earl of Thanet, the Duke of Argyle, Lord George Cavendish, Lord Robert Spencer, Viscount Sidmouth, Lord Erskine, George Canning, and in the train of this phalanx walking humbly, side by side, "the only two men" says Moore, "who had not waited the call of vanity to display itself—Dr. Bain and Mr. Rogers."

He was buried in Poet's Corner, "opposite the monument of his old friend and companion Dr. Goldsmith, and between Handel and Johnson, with Cumberland by his side." Garrick, too, lies close, but Lord Thanet told Moore that Sheridan, "at no part of his life, liked any allusion to his being a dramatic author, and if he could have spoken out when they were burying him, he would have protested loudly against the place where they had laid him, as Poet's Corner was his aversion; he would have liked to be placed near Fox."[2]

---

[1] It is nonsense to say the Prince Regent had no representative. The Lord Chamberlain could attend only in that capacity.

[2] Moore, *Journal*, III, 233.

PART II
APPENDICES AND BIBLIOGRAPHY

APPENDIX THE FIRST
The Duchy of Cornwall

IN 1804 the Prince of Wales appointed Sheridan as Receiver-General of the Duchy of Cornwall, and he held that place, except for an intermission of one year, until his death. The original appointment was attended with certain complications, and the transactions are exhibited as an instance of the Prince's "heartlessness and ingratitude." But he is entirely exonerated from such charges by the remorseless evidence of letters patent and documents in the archives of the Duchy of Cornwall. These have been consulted by permission of H.R.H. the Prince of Wales, and the facts supplied by Sir Walter Peacock, Counsellor of the Duchy.

The accepted summary is that of Mr. Walter Sichel. He instances the affair not only as evidence of the Prince's heartlessness, but also as evidence of "the extremes to which Sheridan pushed his infatuation" when he "was drawn to follow one whom even treachery could not trust most of the journey down his long descent to limbo." Such is the rhetoric: but here are the "facts" by which it is inspired. (i) "In 1805 the Prince conferred upon him the Receivership." (ii) "A post that in good years brought an income of over £900." (iii) For years its benefit was deferred, since "it afterwards transpired that Lord Lake had been promised a reversion of the post, and until his death in 1808, Sheridan surrendered the income." (iv) Moreover "he could only have been appointed Lake's deputy by the Privy Council and obstacles were raised." (v) Sheridan's letters of 1808 to the Prince's secretary, MacMahon, including one for transmission to Lord Lake shortly before his death, show that Sheridan's one object was to shield the Prince from a public misconception of faithlessness; "In one of his letters to his wife he told her on no account to 'suspect or decry' the paragon, who was 'acting as honourably as man can do,' and reposing in Sheridan 'his entire and unqualified confidence.' "[1]

From beginning to end there is hardly a correct statement:

(i) The appointment was made not in 1805, but early in 1804. The Prince notified Sheridan of his intentions on February 20th, 1804, and conferred on him the office "during pleasure" (that is, as revocable by the Prince) by letters patent of March 6th. (ii) Creevey gives the income as about £1,200, with an additional £1,300 in one year; the accounts give the average as about £1,400; the Deputy who performed the duties in the Stannary Courts received fees. (iii) Except during the eleven months when Lord Lake was in office, the income was paid to Sheridan, and there is no evidence that Sheridan made to him any payment whatsoever, which would have nullified the Prince's grant. (iv) The Privy Council had no concern with the appointment, which was solely at the discretion of the Prince, and the obstacles raised were when Warwick Lake claimed the right under power of attorney to act as Deputy for his brother. But certain duties, especially those as Auditor, could only be executed in person by the Receiver-General, and the remainder could be performed only by deputy of the principal in possession after being sworn into office before the Prince's Council. There was never any question of appointing Sheridan as Deputy to Lake. (v) Sheridan's letter to Colonel MacMahon was not written in 1808; not only was Lord Lake in office in March 1807, but the correspondence belongs to February 1804. The letter supposedly written to Lord Lake "shortly before his death" in February 1808 was, moreover, the "Authentic Statement" prepared by the Prince's commands three years before and being addressed to General Lake in India could not have omitted his title after he was made a Peer in September 1804. Sheridan's letter to his wife (Rae, II, 273) refers to some question of Spencer Perceval's relations with the Prince Regent, and therefore is of a much later period, and has no relation to the Duchy.

The records of the Duchy, transmitted by Sir Walter Peacock are:

[1]Sichel, I, 111; II, 319–20, & 364.

1. Date of Sheridan's appointment as Receiver-General of the Duchy of Cornwall.

The following shows the succession of Receivers-General with dates of Letters Patent:

Edward Eliot, Esq., (later Baron Eliot of St. Germans): L.P. 13 May, 1749, by Prince; do 26 June, 1751, by the King; do 23 March, 1761, by the King; died 17 Feb., 1804.

[*Major General Gerard Lake* (first Viscount Lake); L.P. 5 Aug., 1795, during good behaviour, in reversion of Eliot.]

Richard Brinsley Sheridan: L.P. 6 March, 1804, during pleasure.

Major-General Gerard Lake as above; L.P. 12 March, 1807, for life: died 21 Feb., 1808.

Richard Gray, Esq., sign manual Warrant dated 1 April, 1808, during pleasure, "until we shall think fit to grant the same by Letters Patent."

Note in "Receiver's View" from 12 Dec., 1807, to 21 Feb., 1808.

"N.B. No Receiver General from 21st day of February (the day of the death of Lord Lake) to 1st April when Mr. Richard Gray was appointed to the Office *pro tempore*, and who continued to hold it till the appointment of Mr. Sheridan on 20th April, 1808."

R. B. Sheridan: L.P. 20 April, 1808, for life: died 7 July, 1816.

2. The Emoluments of Office.

The figure stated to be eight or nine hundred pounds a year seems to be underestimated.

The salary was	£241 a year
Allowance for riding charges	36
Fees for acquittances on rents about	10
Poundage of 6d. on all monies paid, not claimed in every instance; should have averaged in Sheridan's time	715
Fees for coinage of tin about	400
	£1402

The salary was increased to £341 in 1811.

The estimate of the Receiver-General's fees on tin coinage is based on a Report of the Vice-Warden of the Stannaries in 1785. They depended on the number of slabs of tin, etc., particulars of which are not in this Office. But the Vice-Warden estimated the fees to be worth £400 on average after paying inferior officers and labourers.

The Poundage on money received varied from year to year but the following figures may be taken as approximate, a normal sum having been deducted for unpaid claims;

Period.	Receipts. (exclusive of tin coinage)			Estimated Poundage.		
1803/4 & on to 17 Feb.	£15,475	19	7½	£368	10	0
17 Feb. 1804 to Mich. 1804	16,111	13	3	383	10	0
1804/5	22,368	13	10¾	532	10	0
1805/6	20,765	12	7¾	490	0	0
1806/7	24,585	5	0	585	0	0
12 Dec. 1807 to 21 Feb. 1808	5,285	0	7½	125	15	0
1 to 20 Apr. 1808	8,090	11	9½	192	10	0
20 Apr. 1808 to Mich. 1808	11,925	9	8	284	0	0
1808/9	38,762	6	1½	923	0	0
1809/10	91,550	18	5¾	2,180	0	0
1810/1	35,163	2	8¾	837	0	0
1811/2	24,702	0	11	588	0	0
1812/3	28,704	18	2	683	10	0
1813/4	21,158	14	9½	504	1	0
1814/5	26,389	13	8	652	0	0
Mich. 1815 to 7 July, 1816	20,924	16	0¼	500	0	0

(i) A portion was paid to Lord Lake and his representatives for the period 12 March, 1807, to the 21 February, 1808.

There is no means of ascertaining in this Office whether Sheridan paid over a portion of the receipts from the 6th March, 1804.

(ii) Charles Carpenter of Moditonham Esquire was appointed by Sheridan, 8 September, 1809, as Deputy to the Receiver-General of the Duchy, as Weigher and Prizer of Tin in Cornwall and Devon. As such he received from the Duchy fees for attendance on the Assessionable Manors Commissioners and for attendance at the Audit at Liskeard, but he does not seem to have had a salary, but relied on fees for his remuneration.

The Deputy Receiver in London was Thomas Somers Cocks, Esq., Banker, of Charing Cross appointed by Sheridan, 14 March, 1804; by Lake, 17 December, 1807; by Sheridan, 1 May, 1808, and by John McMahon, Esquire, 22 July, 1816. He received no salary from the Duchy.

Sheridan was a Member of The Prince's Council from 6 March, 1804, and an Assessionable Manors Commissioner in 1805, 1808, 1812 and 1815, but there is no record that he ever went to Cornwall to take an active part at the Assession Courts. Carpenter probably took his place.

WALTER PEACOCK

Duchy of Cornwall Office,
*Buckingham Gate, S.W.*1

APPENDIX THE SECOND
Unpublished Documents

R. B. SHERIDAN TO THE EARL OF SURREY.
Norfolk MSS., Catholic Record Society.

[The reference to the Coalition ministry, in which he had been appointed Secretary to the Treasury on April 2nd, confirms what he said in the House of Commons on his attitude to this Government—"The prejudices of the public all concurred to prevent the Coalition. The middle classes of the people, for whom he had the highest respect, and to whom rather than the great the House must look for support in every emergency, were not the best qualified to judge of nice and refined points of politics. He apprehended that, accustomed to judge of measures by men, they would give themselves no time to examine the principles, motives, and grounds of a Coalition, but would condemn it on the first appearance, merely because it was composed of men who had long been political enemies. On these grounds, he most certainly gave his advice against the Coalition." (*Speeches*, i, 67.) Lord Surrey, by his marriage had acquired a political interest in Herefordshire, and John Rolle had apparently proposed a tax on cider which would apparently have affected adversely their staple industry.]

"London.
"April 23rd. [1783]

"MY DEAR LORD
"The Board is strong in numbers at present, so that a stray member is less miss'd—and now nothing is thought of but the Taxes to provide for the unfortunate loan, which gets abused more and more every Day. There is no chance of Cyder I concieve being meddled with, so your L'ship and the Whigs of Hereford may toast the Defeat of Rolles with

safe consciences. I am afraid no talking will make the Coalition a popular measure, we must do something to convince the People that we are not the worse for it.

"Here is no news. Threats to attack the loan again from
day to day, but nothing attempted.

"Ld. Northington goes to Ireland and Wyndham secretary—

"Yours my Dr. Lord,
"most faithfully,
"R. B. Sheridan.

" I am to thank you for your royal present."

Mrs. Sheridan to Richard Peake.

Salt Library MSS.

[The signature as E[lizabeth] L[inley] Sheridan is curious:
"When married, she sometimes wrote 'E. L. Sheridan' but her
ordinary signature was 'E.A.S.' (Rae, I, 122). Sichel doubts
this, having never seen a letter so signed, but Rae is correct.]

"Sir,

"By Mr. Sheridan's desire I beg you will put Mr.
Charles Meyer's name on the free lists of D. L-Theatre, &
that you will have the goodness to make this properly understood that there may be no mistake about it. When you
can conveniently call, I wish very much to speak with you:
any morning at about eleven or at ½ past five in the afternoon,
you will find me at home,

"Yrs very truly
"E. L. Sheridan.

"Saturday."

Endorsed in her own writing:

Mr. Peake, Drury Lane Theatre From Mrs. Sheridan.

Sheridan's Draft of Thomas Linley's Will, 1788.

Salt Library MSS., Stafford.

[This draft is in Sheridan's hand. According to a short summary in Emanuel Green's *Linley, Sheridan and Mathews at*

Bath, it was "dated August 1788 and proved 1st April, 1789 (Harris, 195)." Some slight changes were made; the freehold estate, a farm called Oldbury at Didmarton, near Badminton, probably his father's home and his own birthplace, was left with reversion—failing issue to Ozias—to William Linley, who dying in 1835 bequeathed to his niece Elizabeth Ann Tickell. By the same will, William gave to Dulwich College, where Ozias was Organist Fellow, the family portraits— among them his picture of Mrs. Sheridan and Mrs. Tickell, by Gainsborough. The influence of Sheridan is shown in the precaution against the alienation of the shares in Drury Lane without the consent of the Sheridans, and the other legatees.]

"Mr. Linley's Intention is to divide the whole of his Property *equally* among his Children—Mrs. Tickell's children to stand in the Place of the late Mrs. Tickell—first charging the whole with an annuity of three hundred Pounds per annum to Mrs. Linley—to whom also He leaves the Furniture Plate and articles which may be in the House & he may be living in Town—except the Harpsichord & MSS. to Mrs. Sheridan—and the Picture of Mrs. Sheridan & Mrs. Tickell to Mr. Sheridan & Tom after Mrs. Linley's Death if *she* wishes to keep it.

"His Musick & Musical instruments between Ozias and Wm. Linley.—

"£600 to Tom Sheridan for books 100—to his Daughter Jane Linley & 100 to his grandaughter E. Tickell.

"The Free Hold Estate at Didmarton to go to Ozias Linley—but liable to the annuity to Mrs. Linley.

"If it should be thought best for the Family not to dispose of the Theatrical Property—The Profits after Paying the Interest of the Mortgagees and the annuity to Mrs. Linley (to be divided equally among the Legatees). This Property is to be estimated. Such Portion of the Dividend as it may not be found necessary to apply towards the Reduction of the Principal Debt to the Executor of Mr. Garrick, or to Dr. Ford or his Executor.

"The property in the Theatre to be valued according to the Rate at which it was purchased by Mr. Linley and if at in order anytime the share of any Legatee can be paid to him and her in money. The other Legatee may purchase at that Price—and no Legatee to part with his or her Interest without first offering it to the others (or 2, the Executor to be empowered to pay off the Claims of the Legatee at the Price above mentioned if they please). For there must be no risk of any part of the Property passing into other hands by marriage settlement."

R. B. SHERIDAN TO JOHN BURGESS.

MSS., Messrs. Birrell and Garnet.

[John Burgess was Sheridan's attorney over a long period. These letters refer to the Polesden estate, of which Metcalfe was the agent for Sheridan.]

(i)

"Farnham, Monday.

"DR. B,

"I entreat you to bear uppermost in your mind the 150 guineas for the Rev. S. Blomfield Dunton, Winslow, Bucks —I shall pant the Hour of your transmitting me the receipt for that to Northcourt—Pray write to me constantly as I will to you—I will write by tomorrows Post to D——[?] & Metcalfe.

"I am happier in my own mind for the measures taken & I thank you sincerely for the alacrity and zeal you have shewn in the business.

"Polesden looks most beautiful to-day—thank God the three farms are not in sight of it. I have two teams at work at Polesden itself, & Wood is doing quite right at Yew Trees. Hudson chearfully guarantees Ironmonsons (?) Rent & taxes—but you must advance him 50 for stock—I shall take as little as I can, I dont want the cows—The Lillies are close to the High Beeches. Truly yours

R.B.S."

(ii)

"Monday.

"Dr. B.

"The only resource I can see at this moment for meeting this day's difficulty is your accepting the enclosed which I can get discounted to take up the other but on the sole condition that He is put into the situation of the present holder that is that the *cognovit* shall be made over to him as a new one given—so that you will stand precisely in the situation you do now without a shilling more risk; send me word where the bill is? Mr. Fairbrother is returned from S—[?] who will finish his business tomorrow & be in town on Wednesday morning to meet Mr. Metcalfe & me—you had better be with us. Yours

" R.B.S.

"W.N. will tell you why I don't go out."

(iii)

[There is nothing to indicate the date, but the letter has probably some connection with the appointment as deputy to John Graham 1813.]

"Dear Burgess

"I ought to have been very angry at your addressing me with 'Sir' but let the past be forgot. You ought to have known me better than ever to have doubted for a moment my sincere desire & persevering efforts to serve you whenever I could. After our long & intimate connexion nothing can be so foolish as doubt or complacency on either side, but you often allow your temper to get the better of your reason—however as I said before, let us look to the future, I wish particularly to see you to night. I shall be alone the whole evening. Yours truly

R.B.S."

R. B. Sheridan to Viscount Addington.

MSS., Messrs. Birrell and Garnet.

["Justice Graham," one of the Westminster magistrates, was for some time manager of Drury Lane. When Lord Robert Spencer was to be appointed Lord Lieutenant of Ireland in 1789 he proposed to take as Secretary "Mr. Graham ye lawyer" (Sichel, II, 425)—Duchess of Devonshire's Diary.]

Addressed. Viscount Addington, One of his Majesty's Principal Secretaries of State &c &c. R. B. Sheridan.

Dated. August 13th, 1813.

"My Dear Lord,
"Some time since I took the liberty of recommending to your Protection my friend Mr. Burgess as a person I was particularly anxious to serve . . . my present application tho' still connected with Mr. Graham is of a different character, —it is that your Lordship would allow Mr. Graham to appoint Mr. Burgess, during his illness to be his Deputy—I am confident this would be a very healing indulgence to poor Graham's mind, who has been a very meritous public servant, as it would show that his recovery is not considered beyond hope. And with respect to Mr. Burgess I pledge myself to be responsible for his ability diligence and integrity. . . ."

R. B. Sheridan to Thomas Westley, 1793.

R. Crompton Rhodes' MSS.

[In 1793, when the Drury Lane company were acting at the King's Theatre in the Haymarket, Sheridan gave two nights a week to Italian Opera, under the direction of Michael Kelly and Stephen Storace, and on those nights the theatrical company acted at the Little Theatre in the Haymarket. The opera season began on January 26th with Madame Mara as *prima donna*: Sheridan wrote this note to Thomas Westley, the treasurer of Drury Lane.]

"Dear Sir,

"Mad. Mara must positively be paid have her weekly salary from the beginning of season immediately or the Opera will be finished up—I will see this money returned from the Opera account.

"R. B. Sheridan.

"Her engagement is £1000.
"To Mr. Westley."
Endorsed; 4th Febry, 1793.

R. B. Sheridan to Mrs. Joseph Lefanu, 1812.

Lefanu MSS.

[Mr. T. P. Lefanu, the owner of the MSS., tells me that "Homan" is Frederick Homan, who ran away with the beautiful daughter of Sheridan's first cousin Louisa Dexter. "There is a pamphlet in existence," he adds, "published, unless I am mistaken, without place or date, and entitled 'A Brief Statement of the Services of Frederick Homan, Comptroller of the British Mail, Dublin, and many years Private Secretary and confidential friend of the late Right Hon. R. B. Sheridan'; but I should be disposed to receive this statement with reserve, as the pamphlet may have been written by Homan, and my father, who remembered him, told me that in his old age he was rather inclined to romance about his career." The paper is watermarked 1810, and 1812 is the only year in which July 24th fell on a Friday. Mr. Lefanu thinks the sister was Alicia —Mrs. Joseph Lefanu, Homan wishing to take her a message on returning to Ireland.]

"Friday night
"July 24th.

"My Dearest Sister,

"Homan makes such a point of being the bearer of a line for me to you that I cannot refuse him tho' I am ashamed to say that it can be only a single line to assure you that you shall hear from me in the course of next week, and that in future I shall endeavour to make up for paſt seeming negleƈt,

"Ever your moſt affeƈtionate

"R. B. SHERIDAN."

THE STAFFORD ELECTION, 1812.

Salt Library MSS., Stafford.

[R. Gouldsmith to a gentleman at Stafford. This lampoon may have been intended for publication.]

"DEAR SIR,

"There is a New Work getting ready for publication wh I think will have a rapid Sale—a great Man a Friend of yours is the Hero of the piece & there are some excellent Caricature Likenesses—I have seen an advertisement prepar'd for the papers to announce it to the world. 'Speedily will be publish'd A right Honble Gentleman's Journey to Stafford—with a *Night's Amusement on the Road* & his arrival at the Huſtings in which will be given *Four Caricatures* superiorly sketch'd & Coloured—Viz Solicitude—Hope—Disappointment & Despair, with a discriptive Poem to each in Hudi-braſtic Verse—likewise a Design for the *Gold Cup*, which the *Merry* Sons of Crispin voted him, inſtead of a *Seat* in the New Parliament—to conclude with the Return to Town & an outline Sketch of the reception at Carlton House. A few copies will be printed on extra fine Paper with Proof Impressions of the Plates.'

"I have seen One of the Drawings juſt finished, replete with Humour & Satire—it is beautifully drawn & composed. The Burlesque Poem annexed to it begins thus—

"'See! Sherry slumbering in his Bed
At once to sense & reason dead,
With Pain & pleasure by his side
And Sloth, rejeƈting ev'ry Guide.

Pain, hugging with a Bear's embrace!
And Pleasure tickling ruby Face.'
        etc etc etc.

Pain—Pleasure—& Sloth are personified—the figure of
Pleasure is beautifully drawn—quite allegro & playful, &
the Caricature likeness of the Rt Honble Gentn is admirable.

"There is not a doubt but he lost his Election at Stafford
thro' Negligence—What a sacrifice of Honr & Independence to Sloth & Indolence! But he has behaved so *extremely
ill to me* that I can hardly be sorry for him— he diserves every
disappoint^t he meets with—I have not been able to obtain a
Moment's audience of him these *Eight Months* tho' I think
I had some claims—I've called a Hundred times by Ap-
point^t & never could see him—I consider myself insulted &
very unhandsomely treated. My motive for call'g so often
was to have render'd him a service—Some Friends of mine
are intimately acquainted with some of the lead'g people in
Stafford—& believing me a Friend of the Rt. Honble
Gentleman—informed me of the Estimation he was held in at
Staffd & of the State of the Parties there—I saw the necessity
of some exertion & attention on his part & called to shew
him a Letter or two I had received in July & the begin'g of
August—I suppose I called 50 times but all in vain—I
never could see him or obtain an answer—I told my friend,
how I was treated & beg'd they would use their interest as
they thought proper I should have felt a pleasure in going
down, or doing anything in my power to serve him—had
been treated even decently,
        "I remain
            " Dear Sir
            "Yrs Truly
                "R. GOULDSMITH.
"Nov. 12th, 1812."

"There is a single caricature just ready, but it is not intended to publish till a Day or two before the meet'g of
Parliament, it is entitled *Promises* or *Sherry & Crispin* it is an

excell^t likness. The great Man is seen bareheaded & bare-footed, trundling down to Stafford with his speeches all ready cut & dried—& several laughable Incidents about it —& the following Lines are annex'd

" 'Sherry, to Stafford lately hied,
Stafford! the great St Crispins' pride,
He smooth'd his Face—he went unshod,
No shoes like their's—he swore, By God!
He had the Regent's dread Commands:
Shoes, should be worn on Feet & Hands,
The Court, had held the Fashion meet—
That Men should walk on Hands & Feet.
Give your Votes!—I'll do such things!
Shall make you great—as little Kings!
Crispin—who erst did Britons shield
On Agincourt's most glorious Field!—
Look'd from a Cloud with fierce disdain
And sent him back to Court again.'

"I have heard y^r Friend has got a Borough—I hope 'tis true."

R. B. SHERIDAN TO RICHARD WILSON, 1815.

Salt Library MSS., Stafford.

[Richard Wilson was an old friend of Sheridan's, and went with him to the funeral of Joseph Richardson. The principal actors and officers of Drury Lane were dining at his house on February 24th, 1809, when his younger daughter, afterward Mrs. Montague Bellenden, brought the news that the theatre was in flames (Kelly, 2nd Edition, II, 252).]

"Saville Row.
"Sat. May 27th.

"MY DEAR DOMINE,
"Having been from Town I did not get your note till last Night—I should be most happy to be of your Party to Day —but I have a formal engagement of a fortnights standing to

dine with Lord Essex. You are wrong as to *St. John's* it is *Trinity* Charles goes. Do I read aright in the newspaper that there is a grand-daughter produced at Lincoln's Inn? If so I wish you and Mrs. Wilson joy—why would you not be a fifth in the new direction of old Drury? by the way I wish to see you on matters connected with this subject—I will call in a Day or two

> "ever yours
> "R. B. SHERIDAN."

Addressed; Richard Wilson Esqr
Lincoln's-Inn-Fields.
Endorsed; May 1815.

A LOST PASSAGE IN ST. PATRICK'S DAY, 1775.

MSS. Larpent, Huntingdon Library, California. Transcribed by Mr. F. W. Bateson.

[In *Plays and Poems* (I, 141) I wrote that *St. Patrick's Day*, like so many Benefit Plays, was generally ignored by the Periodical Press; *The Whitehall Evening Post* for May 6th, 1775, however, makes it clear that one scene has been lost, no doubt beyond recovery. It says:

"The recruiting party reappear beating up for recruits; a drunken cobler and a countryman in vain are attempted to be enlisted, the former declaring himself to be perfectly sober, and swearing that his companion has never any courage till he is drunk; if he was made a General, it would cost Government five shillings a day to find him in valour."

This passage, however, is found in the copy submitted for license to the Lord Chamberlain's department, dated April 24th, 1775, and now in the Huntingdon Library.]

Enter a BLACKSMITH, *& an* IRISHMAN, *drunk.*

Serjt. Hah! my fine fellows—Come, now for the honour of St. Patrick—will ye be after serving his Majesty?—and instead of drowsy beer, have Seas of Punch, and Shambrogue Islands, all your lives after.

Irish. Come, Neighbour, what say you?—shall we make a Friend of his Majesty? I feel as if I could handle a Musket.

2d. Man. Taddy you're drunk—but I who am sober know better—sometimes when I'm merry I thinks how I could make a Soldier, but when I'm sober, I knows that I am fit for nothing but a civil employment.

Irishmn. Aye! Neighbour, but I feel bould at all times.

2d. Man. Taddy, you're a Fool, I tell ye, You're brave only when you are drunk: and if you were a General, 'twould cost his Majesty five Shillings a day to keep you in Courage: so, come along—Good liquor and a whole Skin to put it in for ever—

Exeunt IRISHMAN & BLACKSMITH.

JOHN EWART TO R. B. SHERIDAN, 1772.

R. Crompton Rhodes' MSS.

[This letter, formerly in the collection of the late Dr. Selfe Bennett, of London, appears to be a forgery, though no account of Sheridan gives, so far as I know, the name of "Old Ewart" as John. As the date of leaving Bath was Wednesday, March 18th, and that of the great storm was the 23rd, it does not seem likely that Ewart could have hoped that they had a good passage, unless he meant after their disembarkation at Margate. The assumed name of "Harlow" is curious, for in the forged letter from "Miss Linley to Miss Saunders" it is given as "Harley," and it would be interesting to know if some genuine assumed name is echoed in both these letters. "The newspapers" may corroborate this rumour as to the elopement, but none of the several I have seen do.]

"To Mr. Richard Sheridan, To the Care of Mr. Paul Possell, Merchant in Dunkirk.

"London, March 27, 1772.

"MR. SHERIDAN,

"I have pleasure to hear this day by Mr. Havers of your safe Arivall with Miss Harlow at Dunkirk. Inclos'd is

T

severall letters I received from your sister who recommends the speedy delivery to *Miss* as they are of some consequence. I make no doubt of Mr. & Mrs. Possell receiveing you politely, and dare say will serve you as much as is in their power. I forget to mention in the Coppy of the Notes or bills you may draw *to insert (for the use of Miss Harlow)* which you [may pl]ease to do. I hope you have settled miss in the Country agreeable to her inclinations, the news papers say Mr. Sheridan Senr. was gon to Scotland upon a matrimoniall Scheem, others that the young Mr. Sheridan was gon off to France with Miss Linley. I hope you had a good passage & also that the Captain behaved equall to my recommendation. I beg my Compliments to Miss and asure her anything in my power she may freely comand.

"I am Sir your most obedient

"Humble Servant

"John Ewart."

APPENDIX THE THIRD

Sheridan's Eulogium on the Death of Charles Fox 1806

Birmingham Reference Library.

[No edition of this speech has hitherto been recorded, although some sentences from it were given by Watkins—and borrowed by Moore, without acknowledgment.]

DEATH OF MR. FOX.
An
EULOGIUM
on the
RIGHT HONOURABLE C. J. FOX,
Delivered
BY THE HONOURABLE
MR. SHERIDAN
At a meeting convened at the
CROWN AND ANCHOR TAVERN,
On THURSDAY, SEPTEMBER 13th, 1806,
To consider of a proper person to succeed that GREAT MAN,
IN THE REPRESENTATION OF THE
CITY OF WESTMINSTER.
NOTTINGHAM:
PRINTED BY E. B. ROBINSON,
and sold by the booksellers.
1806.
Price Twopence.

A SPEECH, &c.

Gentlemen, Electors of Westminster, in addressing you upon this occasion, I am afraid that before I proceed to the few observations which I feel it my duty to submit to you, I shall be obliged to commence with a request which I am almost ashamed to make—for your indulgence, if in consequence of a short, but sharp indisposition, from which I am just recovering my voice should not be strong enough to be clearly audible to the full extent of this large Assembly. (Applause.) Upon that subject which must fill all your minds—upon the merits of that illustrious man, whose death has occasioned the present meeting I shall, I can say but little. There must be some interval between the heavy blow that has been struck, and the consideration of its effect, before any one (and how many are there of those) who have loved and revered Mr. Fox as I have done, can speak of his death with the feeling but manly composure which becomes the dignified regret it ought to inspire. (Applause.) To you, however, Gentlemen, it cannot be necessary to describe him—for you must have known him well. To say any thing to you at this moment in the first hours of your unburthened sorrow, must be unnecessary and almost insulting. His image is still present before you—his virtue is in your hearts—his loss is your despair, (loud applauses) I have seen in one of the Morning Papers, what are stated to have been the last words of this great man—"I die happy;" then, turning to the dearest object of his affection, "I pity you." But had another moment been allowed him, and had the modesty of his great mind permitted him, well might he have expressed his compassion, not for his private friends only, but for the world—well might he have said "I pity you, I pity England, I pity the human race."—(loud plaudits). For to mankind at large his death must be a scource of regret, whose life was employed to promote their benefit. He died in the spirit of peace struggling to extend it to the world. Tranquil in his own mind he cherished to the last, with a parental solicitude, the consoling hope to give tranquillity to nations. Let us trust that that stroke of death which has borne him from us, may not have left peace, and the dignified charities of human nature, as it were, orphans upon the world. (applause). From this afflicting consideration, I pass to one comparatively insignificant, yet it is the question we are met this day to consider namely, that the pretensions of those who have the presumption to aspire to succeed him. An Honourable Friend has proposed me as a person worthy of that proud distinction. I cannot deny but that it is an object of ambition, unmixed I think with one unworthy motive, very near to my heart. I have received a friendly, though public caution, that I may risk the confidence and attachment of my friends at Stafford by such a pursuit. I thank my monitor for his anxiety on that account, but he may rest assured that I know my constituents better. I have before declined an offer of support for this city upon a general election. My gratitude and devotion to my friends at Stafford binds me to seek no other. I have been six times chosen by them, which is a proof, at least, that when once elected I am not quarrelsome with my constituents. To attend to their wishes must of course be an object of my peculiar solicitude, and to continue to represent them, the favourite pursuit of my ambition, even more, perhaps, than that of Westminster. But it is not inconsistent with that sentiment, nor can it be offensive to the feelings of my constituents that I should have offered myself to your notice upon this occasion. For my constituents must feel that it is one thing to be the representative of Westminster, and another to be the successor of Mr. Fox. That, I own, I cannot but consider as an object of the highest importance, of which, if I were not ambitious, I must be insensible.— (Applause.) Upon the present awful occasion, with such feelings as I know are clinging to your minds, hoping at most to palliate a loss irreparable—yet searching with affectionate diligence how best to do so, to have been the object of your deliberate selection, would, I feel, have been to me an inspiring motive, beyond all ordinary encouragement, to have shewn myself not unworthy of the proud preference you had bestowed upon me. I fear not but that my friends at Stafford would have fully entered into this feeling, and not have considered my elevation by you as a desertion of them. Having thus avowed my ambition, or my presumption, as some have been heard to call it, I have now to speak of my pretentions. Egotism is always offensive, and I am happy that my Learned Friend has left me little or nothing to say on this head. He has stated, and I vow and adopt his statement, that my claim to your favour rests on the fact that I have step by step followed Mr. Fox through the whole course of his political career, and to the best of my poor abilities, supported him in every one of those measures, and in the maintenance of every one of those principles which originally recommended him to, and so long continued him in your confidence and esteem. It is true there have been occasions upon which *I have differed from him*—painful recollection of the most painful moments of my political life! Nor were there wanting those who endeavoured to represent those differences as a departure from the homage which his superior mind, though unclaimed by him, were entitled to, and the allegiance of friendship which our hearts all swore to him: but never was the genuine and confiding texture of his soul more manifest than on such occasions; he knew that nothing on earth could separate or detach me from him; and he resented insinuations against the sincerity and integrity of a friend, which he would not have noticed had they been pointed against himself. With such a man to have battled in the cause of genuine liberty—with such a man to have struggled against inroads of oppression and corruption—with such an example before me, to have to boast that I never in my life gave one vote in Parliament that was not on the side of freedom, is the congratulation that attends the retrospect of my public life. His friendship was the pride and honour of my days. I never, for one moment, regretted to share with him the difficulties, the calumnies, and sometimes even the dangers that attend an honourable course. And now reviewing my past political life, were the opinion possible that I should retread the path, I solemnly and deliberately declare, that I would prefer to pursue the same course—to bear up under the same pressure—to abide by the same principles—and to remain by his side, an exile from power, distinction and emolument, rather than be at this moment, a splendid example of successful servility, or prosperous apostasy—though clothed with power, honours, titles, and gorged with sinecures and wealth obtained from the plunder of the people (a tumult of applause).—Grateful as I am for the manner in which you are pleased to receive my sentiments and espouse my cause, I think it must have been obvious that I have in my mind an eager desire that contest and dissention should be avoided on the occasion of the present vacancy. How is this to be effected but by one of the candidates retiring? A man's pride may be piqued without his mind being induced to swerve from the cause he ought to persevere.— Illiberal warnings have been held out—most unauthoritively I know—that by persevering in the present contest I may risk my official situation: and if I retire, I am aware that minds as coarse and illiberal may assign the dread of that as my motive. To such insinuations I shall scorn to make any other reply than a reference to the whole of my past political life. I consider it as no boast to say, that any one who has struggled through such a portion of life as I have, without acquiring an office, is not likely to abandon his principles to retain one when acquired. To be at all capable of acting upon principle, it is necessary that a man should be independent: and to independence, the next best thing to that of being very rich, is to have been used to be very poor. (loud applause.) Independence, however, is not allied to wealth, to birth, to rank, to power, to titles, or to honours.—Independence is in the mind of man, or it is no where. On this ground were I to decline the contest, I should scorn the imputation that should bring the purity of my purpose into doubt. No minister can expect to find me a servile vassal. No minister can expect from me the abandonment of any principle I have avowed, or any pledge I have given. I know not that I have hitherto shrunk in place from opinion that I have maintained while in opposition. Did there appear a Minister of different cast from any I know existing—were he to attempt to exact from me a different con-

duct, my office should be at his service to-morrow. Such a
Minister might strip me of a situation, in some respect of
considerable emolument—but he could not strip me of the
proud conviction that I was right—he could not strip me of my
own self esteem—he could not strip me, I think, of some portion of the confidence and good opinion of the people.   But I
am noticing the caluminous threat I have alluded to more than
it deserves.   There can be no peril to assert, under the
present Government, in the free exercise of a discretion, such
as belongs to the present question: I therefore disclaim the
merit of putting any thing to hazard. If I have missed the
opportunity of obtaining all the support I might, perhaps, have
had on the present occasion, from a very scrupulous delicacy,
which I think became, and was incumbent upon me, but which
I by no means conceive to have been a fit rule for others, I
cannot repent it. While the slightest asperation of breath remained on those lips, so often the channel of eloquence and
virtue—while one drop of life's blood beat in that noble heart,
which is now no more, I would not suffer any friend of mine,
in anticipation of the melancholy event that has occurred, to
institute a canvass. I could not, I ought not to have acted
otherwise than I have done. Now, Gentlemen, I come, with a
very embarrassed feeling, to that declaration which I yet
think you must have expected from me, but which I make
with reluctance, because, from the marked approbation I have
experienced from, I fear with reluctance you will receive it.
I feel myself under the necessity of retiring from this contest. (Here
Mr. Sheridan was interrupted for many minutes by loud cries
of No, no, no.) I beseech you, resumed the Right Hon. Gentleman, to hear me with patience, and in the temper with
which I address you. There is in true friendship this advantage.
The inferior mind looks to the presiding intellect as its guide
and landmark while living, and to the engraven memory of its
principles, as a rule of conduct, after his death. Yet further,
still unmixed with idle superstition, there may be gained a
salutary lesson from contemplating what would be grateful to
the mind of the departed, were he conscious of what is passing

here. I solemnly believe, that could such a consideration have
entered into the mind of Mr. Fox's laſt moments, there is
nothing his waſted spirits would have deprecated more than a
conteſt of the nature I now disclaim and relinquish. It was not
ascertained to me until Monday laſt, after this meeting had
been fixed, that Lord Percy would certainly be a candidate. My
friends hesitated in the hope that it might be left to arbitration
which candidate should withdraw. That hope has failed. I
claim the privilege of neareſt and deareſt friendship, to set the
example of a sacrifice—comparatively how small to what it
demands—nothing could ever have induced me to have proceeded to a disputed poll on this occasion.—The hour is not far
diſtant when an awful knell shall tell you that the unburied
remains of your revered patriot are passing through the ſtreets
to that sepulchral home, where your kings—your heroes—
your sages—and your poets lie, and where they are to be
honoured by the association of his noble remains; that hour
when, however the splendid gaudiness of public pageantry may
be avoided, you—you—all of you will be self-marshalled in
reverential sorrow, mute and reflecting on your mighty loss.—
At that moment shall the disguſting conteſt of an election
wrangle, break the solemnity of the scene?—Is it fitting that
any man should overlook the crisis, and risk the rude and
monſtrous conteſt?—Is it fitting that I should be the man?
Allow me to hope from the manner in which you have received
the little I have said on this subject, that I need add no more.
Yet ſtill would my purpose be incomplete and my remon-
ſtrance inconsiſtant, if I did not at the same time that I withdraw myself, urge to you to take the measures moſt propitious
to prevent the tranquillity we purpose from being deſtroyed by
others. To me there seems no mode so obvious and decisive as
adding your suffrages to the countenance given to the noble
Earl who has the support of those Miniſters with whom your
late illuſtrious representative lived and died in the moſt perfect confidence and amity. I turn to him rejoicing that I shall
not be his antagoniſt—I turn to him with respect due to an
early character of the higheſt promise—with the ſtrong assur-

ance of those qualities which engage affection and command respect—on these grounds, I, for one, shall give him my cordial support. Gentlemen, I have now executed a difficult and painful task—yet one duty more remains—not a painful but a grateful one—yet one more difficult, perhaps, than that which I have left—it is to endeavour to express to you those sentiments of sincere and eager gratitude which your voluntary proffered support, and your indulgent acceptance of what I have this day submitted to you, and which is indelibly imprinted on a heart not formed to be unthankful, inspires. As a public man I feel that your approbation rewards my past efforts and it shall be the animation of my future endeavours.

Bibliography

THE most comprehensive bibliography of Sheridaniana is that which was compiled by John P. Anderson for the *Life of Richard Brinsley Sheridan* by Lloyd C. Sanders (1896), to which however considerable additions are now made. The *Biographical Dictionary* here cited is *A Biographical Dictionary of the Living Authors of Great Britain and Ireland*, London, Colburn (1816); according to my copy the compiler was Frederick Shoberl, who took over from William Upcott, the author of the lives under the letters A to C.

1. POLITICAL PAMPHLETS AND SPEECHES

i. By Sheridan

[*May 30th, 1785. House of Commons. Legislative Independence of Ireland.*]

The/Legislative Independence/of Ireland Vindicated./In/a/ Speech/of/Mr. Sheridan's/on the/Irish Propositions,/In the/ British House of Commons./

To which/is annexed an Authentic Copy/Of the Twenty Resolutions,/On the Irish Commercial Intercourse,/As they/ Passed that House, on the 30th of May, 1785; and were/sent up to the House of Lords./Taken from the Votes of the English House of Commons./Dublin,/Printed by P. Cooney/at the Hibernian Printing Office, Essex Street./M.DCC.LXXXV.

Half-title:

The/Legislative Independence/of/Ireland Vindicated./In a/. Speech/of/Mr. Sheridan's/on the/Irish Propositions,/in the/ British House of Commons,/on Monday, the 30th of May 1785./Also an Authentic Copy of the/Twenty Resolutions/On the/Irish Commercial Intercourse;/being taken from the votes of the/English House of Commons./Price A British Sixpence.

8vo. *Pagination:* [i] *half title.* [ii] *blank.* [1] *title* [2] *blank* 3-26 *text.*

[February 7th, 1787. House of Commons. Against Warren Hastings.]

*The/Genuine Speech/of/Mr. Sheridan,/Delivered in the House of Commons,/on a charge of/High Crimes and Misdemeanours,/Against/Warren Hastings, Esq./Late Governor General of Bengal/for/Extortion, Perfidy, and Cruelty,/to the/ Princesses, and other Branches of the Royal Family of Oude./ London:/Printed for W. Richardson, Bookseller, under the Royal-Exchange.

Pagination: [i] *title.* [ii] *blank.* [iii & iv] *preface.* 1-82 *text.* 83-4 Copy of the Treaty of Chunar. Cut copy $8\frac{1}{4}''$ × $5\frac{1}{8}''$ fair margins.

Mr. Percival F. Hinton's copy and collation. The Preface states:
"Several gentlemen who took notes have cordially produced them, for rendering this report as complete as possible. They presume to call the result of their united cordrilentians genuine with the greater confidence, that though much statement and reference is necessarily omitted, all the most brilliant passages are preserved in their native purity. Most of these Mr. Sheridan could not give more exactly as delivered. Nor have they any where fastidiously avoided his language, merely because it may have found its way into a newspaper. It is one proof among others of its excellence that the reports of the day were in general so replete with his identical phraseology."
Mr. Iolo A. Williams could trace no copy of this report. Sichel, II, 127, reproduces a title page of "The Second Edition. Faithfully Reported" and a passage from the Preface which corrects "cordrilentians" to "contributions", so it was a printer's error, not an effort in neology.

*Speech of Richard Brinsley Sheridan Esquire, on Wednesday, February 7, 1787. 2nd Edition, Revised, Corrected, and Enlarged. Reported by a Member of the House of Commons. London. Printed for J. French. 1787.

From Sichel, II, 126. According to Mr. Sichel, Adolphus, *History of the Reign of George III* (IV, 256), calls this "rather a narrative or review than a speech." Iolo A. Williams, *Seven XVIII Century Bibliographies,* failed to discover any copy of French's edition in British Libraries. Mr. Richard L. Purdy tells me there is one in the library of Yale University. Possibly this is the "Speech upon the fourth charge relative of the Begums of Oude, 8vo 1787," listed by Anderson.

[March 14th, 1788. House of Commons. East India Bill.]

A/Comparative Statement/of the two bills,/for the better government of the/British Possessions in India,/brought into Parliament by/Mr. Fox and Mr. Pitt./With Explanatory

Observations./By R. B. Sheridan, Esq./London:/Printed for
J. Debrett, removed to No. 179, opposite Burlington-House,/
Piccadilly; and T. Becket, Pall-Mall/MDCCLXXXVIII./
Pagination:[1] *half title.*/Comparative Statement/of the Two
Bills/for the better government of the/British Possessions in
India./Price one shilling./ [2] *blank.* [3] *title.* [4] *blank.* [5] &
6-10 *Preface.* To J—— M——, Esq. *Signed* Richard Brinsley
Sheridan, Bruton-Street, March 24th, 1788. 11-17 Copy of a
Paper read by Mr. Sheridan in the House of Commons on
Friday the 14th Day of March, 1788. 18-39. Observations.
[40] *blank.*

Third Edition 1788.

[*June 3rd, 6th,* 10*th, and* 13*th June,* 1788. *Westminster Hall.*
Against Warren Hastings.]

*The Celebrated/Speech/of/Richard Brinsley Sheridan, Esq;
/in/Westminster-Hall/, on the/3d, 6th, 10th, and 13th of June,
1788, on his summary of/the Evidence/on the Begum Charge/
against Warren Hastings, Esquire./
London:/Printed for C. Foster, Poultry; and sold/ by the
Booksellers in Picadilly./M.DCC.LXXXVIII.
Price Two Shillings./Entered at Stationers Hall.
Pagination: [i] *title.* [ii] *blank.* [iii-iv] *Advertisement dated*
16th June 1788. [5] & 6-59 *text.* [60] *blank.*

Mr. Percival F. Hinton's copy.

The/Speech/of/R. B. Sheridan, Esq./(Which continued
Four Days)/Before the/High Court of Parliament,/On/
Tuesday 3rd, Friday 6th, Tuesday 10th, and/Friday 13th of
June 1788./
London: Printed for W. Richardson, No 91 Royal Ex-
change. M.DCC.LXXXVIII. Price Eighteen-Pence./
Pagination: [i] *title.* [ii] *blank.* [1] & 2-70 *text.*

[*Regency Restrictions,* 1789.]
Authentic Copy/of/A Letter/From/Mr. Pitt/To His Royal

Highness/The Prince of Wales,/containing the/Restrictions on the Intended/Regency;/with his/Royal Highness's Answer./ (double rule across page)/London:/Printed for J. Ridgway, No. 1, York-Street,/St. James's-Square./ MDCCLXXXIX.

Pagination: [i] *half title* Authentic Copy &c. Price Six-Pence [ii] *blank.* [iii] *title.* [iv] *blank.* [1] & 2-22: *text.* 23-4: New Publications on the Subject of the Regency &c Printed for J. Ridgway.

Sichel listed this as unpublished—that is, in pamphlet form, for it was printed in the *St. James's Chronicle* of Saturday, January 24–Tuesday 27, 1789, which Mr. Sichel reprinted (II, 393-6). It was also printed in *The Town and Country Magazine,* 1789. This copy was discovered by Mr. Percival F. Hinton. In spite of Mr. Sichel's arguments, it cannot be doubted that the author was Burke, with minor corrections by Sheridan.

[*April* 21st, 1798. *House of Commons. Affairs of the Nation.*]

Speech/of/Mr. Sheridan,/in the House of Commons,/on Friday the 21st. of April, 1798,/On the motion to address His Majesty,/on the present alarming State of Affairs.

Pagination: [1] & 2-13 *text.* 14-16 *blank.*

8vo. This pamphlet has no imprint, and the text begins under the heading on the first page.

[*January* 31st, 1799. *House of Commons. Union with Ireland.*]

Speech/of/Richard Brinsley Sheridan, Esq./in the/House of Commons of Great Britain,/on Thursday, January 31st, 1799/ in/Reply to Mr. Pitt's Speech/on the/Union with Ireland./ Dublin: Printed for James Moore,/No. 45 College-Green,/ 1799.

Pagination: [i] *title.* [ii] *blank.* [1] & 2-26 text.

[*December* 8th, 1802. *House of Commons. Army Estimates.*]

The/Speech/of/Richard Brinsley Sheridan, Esq.,/in the/ House of Commons (8th December 1802) on the Motion for/ the Army Establishment/for the ensuing year./ London:/Printed for John Stockdale, Piccadilly./1802./

Price Sixpence,/or per Hundred, One Guinea and a Half.
Pagination: [1] *title.* [2] *small imprint at foot:* T. Gillett,. Printer Salisbury-Square. [3] & 4-20, text. [21,] 22, [23-4] *Advertisements.*

Other copies have slightly varying imprints. A "New Edition Corrected" is dated 1803. The British Museum and the Birmingham Reference Library have copies of the same speech with the imprint of "Birmingham, Knott and Lloyd" [1802?]. The Bradshaw Collection in the Cambridge University has another with the imprint "Birmingham. T. A. Pearson" [1802?].

[*September* 13*th,* 1806. *Crown and Anchor Tavern. On the Death of Fox.*]

*Death of Mr Fox/An/Eulogium/on the/Right Honourable C. J. Fox,/Delivered/By the Honourable/Mr. Sheridan/At a meeting convened at the/Crown and Anchor Tavern,/On Thursday, September 13th, 1806,/To consider of a proper person to succeed that Great Man,/in the Representation of the/City of Westminster./
Nottingham:/Printed by E. B. Robinson,/and sold by the booksellers. 1806./Price Twopence.

8vo. Birmingham Reference Library. The text is reprinted in full for the first time in this edition.

———

Speeches of the late Right Honourable Richard Brinsley Sheridan (several corrected by himself.) Edited by a Constitutional Friend. 5 vols. London. P. Martin. 1816.

The speeches were reprinted in 3 vols. 1842.

———

A Short Memoir of Sheridan, etc., to which is added a Report of his Celebrated Speech delivered, etc., in Westminster Hall. Booth. 8vo. 1816.
Speeches in the Trial of Warren Hastings. Edited by E. A. Bond, (from Gurney's original shorthand notes). 4 vols. 8vo. 1859-1861.

Sheridan's speeches are in Vols. I and IV.

ii. By other Authors

An Epistle from Joseph Surface, Esq. to Richard Brinsley Sheridan, Esq. of Great Queen Street. London. Printed for G. Kearsley, No. 46 in Fleet Street Price One Shilling and Six Pence. 1780.

Mr. Sichel, who gives this title, describes the pamphlet as "very rare".

Independence: A Poem in Hudibrastic Verse. Addressed to Richard Brinsley Sheridan, Esq. Printed for the Author and Sold by W. Flexney, opposite Gray's-Inn Gate, Holborn. 1783.

Lord George Germaine, General Washington and the King of France are among the principal characters under pseudonyms like Sir Pigmy Spitfire. It has little to do with Sheridan.

Observations upon Mr Sheridan's Pamphlet intituled "Comparative Statement of the Two Bills for the better government of the British Possessions in India." By John Scott. London, 1788. 4to.

Second edition, London 1788, 4to. Third Edition, London 1789, 4to.

The Struggles of Sheridan, or The Ministry in Full Cry. London. 1790. 4to.

A satire in verse.

*A Letter to Mr Sheridan on his conduct in Parliament. Bury St. Edmunds, 1794.

London Library. The author is given as the Rev. Charles Edward Stewart, Rector of Reed in Suffolk, but it is not included among his works in the *Biographical Dictionary* of 1816.

A Second Letter to Mr Sheridan. With strictures on the general conduct of the Opposition. By a Suffolk Freeholder. Bury St. Edmunds, 1796.

Also ascribed to C. E. Stewart.

The Political Dramatist in November 1795. A Poem.

London: Printed for J. Parsons, No. 21 Paternoster-row. Price One Shilling and Sixpence.

8vo. *Pagination:* (i) *title.* (ii) *blank.* 5 & 6-18 *Text.*

Apparently a half-title is missing. Under "Thomas James Mathias, Esq. treasurer of her Majesty's Household", The *Biographical Dictionary* of 1816 gives "The Political Dramatist of the House of Commons 8vo 1795." Anderson gives "The Political Dramatist of the House of Commons in 1795, 8vo, 1796." How many issues this implies is uncertain.

An Epistle from R - ch - - d Br - n s - - y Sh - - - d - an, Esqre. to the Right Honourable H - n - y D - nd - s. London. Printed for J. Owen, Piccadilly. 1796.

From Sichel, II, 253-4, where it is described as "a rhymed satire, rare and absent from the British Museum, twitting Sheridan on his change of front" as to the French Revolution. It is entered in the *Biographical Dictionary* 1816 under Sheridan as if it was a genuine work of his own.

The Political Proteus. A View of the Public Character and Conduct of R. B. Sheridan, Esq. By William Cobbett. London, 1804. 8vo.

Mr. Fox's title to Patriot disputed, and the Political Conduct of Mr. Sheridan scrutinised. London. 1806. 8vo.

An Address to Richard Brinsley Sheridan on the public and private proceedings during the late Election at Westminster. By the author of Mr. Fox's title to Patriot disputed. London, 1807. 8vo.

History of the Westminster and Middlesex Elections in the Month of November 1806. London 1807. 8vo.

The contents of this amusing volume are analysed in Chapter XIX of this book.

The Literary Bazaar. By Peter Pepperpod. With a Pic-Nic Elegy on Richard Brinsley Sheridan. London. 1816. 8vo.

Lines on the Death of ********. From the *Morning Chronicle* of Monday, August 5, 1816. Ascribed to a personage

U

of the highest poetical talent and to gratify the anxious curiosity of the public, re-published without note or comment. Price Sixpence. Hone. 1816.

"Mr. Moore's Lines (if they are Mr. Moore's Lines) are very pretty and sparkling." *Theatrical Inquisitor* for November 1817. Cf. Moore, *Sheridan*, 698, quoting six stanzas.

Lines supposed to be written on the Death of the late R. B. Sheridan, Esq. With Additional Lines Addressed to Friendship. London [1816].

Folio. By Matthew Concanen.

The Life of R. B. Sheridan. With the Remarks of Pitt, Fox, and Burke on his most celebrated Speeches. Second edition, including an account of the funeral. J. Fairburn: London [1816]. 8vo.

Monody: to the Memory of the Right Honourable Richard Brinsley Sheridan. By Thomas Gent. London. 1816. 8vo.

Authentic Memoirs of the Life and Death of the Right Honourable Richard Brinsley Sheridan. With an estimate of his Character and his Talents. London. William Hone. 1816.

Quin, almost verbatim, with a few unimportant additions.

Monody on the Death of the Right Honourable R. B. Sheridan, Written at the Request of a Friend, To be Spoken at Drury Lane Theatre. London. Murray. 1816. 8vo.

By Lord Byron. The monody as delivered omitted some of the more violent passages.

A Garland for the grave of Richard Brinsley Sheridan. By Charles Phillips, Esq., Barrister at Law. Second Edition. London. 1816. 8vo.

From Lowe's *Bibliography of Theatrical Literature.*

Patronage A Poem suggested by the Prince Regent's treatment of the late Mr. Sheridan. By J. Brown, Esq. Author of the Stage.

From a list of books published, dated 1820, in the Salt Library Collection. I have not seen this.

Thoughts/on the/Greek Revolution./By/Richard Brinsley
Sheridan, Esq./La sagesse n'est que la mesure.—Mad. de Stael./
London: John Murray, Albermarle-Street. MDCCCXXII.
[i] *half title*. Thoughts on the Greek Revolution. [ii] *blank*.
[iii] *title*. [iv] London. Printed by William Clowes. Northum-
berland-Court. [v] & vi, vii, viii, Preface. Pp. [1] & 2, 80
Text. [81] 82, 92, Notes.

Birmingham Reference Library, P. vii has this curious note: "I should have been
more diffident in passing judgments, if I had originally meant to prefix to these pages
a name, which forms their sole chance of attracting attention."
The author was, of course, Sheridan's son Charles, and the name seems to have been
added by the publisher, when it was decided that the pamphlet should not be anonymous. A second edition followed, entirely reset, with the correct name on the title-page.

The/Maid of Bath,/a/comedy/of three acts,/as it is per-
formed at the/Theatre-Royal, in the Hay-Market./By Samuel
Foote, Esq./with the/original prologue,/as written/By Mr.
Garrick,/and spoken/By Mr. Foote;/The Epilogue, spoken by
Mrs. Jewell./London:/Printed for George Allen, No. 59,
Pater-Noster Row/
Pp. i-vii & 1-68, 69-70.

This edition was unauthorized, as is determined by its dedication (iii, Sig A 3) to
"Samuel Foote, Esq." This shows that it was published before Foote's death, while the
supposed "first edition" by Wheble, 1778, also piratical, was posthumous.
The only copy I know, in the City Library, Bristol, formerly belonged to
Emanuel Green, who dated it as 1771. The actual year may have been cropped in
binding, but it is equally possible that it was undated.

2. BIOGRAPHICAL AUTHORITIES

Watkins: Memoirs of the Public and Private Life of R. B. Sheridan, with a particular account of his Family and Connexions. By John Watkins, LL.D. 2 vols. 1817.

Lefanu: Memoirs of Mrs. Frances Sheridan, with remarks upon a late life of R. B. Sheridan. By her grand-daughter Alicia Lefanu. 1824.

This was partly a reply to Watkins. It contains *The Travellers,* a poem by the Rev. Walter Chamberlaine, Sheridan's uncle, which includes the *Stanzas on Fire* printed as Sheridan's in the edition of *An Ode to Scandal,* 1816. The poem appeared first in *The Dublin Magazine, or The Gentleman's New Miscellany,* 1733, so Sheridan has no claim to it, except for one verse.

Moore: Memoirs of the Life of Richard Brinsley Sheridan. By Thomas Moore. 1 vol. large 4to. 1825. 2 vols. 4to. 1825.

The large single-volume edition was the first. The 5th Edition, 2 vols., 1827, contains a new preface making some important corrections.

Sheridaniana: Sheridaniana or Anecdotes of Sheridan, his Table Talk & Bon Mots. 1826.

While some of the stories are apocryphal, and others borrowed from Michael Kelly and from Moore, it contains some important extracts from contemporary periodicals.

Smyth: Memoir of Mr. Sheridan. By William Smyth [*privately printed*] Leeds. 1840.

Fitzgerald: Lives of the Sheridans. By Percy Fitzgerald. 2 vols. 1887.

Contains little new material, but uses the Garrick Correspondence for the first time.

Rae: Sheridan, A Biography. By W. Fraser Rae. 2 vols. 1896.

Written to order, at the suggestion of Sheridan's grandson, the Marquis of Dufferin. Contains much material from the Frampton Court MSS., but the author suppressed a great amount of evidence which did not suit his brief.

Green: Linley, Sheridan and Mathews at Bath, by Emanuel Green. Bath 1903.

A neglected book, including much material from the files of *The Bath Chronicle,* and other newspapers.

Sichel: Sheridan From New & Original Material. By Walter Sichel. 2 vols. 1909.

Sadleir: The Political Career of Richard Brinsley Sheridan by M. T. H. Sadleir. Oxford. 1912.

Butler: Sheridan: A Ghost Story. By E. M. Butler. 1931.

EARLY PERIODICAL ARTICLES

"Account of Richard Brinsley Sheridan" in *The London Magazine.* 1778.

"Account of Richard Brinsley Sheridan" in *The European Magazine.* 1782.

"Mr Sheridan" in *The British Magazine and Review.* September. 1783.

"Mr Sheridan" in *Public Characters of* 1799. [1800].
By Edward Quin, who received some information from Samuel Whyte of Dublin.

Le Beau Monde: the Fashionable Literary and Magazine. November. 1808.
Biographical Dictionary of Living Authors. 1816.
Quin abridged, with a misleading bibliography.

3. REJECTED AUTHORITIES

[Mr. Walter Sichel and other writers have accepted as genuine certain "authorities", which, after long and careful consideration, I have ignored. The reasons for rejection are briefly summarized below, but they do not exhaust the evidence upon which I have acted.]

1. *Miss Linley to Miss Saunders*. Dated May 2, 1772.

This letter was printed in *The Gentleman's Magazine* for [the end of] October 1825 being described as "A Letter from Miss Linley (afterwards Mrs. Sheridan) to her confidential friend, Miss Saunders." It was reprinted in full by G. G. Sigmond, with a proviso that it might not be authentic, in his edition of *Sheridan's Works*, 1848, and by "An Octogenarian" in *Sheridan and His Times*, 1859, with the omission of a postscript. What appears to be a later transcript, dated "May 2, 1770" was examined by Fraser Rae, and a facsimile of the first page was given in his *Sheridan*, with an argument against its genuineness. He did not name the owner, but it was apparently one of the documents discussed below, which were purchased by Augustin Daly from James MacHenry. There is, however, no reason to suppose it was the original transcript sent to *The Gentleman's Magazine*, and its provenance is irrelevant to the consideration of that article.

Thomas Moore in his 5th Edition rejected it as "a clumsy forgery". After its dismissal by Rae (I, 420-422), the arguments were traversed by Sichel (I, 329-33), who described the letter in *The Gentleman's Magazine* as "a transcript, however garbled, from a genuine document," and as "embellished, but containing first hand information." An admission that it is "garbled" and "embellished" in parts is of itself a sufficient reason for rejection, and Miss Butler—echoing Mr. Sichel to the extent of saying that it was "the product of somebody in the know" (whatever that may mean)—is afterwards constrained to admit that "the facts are true, but they wear a spurious air, and seem more imaginary than real." But *are* the facts true?

Miss Butler, and Miss Black in *The Linleys of Bath* agree with Mr. Sichel that the "details have been substantiated by unpublished sources inaccessible to the supposed forger"— that is, from private papers not published before Rae's biography of 1896. All this supposed "first hand information" is nevertheless to be found in Moore's *Memoirs of Sheridan*. Mr. Sichel says that the letter mentions "Linley's intended lawsuit omitted by Moore, but noticed by Alicia in a part of her story as yet unpublished". Apart from the fact that the story of the lawsuit was common property, this sentence contains three errors of fact: (i) it is not "omitted by Moore", who says that "Long indemnified the father, who was proceeding to bring the matter into Court, by settling £3,000 on his daughter": (ii) it was not "as yet unpublished", for Rae printed the original statement by Mrs. Henry Lefanu, who wrote that "Mr. Linley immediately declared his intention of prosecuting Mr. Long for breach of contract", and that "Long voluntarily gave Mr. Linley three thousand pounds to be lodged in the hands of trustees for the use of his daughter": and (iii) it was not written by Alicia, the elder sister, but by Elizabeth, the younger. Similarly, Mr. Sichel says that Moore omits to mention Mathews's "repeated menaces of suicide", yet he speaks of him using "the threat of self-destruction, often tried with effect in these cases." It is probable, of course, that these threats only existed in the imagination of Sheridan's young sister.

Mr. Sichel is equally unhappy in his other instances. He says that the letter speaks of Miss Saunders as at "D——", and the Yorkshire border of Derby was the Linley's "original home". It is evident that "D——" was intended to represent a town, and from the context that town was Dublin, where a certain Mr. R. had spoken "disrespectful things" of Elizabeth. The writer of the letter says that "at the age of twelve I was brought up from the country where I had been all my life". Mr. Sichel comments that Elizabeth and Mary were brought up at a boarding school "not far from Wells", but the school was near Brandon's Hill, which was not, as Mr. Sichel thinks, near Wells, but is the hill overlooking Bristol from which, according to tradition, "Oliver Cromwell battered the Cathedral and town." In short, not one of his reasons for supposing this letter to be authentic is valid.

The confusion between the two sisters adds to Mr. Sichel's difficulties, and overwhelms his chapter. The elder sister, Mrs. Joseph Lefanu, wrote to Sheridan's widow a short letter dated "Dublin, November 9th, 1816," printed in part by Moore, and in full by Rae (I, 73-77). The younger sister, Mrs. Henry Lefanu, wrote Moore about 1818 a long account of the duels and the elopement which he paraphrased and corrected, while Rae printed it in full, though dispersedly (I, 161-199). The elder sister, Mrs. Joseph, was Alicia: the younger sister, Mrs. Henry, was Elizabeth. But as Mrs. Henry's account was written, it appears (Moore, VIII), by her daughter acting as her amanuensis, it may have been signed, or the covering letter, by "Alicia Lefanu", Sheridan's niece. But this does not warrant Mr. Sichel speaking of it as a "long narrative of the events, forwarded four months after Sheridan's death," and written by "the elder sister, Alicia". In short, the narrative was not written by Mrs. Joseph Lefanu in 1816, recollecting events when she was just nineteen, but by Mrs. Henry Lefanu in 1818, recollecting events of forty-six years before, when she was a child of thirteen. This account has several demonstrable errors of fact, such as making Charles Sheridan the second in the first duel instead of Simon Ewart, and placing the second on Claverton Hill instead of Kingsdown. But through Moore, it inspired the "Letter to Miss Saunders", which was written by somebody with a theory that Elizabeth was the incarnation of Lydia Languish. It is a ridiculous forgery.

2. *Sheridan and His Times. By an Octogenarian, who stood by his knee in youth and sat at his table in manhood. In Two Volumes. London. J. F. Hope. MDCCCLIX.*

Whoever the author was, and whatever his relations to Sheridan, this book is utterly valueless, for the most credulous

of its supporters have not dared to claim exactitude for its
florid "verbatim" records of conversations that were supposed
to have taken place forty to sixty years before. Fraser Rae,
giving no authority, ascribed it to one William Earle. E. M.
Butler says that "Earle was introduced into Sheridan's household in 1790, when he was ten years of age: he remained there,
probably in some menial capacity, until his master's death."
She again gives no authority, and her "probably" points to
guessing. The only known William Earle, or Earl, who can be
traced is the author of *The Welshman*, a romance, 1801;
Welsh Legends, 1801; *Trifles in Verse*, 1803; and *Obi, or the
History of Three-Fingered Jack* [n.d.], who was fined and imprisoned in February 1814 for a "scurrilous and malignant
libel" (*Dictionary of Living Authors*, 1816). He seems also to
have written *Outwitted at Last*, a comedy acted in 1817. No
reliance can be placed upon any of the statements that the
"Octogenarian" did not borrow from other books, and his two
volumes are rubbish.

3. *The English Illustrated Magazine, April 1887. "Sheridan and
Miss Linley." By Maria Stoker.*

This contains twenty-four letters, purporting to be written
by Elizabeth Linley to Sheridan, alleged to have been found
among a "heterogeneous mass of papers," which, on the
destruction of the theatre in 1809, were "hurriedly packed in
barrels" and "in the confusion thrust into neighbouring
cellars, where they remained undisturbed for over sixty years."
This romantic story of their *provenance* appears to have been
nonsense, and Percy Fitzgerald in his *Memoirs of an Author*
denounced the collection as "a literary imposture." Moy
Thomas traced the owner, whose name is not given, but he was
a dealer of dubious reputation, James MacHenry. He mentioned that they had been bought at "Mr. Lacy's sale"—and
I have found them in a priced catalogue of the sale of Thomas
Hailes Lacy, the theatrical publisher, 1873, as "*Sheridan, R. B.*
Various autograph letters and other papers etc relating to him.
Harvey £2. 2. 0.".

They were purchased from MacHenry by Augustin Daly, after whose death they were sold and disappeared, but Mr. Richard L. Purdy, of Yale, has recently ascertained for me that they are in an extra-illustrated copy of Moore's *Sheridan*, now in the library of Harvard University. Daly lent them to Rae, who transcribed a number of them, with characteristic suppressions. Supplementing his extracts with Matilda Stoker's, they prove (if genuine) to give an unflattering portrait of Sheridan in his conduct to Elizabeth—as a seducer vaunting his conquests, and refusing to surrender certain correspondence of hers, some of which was eventually "made public" by him, in such a way as to turn her into "the sport of his idle hours, and the subject of his wit with every milliner's apprentice in Bath." The one correspondence to which this can allude, to the best of my knowledge, is the correspondence with Lord Grosvenor, printed in *The Bath Chronicle*—of which an undated extract from her letter was given by Moore, though actually they were published at the time of Sheridan's marriage.

Nevertheless, some of the later letters—almost all undated, but covering the period between 1781 and 1792—have every appearance of being authentic, for in 1887, when they were published, there was no ordinary source of information— Watkins or Moore, Lefanu or Smyth—which could account for certain references, as to Sheridan's house at Heston, to "Jen" meaning Jenny Linley, and "George," meaning George Edwards, Sheridan's manservant. Yet as the extracts are incomplete, and require to be collated with the MSS., I have made no use of them, preferring to ignore all doubtful documents. Mr. Sichel supports their authenticity by their similarity of style to the "Letter to Miss Saunders"—which is another reason for their re-consideration.

"*Sheridan Whitewashed*, An Examination of the New Life by Fraser Rae With an Account of the Linley Letters, said to have been found in Barrels in Drury Lane," by Percy Fitzgerald [1897] is, of course, very much on the defensive, and by no means final.

Index of Persons and Books

Index of Plays

305

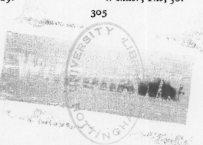